Other Books and Series by Jeff Bowen

Applications for Enrollment of Choctaw Newborn Act of 1905 Volumes I thru XX

Choctaw By Blood Enrollment Cards 1898-1914 Volumes I thru XVIII

Visit our website at **www.nativestudy.com** to learn more about these
and other books and series by Jeff Bowen

CHOCTAW BY BLOOD

ENROLLMENT CARDS

1898-1914

VOLUME XVIII

TRANSCRIBED BY

JEFF BOWEN

NATIVE STUDY
Gallipolis, Ohio
USA

Other Books and Series by Jeff Bowen

1901-1907 Native American Census Seneca, Eastern Shawnee, Miami, Modoc, Ottawa, Peoria, Quapaw, and Wyandotte Indians (Under Seneca School, Indian Territory)

1932 Census of The Standing Rock Sioux Reservation with Births And Deaths 1924-1932

Census of The Blackfeet, Montana, 1897- 1901 Expanded Edition

Eastern Cherokee by Blood, 1906-1910, Volumes I thru XIII

Choctaw of Mississippi Indian Census 1929-1932 with Births and Deaths 1924-1931 Volume I
Choctaw of Mississippi Indian Census 1933, 1934 & 1937, Supplemental Rolls to 1934 & 1935 with Births and Deaths 1932-1938, and Marriages 1936-1938 Volume II

Eastern Cherokee Census Cherokee, North Carolina 1930-1939 Census 1930-1931 with Births And Deaths 1924-1931 Taken By Agent L. W. Page Volume I
Eastern Cherokee Census Cherokee, North Carolina 1930-1939 Census 1932-1933 with Births And Deaths 1930-1932 Taken By Agent R. L. Spalsbury Volume II
Eastern Cherokee Census Cherokee, North Carolina 1930-1939 Census 1934-1937 with Births and Deaths 1925-1938 and Marriages 1936 & 1938 Taken by Agents R. L. Spalsbury And Harold W. Foght Volume III

Seminole of Florida Indian Census, 1930-1940 with Birth and Death Records, 1930-1938

Texas Cherokees 1820-1839 A Document For Litigation 1921

Starr Roll 1894 (Cherokee Payment Rolls) Districts: Canadian, Cooweescoowee, and Delaware Volume One
Starr Roll 1894 (Cherokee Payment Rolls) Districts: Flint, Going Snake, and Illinois Volume Two
Starr Roll 1894 (Cherokee Payment Rolls) Districts: Saline, Sequoyah, and Tahlequah; Including Orphan Roll Volume Three

Cherokee Intruder Cases Dockets of Hearings 1901-1909 Volumes I & II

Indian Wills, 1911-1921 Records of the Bureau of Indian Affairs Books One thru Seven
Native American Wills & Probate Records 1911-1921

Turtle Mountain Reservation Chippewa Indians 1932 Census with Births & Deaths, 1924-1932

Other Books and Series by Jeff Bowen

Chickasaw By Blood Enrollment Cards 1898-1914 Volume I thru V

Cherokee Descendants East An Index to the Guion Miller Applications Volume I
Cherokee Descendants West An Index to the Guion Miller Applications Volume II (A-M)
Cherokee Descendants West An Index to the Guion Miller Applications Volume III (N-Z)

Applications for Enrollment of Seminole Newborn Freedmen, Act of 1905

Eastern Cherokee Census, Cherokee, North Carolina, 1915-1922, Taken by Agent James E. Henderson   *Volume I (1915-1916)*
                                        Volume II (1917-1918)
                                        Volume III (1919-1920)
                                        Volume IV (1921-1922)

Complete Delaware Roll of 1898

Eastern Cherokee Census, Cherokee, North Carolina, 1923-1929, Taken by Agent James E. Henderson   *Volume I (1923-1924)*
                                          Volume II (1925-1926)
                                        Volume III (1927-1929)

Applications for Enrollment of Seminole Newborn Act of 1905 Volumes I & II

North Carolina Eastern Cherokee Indian Census 1898-1899, 1904, 1906, 1909-1912, 1914 Revised and Expanded Edition

1932 Hopi and Navajo Native American Census with Birth & Death Rolls (1925-1931) Volume 1 - Hopi
1932 Hopi and Navajo Native American Census with Birth & Death Rolls (1930-1932) Volume 2 - Navajo

Western Navajo Reservation Navajo, Hopi and Paiute 1933 Census with Birth & Death Rolls 1925-1933

Cherokee Citizenship Commission Dockets 1880-1884 and 1887-1889 Volumes I thru V

Applications for Enrollment of Chickasaw Newborn Act of 1905 Volumes I thru VII

Cherokee Intermarried White 1906 Volume I thru X

Applications for Enrollment of Creek Newborn Act of 1905 Volumes I thru XIV

Native Study LLC
Gallipolis, OH
www.nativestudy.com

Library of Congress Control Number: 2020911767

ISBN: 978-1-64968-114-0

Made in the United States of America.

This series is dedicated to
Mike Marchi,
who keeps my spirits up.

CREEK CENSUS.

SECOND NOTICE.

Members of the Dawes Commission will be present at the following times and places for the purpose of enrolling Creek citizens, as required by Act of Congress of June 10, 1896:

At Muskogee, Nov. 8 to 30, 1897, inclusive.
At Wagoner, Nov. 8 to 13, " inclusive.
At Eufaula, Nov. 8 to 13, " inclusive.
At Sapulpa, Nov. 15 to 20, " inclusive.
At Wetumpka, Nov. 15 to 20, " inclusive.
At Okmulgee, Nov. 22 to 30, " inclusive.

All persons who have not heretofore enrolled before the Dawes Commission should appear and enroll. Parents and guardians can enroll their families and wards.

TAMS BIXBY,
FRANK C. ARMSTRONG,
A. S. McKENNON,
THOS. B. NEEDLES,
Commissioners.

The above illustration is similar in nature to what was found throughout Indian Territory for different tribes as far as postings on bulletin boards, public centers, or wherever they could be read so people would be notified of where and when they needed to be for enrollment with the Dawes Commission.

This is a picture of the Dawes Commission at Camp Jones in Stonewall, Indian Territory on September 8, 1898.

The images below are of two of the original cards given on the microfilm. The cards given in this book have been formatted to fit on one page and still give all the information found on the original cards.

Introduction

This series of Choctaw Enrollment Cards for the Five Civilized Tribes 1898-1914 has been transcribed from National Archive Film M-1186 Rolls 39-46.

The series contains more than 6100 Choctaw enrollment cards. All of the cards list age, sex and degree of blood, the parties' Dawes Roll Numbers, and date of enrollment by the Secretary of Interior for each person. The contents also give the enrollee's parents' names as well as miscellaneous notes pertaining to the enrollee's circumstances, when needed. Most entries indicate whether or not a spouse is an Intermarried White, with the initials I.W.

Enrollment wasn't as simple a process as most would think just by going through these pages. The relationships between the Five Tribes and the Dawes Commission were weak at best. There were political battles going on between the tribes and the U.S. Government as it was, but the struggles didn't stop there. Each tribe had its own political factions pulling it from every direction. On top of everything else, people from every corner of the United States were trying to figure how to get in on the spoils (Money and Land Allotment) by means of political favor. Kent Carter, author of *The Dawes Commission*, describes the continuous effort required to enroll the different tribes and the pressure the Commission incurred from people all over the country who tried to insinuate themselves into the equation:

"In May 1896 the Dawes Commission Returned To Indian Territory for its third visit, establishing its headquarters at Vinita in the Cherokee Nation. It now had to process applications for citizenship in addition to negotiating allotment agreements; these circumstances make the narrative of events more confusing because the commission attempted the two tasks concurrently. The commissioners resumed making their usual speeches to tribal officials and public gatherings to promote negotiations, but now they inevitably had to respond to questions about how the application process for citizenship would work. They also began receiving letters from people all over the United States asking how they could 'get on the rolls' so they could 'get Indian land'."[1]

For the actual process of Choctaw enrollment, "A commission was appointed in each county of the Choctaw Nation under an act of September 18 to make separate rolls of citizens by blood, by intermarriage, and freedmen; it was to deliver them to recently elected Chief Green McCurtain by October 20, but he rejected them even before they were completed because of charges that people were being left off for political reasons. On October 30, the National Council authorized establishment of a five-member

---

[1] *The Dawes Commission* by Kent Carter, page 15, para. 1

commission to revise the rolls within ten days and then directed McCurtain to turn them over to the Dawes Commission on November 11, 1896. The Choctaws hired the law firm of Stuart, Gordon, and Hailey, of South McAlester to represent the tribe at all proceedings held by the Dawes Commission,"[2] another indication that throughout the Commission's efforts there was always controversy between the tribes and the negotiators.

When completed, this multi-volume series will contain thousands of names, all of them accounted for in the indexes carefully prepared by the author. Hopefully this work will help many researchers find their ancestors and satisfy the questions that so many have had about their Native American heritage.

Jeff Bowen
Gallipolis, Ohio
NativeStudy.com

---

[2] *The Dawes Commission* by Kent Carter, page 16, para. 5

Choctaw By Blood Enrollment Cards 1898-1914

RESIDENCE:	Chickasaw Natn
POST OFFICE:	Wilson I.T.

Choctaw **Nation**   Choctaw **Roll**

CARD No. **5101**
FIELD NO.

Dawes' Roll No.	NAME	Relationship to Person First Named	AGE	SEX	BLOOD	TRIBAL ENROLLMENT		
						Year	County	No.
✓	1 Pearcy James W	Named	22	M				
✓	2 " Rosa B	Dau	3	F				
O	3 " John D	Son	1	M				
	4 " Joseph Elijah	Son	4mo	M				
	5							
No4	DISMISSED							
	8	SEP 15 1904						
	9							
	10							
	11	DISMISSED						
	12	MAR -4 1907						
	13							
	14							
	15							
	16							
	17							

TRIBAL ENROLLMENT OF PARENTS

Name of Father	Year	County	Name of Mother	Year	County
1 Joseph A Pearcy		Non Citz	Betty Pearcy		Non Citz
2 No1			Bertie Pearcy		" "
3 No1			" "		" "
4 No.1			" "		" "
5					
6					
7 Nos1&2 denied in 1896, case # 299					
8 Admitted by the U.S. Court Ardmore, I.T. Feb 1st 1898 Case # 134					
9					
10					
11					
12	No.4 Enrolled May 24, 1900				
13	DENIED CITIZENSHIP BY THE CHOCTAW AND				
14 No1 2	CHICKASAW CITIZENSHIP COURT				
15					
16			Date of Application for Enrollment	9-22-98	
17					

1

Choctaw By Blood Enrollment Cards 1898-1914

RESIDENCE: Chickasaw Natn
POST OFFICE: Comanche I.T.

Choctaw **Nation**   Choctaw **Roll**

CARD NO. 5102
FIELD NO. 147

Dawes' Roll No.	NAME	Relationship to Person First Named	AGE	SEX	BLOOD	TRIBAL ENROLLMENT		
						Year	County	No.
✓	1 Taylor, George W	First Named	36	M				
✓	2 " Fanny	Wife	36	F				
✓	3 " William H	Son	18	M				
✓	4 " James G	Son	16	M				
✓	5 " Ezell	Son	9	M				
✓	6 " Louis	Son	5	M				
	7							
#1-2-3-	8							
4-5-6-	9							
	10							
	11							
	12							
	13							
	14							
	15							
	16							
	17							

TRIBAL ENROLLMENT OF PARENTS

	Name of Father	Year	County	Name of Mother	Year	County
1	Wm H Taylor	Dead	Non Citz	Elizabeth Taylor		Non Citz
2	Green B Brown		" "	Kittie Brown	Dead	" "
3	No1			No2		
4	No1			No2		
5	No1			No2		
6	No1			No2		
7						
8	Nos 1 to 6 denied in 1896, case # 296					
9	Admitted by the U.S. Court at South McAllister[sic], I.T.					
10	Jan 18 - 1898 Court Case 89					
11						
12						
13						
14						
15						
16				Date for		9-22-98
17						

Choctaw By Blood Enrollment Cards 1898-1914

RESIDENCE:	Chickasaw					CARD NO.	**5103**
POST OFFICE:	Tatums Ind. Terr	Choctaw **Nation**	Choctaw **Roll**			FIELD NO.	C 148

Dawes' Roll No.	NAME	Relationship to Person First Named	AGE	SEX	BLOOD	TRIBAL ENROLLMENT		
						Year	County	No.
1	Jones Walter W		38	M				
2	" Jennie	Wife	22	F	IW			
3	" Fitzhugh L	Son	8	M				
4	" Ruby E	Dau	4	F				
5	" Minnie C	"	2	F				
6	" Maud	"	2mo	"				
7								
8	#6- DISMISSED							
9	JAN							
10								
11								
12	See Leula West case C108							
13								
14								
15	#2- DISMISSED							
16								
17								

TRIBAL ENROLLMENT OF PARENTS

	Name of Father	Year	County	Name of Mother	Year	County
1	Brinkley Wilburn		Non Citz	Mildred Wilburn		Non Citz
2	Wᵐ Covington		" "	Mary Covington		" "
3	No 1			No2		
4	No 1			No2		
5	No1			No2		
6	No1			No2		
7	Nos 1 to 5 inclusive denied in 1896, case # 56					
8	Admitted by the U.S. Court Ardmore, I.T.					RETARY OF INTERIOR.
9	Jan 19 1898 Court Case No 148			DEPARTMENTAL ACTION		FEB 20 1907
10	Judgment of U.S. [remainder illegible]			FORWARDED ATTORNEYS FOR		07
11				NOTICE OF DEPARTMENTAL		
12	DENIED CITIZENSHIP BY THE CHOCTAW AND			ACTION MAILED APPLICANT.		
13						
14	Nos 1,3,4,5 CHICKASAW CITIZENSHIP COURT					
15				No6 enrolled Oct 30/99		
16	For children of Nos 1&2 see NB #1036 (Act Apr 26'06)			Date of Application for Enrollment 9-22-98		
17						

3

Choctaw By Blood Enrollment Cards 1898-1914

RESIDENCE: Chickasaw Natn
POST OFFICE: Velma   I.T.

Choctaw **Nation**   Choctaw **Roll**

CARD NO. **5104**
FIELD NO. C 149

Dawes' Roll No.	NAME	Relationship to Person First Named	AGE	SEX	BLOOD	TRIBAL ENROLLMENT		
						Year	County	No.
1	Gordon Harriet		47	F				
2	McFatridge William	Son	18	M				
3	Gordon George	Son	13	M				
4								
5								
6								
7								
8								
9								
10								
11								
12								
13								
14								
15								
16								
17								

TRIBAL ENROLLMENT OF PARENTS

	Name of Father	Year	County	Name of Mother	Year	County
1	Carrolton Tucker	Dead	Non Citz	Jane Tucker	Dead	Non Citz
2	Geo McFatridge	Dead	" "	No 1		
3	William Gordon		" "	No 1		
4						
5			Nos 1,2 & 3 denied in 1896 case # 1005			
6			Admitted by U.S. Court Ardmore I.T. Jan 20 1898 Court Case 93			
7						
8						
9			No.1 denied by C.C.C.C. as Harriet Gordon or Hariet Gordon			
10			For children of No2 see NB #1062 (Act Apr 26 '06)			
11						
12						
13						
14						
15						
16				9-22-98		
17						

Choctaw By Blood Enrollment Cards 1898-1914

RESIDENCE: Chickasaw Natn	CARD NO. 5105
POST OFFICE: Velma I.T.	FIELD NO. 150

Choctaw **Nation**   Choctaw **Roll**

Dawes' Roll No.	NAME	Relationship to Person First Named	AGE	SEX	BLOOD	TRIBAL ENROLLMENT Year	County	No.
1	McFatridge James	Named	26	M				
2	" Eliza	Wife	22	F				
3	" Maude	Dau	4	F				
4	" Myrtle	Dau	11mo	F				
5	" Robert	Son	6mo	M				
6	" William Edward	Son	2mo	M				
7								
8								
9	Nos 1,2&3 denied by C.C.C.C. under surname of McPhetridge							
10	No 3 denied as Maude							
11	or Maud							
12								
13								
14	#4-5-6-							
15								
16								
17								

TRIBAL ENROLLMENT OF PARENTS

	Name of Father	Year	County	Name of Mother	Year	County
1	Geo McFatridge	Dead	Non Citz	Harriet McFatridge		Non Citz
2	Dan Wise		" "	Nettie Wise		" "
3	No1			No2		
4	No1			No2		
5	No.1			No. 2		
6	No1			No2		
7						
8						
9	Nos 1,2&3 admitted in 1896 case #547					
10						
11	No5 Enrolled May 24, 1900					
12	No.6 Born Feby 17, 1902; Enrolled April 8 1902					
13						
14						
15	No1				Date of Application	
16					9-22-98	
17						

5

Choctaw By Blood Enrollment Cards 1898-1914

RESIDENCE: Blue County
POST OFFICE: Fulsom Ind. Terr.

Choctaw **Nation**   Choctaw **Roll**

CARD NO. **5106**
FIELD NO. C 151

Dawes' Roll No.	NAME	Relationship to Person	AGE	SEX	BLOOD	TRIBAL ENROLLMENT		
						Year	County	No.
✓	1 Askew William T	First Named	38	M	1/16			
	2 " Bettie	Wife	36	F	IW			
✓	3 " Thane	Dau	15	F				
✓	4 " Perry	Son	14	M				
✓	5 " Tommy	Son	12	M				
✓	6 " Lillie	Dau	8	F				
	7 " Gilbert	Son	6	M				
	8 " Lizzie	Dau	4	F				
	9 " Ethel	"	2mo	F				
	10 Shipman, Robert Floy	Grandson	1mo	M				
	11 Askew Robert	Son	1mo	M				
	12	Bettie Askew admitted as an intermarried citizen by supplemental						
	13	judgment U.S. Court Mch 12th 1898			No9 Enrolled Oct. 13, 1900			
	14			DECISION RENDERED				
	15	Nos1 to 8 denied in '96, case # 1						
#9-10-11- DISMISSED								
	17		RECORD FORWARDED DEPARTMENT.					

DISMISSED
DISMISSED
NOV 12 1904
TRIBAL ENROLLMENT OF PARENTS

	Name of Father	Year	County	Name of Mother	Year	County
1	Wm [?] Askew		Non Citz	Martha Askew	Dead	Non Citz
2	Perry Tolbert	Dead	" "	Lizzie Tolbert		" "
3	No1			No2		
4	No1			No2		
5	No1			No2		
6	No1			No2		
7	No1			No2		
8	No1			No2		
9	No1			No2		
10	T. D. Shipman		non-citizen	No.3		
11	No1			No2		
12	Nos 1,3,4,5,6 and 7 admitted by U.S. Court, Ardmore, I.T. Dec 21,1897: Court case 71					
13	No10 born Oct 26,1901 Enrolled Nov 30,1901 } No1 denied by CCCC as William Thomas Askew					
14	No 11 Born July 19, 1902; enrolled Aug 16,1902 } For child of No3 see NB (Apr 26'06) #1222					
15	No.3 denied by C.C.C.C. as Thane Shipman or Askew					
16	No.5 denied by C.C.C.C. as Tommie Askew or Tommy Askew					
17	No.6 denied " " " Lily Askew or Lillie Askew					

DENIED CITIZENSHIP BY THE CHOCTAW AND
CHICKASAW CITIZENSHIP COURT

Da... for Enrollment ... 9-22-98

Children of #1 will be found on other side [no children listed on reverse side]

6

Choctaw By Blood Enrollment Cards 1898-1914

RESIDENCE:	Chickasaw Natn			CARD NO.	**5107**
POST OFFICE:	Foster I.T.	Choctaw **Nation** Choctaw **Roll**		FIELD NO.	152

Dawes' Roll No.	NAME	Relationship to Person First Named	AGE	SEX	BLOOD	TRIBAL ENROLLMENT		
						Year	County	No.
1	Leonard Sarah	Named	28	F	1/16			
2	" William F	Son	8	M	1/32			
3	" Emma J	Dau	4	F	1/32			
4	" Gracie A	Dau	1	F	1/32			
5	" John Roy	Son	7m	M	1/32	No4 born Aug 13th 1897		
6								
7								
8								
9	NOS 4 & 5 DISMISSED							
10	SEP 15 1904							
11								
12								
13								
14								
15								
16								
17								

TRIBAL ENROLLMENT OF PARENTS

	Name of Father	Year	County	Name of Mother	Year	County
1	Wm SJ Forsyth		Non Citz	Caroline Forsyth	Dead	Non Citz
2	John R Leonard		" "	No1		
3	" " "		" "	No1		
4	" " "		" "	No1		
5						
6						
7						
8	enrolled into the Indian of Aug 1898					
9	Parents of No5 are No1 and John R Leonard					
10	No5 Enrolled March 21 1901					
11	Post Office address of No1 Dixie I T March 21, 1901					
12						
13	Nos 1,2 &3 denied in 1896 case #465					
14						
15						
16					Date of for Enrollment.	9-22-98
17						

Present P.O. seems to be Dixie 3/21/0

7

RESIDENCE: Chickasaw
POST OFFICE: Chickasha   I.T.

Choctaw **Nation**   Choctaw **Roll**

CARD NO. **5108**
FIELD NO.

Dawes' Roll No.	NAME	Relationship to Person First Named	AGE	SEX	BLOOD	TRIBAL ENROLLMENT		
						Year	County	No.
1	Armstrong W. G.		46	M	IW	1896	Chick Dist	14272
2	" Mattie L	Wife	34	F	1/4	1896	" "	561
3	" Layton B	Son	10	M	1/8	1896	" "	562
4	" Bonnie D	Dau	12	F	1/8	1896	" "	563
5	" Rebecca W	Dau	4mo	F	1/8			

No2 Denied by C.C.C.C. as

" 3   7 " " " " " "Layton Buford Armstrong

8   or Layton Bufo[illegible]

4   9 " " " " " "Bennie Durant Armstrong

10   or Bonnie Durant Armstrong"

11 ---------------- Nos 2,3,4&5

12

13   No1

ACTION APPROVED BY
SECRETARY OF INTERIOR

JUL -9

JU

FORWARD

14

15

DENIED CITIZENSHIP BY THE CHOCTAW AND
CHICKASAW CITIZENSHIP COURT

Nos 2,3,4

TRIBAL ENROLLMENT OF PARENTS

	Name of Father	Year	County	Name of Mother	Year	County
1	W. H. Armstrong	Dead	Non Citz	Rebecca A Armstrong		Non Citz
2	W^m H Cundiff	" "		Nancy L Cundiff		Choctaw Ind
3	No1			No2		
4	No1			No2		
5	No1			No2		

6   Nos1 to 4 denied in 1896, cases # 477 & 478

7   No5 was born May 20th 1898

8   W.G. Armstrong admitted as an intermarried citizen

9

10 Admitted by the U.S. Court Ardmore, I.T. Aug 12- 1897 Court Case 129

11

12   No2 on 1896 roll as Mollie L Armstrong 10/10/99

13   No3 " 1896 " " Benny D "   "

14   No4 " 1896 " " Laten B "   "

This notation is an error
N°2 appears on 1896
Choctaw Roll as
Mollie L Anderson

15

16   9-22-98   2/109

17   Date of Application for Enrollment.

RESIDENCE:	Chickasaw Natn		Choctaw **Nation**			Choctaw **Roll**		CARD NO.	**5109**
POST OFFICE:	Ardmore I.T.							FIELD NO.	C 154

Dawes' Roll No.	NAME	Relationship to Person	AGE	SEX	BLOOD	TRIBAL ENROLLMENT		
						Year	County	No.
✓✓* 1	Shockly Ephraim E	First Named	29	M	1/16			
✓✓* 2	" Ava	Wife	24	F	IW			
✓✓* 3	" Mattie	Dau	6	F	1/32			
✓* 4	" Leverett	Son	2	M	1/32			
✓ 5	" Elva May	Dau	1 mo	F	1/32			
6								

DISMISSED
MAY 27 1904

DECISION RENDERED MAR 19 1906

Nos 1,2,3,4,5 GRANTED

NOTICE OF DECISION FORWARDED APPLICANT

NOTICE OF DECISION FORWARDED ATTORNEY FOR APPLICANT

COPY OF DECISION FORWARDED ATTORNEYS FOR CHOCTAW AND CHICKASAW NATIONS

RECORD FORWARDED DEPARTMENT

	TRIBAL ENROLLMENT OF PARENTS						
	Name of Father	Year	County	Name of Mother	Year	County	
1	John Shockly	Dead	Choctaw I&d	Fatima Shockly	Dead	Non Citz	
2	John Townsend	"	Non Citz	Mattie Townsend	"	" "	
3	No1			No2			
4	No1			No2			
5	No.1			No.2			

DENIED CITIZENSHIP BY THE CHOCTAW AND CHICKASAW CITIZENSHIP COURT

6	
7	Nos 1 to 4 inclusive admitted by Com in 1896 case
8	Admitted at South M'Allester[sic] by U.S. Court
9	Ava Shockly admitted as a citizen by intermarriage
10	No.5 enrolled November 12th 1900
11	For child of Nos 1&2 see NB (Apr 26-06) Card #773
12	[On back of page]
13	Mar 19 1906 Commissioner renders decision in accordance with the opinions of the Assistant
14	Atty General of Feby 10, 1905 (I.T.D. 10353-1904) and Dec 8 1905 (I.T.D. 3695-1905) in the
15	case of Lula West enrolling Nos1,3,4 and 5 as citizens by blood [Illegible] No.2 as a citizen by
16	intermarriage of the Choctaw Nation.

		Date of Application for Enrollment.	9-22-98	2/158

| 17 | |

Choctaw By Blood Enrollment Cards 1898-1914

RESIDENCE: Chickasaw Natn   Choctaw **Nation**   Choctaw **Roll**   CARD NO. **5110**

POST OFFICE: Ardmore   I.T.   FIELD NO.

Dawes' Roll No.	NAME	Relationship to Person First Named	AGE	SEX	BLOOD	TRIBAL ENROLLMENT Year	County	No.
1	Cude Lucy		19	F				
2	" Clayton	Son	1	M				
3	" William	Son	15 Days	M				
4	" Clarence	Son	2 wk	M				
5	" Vera	Dau	3 wks	F				
6								
7	#2-3-4-5-							
8								
9								
10								
11								
12								
13								
14								
15								
16								
17								

TRIBAL ENROLLMENT OF PARENTS

	Name of Father	Year	County	Name of Mother	Year	County
1	J. W. Hoffman		Non Citz	Mary Hoffman		Non Citz
2	G. W. Cude		" "	No 1		
3	" " "		" "	No 1		
4	" " "		" "	No 1		
5	" " "		" "	No.1		
6	No.1 denied in 1896, case # 1345					
7	Admitted by U.S. Court Ardmore I.T. Dec 22- 1898					
8						
9	No.4 Enrolled Oct 2nd. 1900					
10	No.1 is the wife of Green W Cude on Choctaw card #11391					
11	No 5 Born March 2, 1901; enrolled March 24, 1902					
12						
13	DENIED CITIZENSHIP BY THE CHOCTAW AND					
14	CHICKASAW CITIZENSHIP COURT					
15						
16				Date of Application 9-22-98		
17						

Record in Choctaw #5078

10

Choctaw By Blood Enrollment Cards 1898-1914

RESIDENCE:	Chickasaw Natn				CARD NO.	**5111**
POST OFFICE:	Earl I.T.	Choctaw **Nation**	Choctaw **Roll**		FIELD NO.	C 156

Dawes' Roll No.	NAME	Relationship to Person First Named	AGE	SEX	BLOOD	TRIBAL ENROLLMENT Year	County	No.
✓ *	1 Sessums Reuben L A	Named	26	M				
✓	2 " Lela E ✓	Dau	3mo	F				
✓	3 " Dora E	Dau	6wks	F				
	4							
	5							
	6							
	7 #2&3 DISMISSED							
	8 MAY 27 1904							
	9							
	10							
	11							
	12							
	13							
	14							
	15							
	16							
	17							

TRIBAL ENROLLMENT OF PARENTS

	Name of Father	Year	County	Name of Mother	Year	County
1	W R Sessums		Non Citz	Eliza A Sessums		Non Citz
2	No1			Ludie Sessums		" "
3	NO.1			" "		" "
4				" "		" "
5						
6						FEB 21 1907

7 No 1 denied in 1896, case # 452   NOTICE OF DEPARTMENTAL ACTION

8 Admitted by U.S. Court at South McAllester[sic] Jan 20th 1898 FORWARDED ATTORNEYS FOR CHOCTAW AND CHICKASAW NATIONS.

9 Court Case 10   MAY 18 1907

10   NOTICE OF DEPARTMENTAL ACTION

11 No2 enrolled Dec 14/99 subj to receipt of evidence of marriage FORWARDED ATTORNEY FOR APPLICANT.

12 of parents. [Illegible...] Received Feby 19, 1900   MAY 18 1907

13 No.3 Born Sept 6, 1901; and enrolled Oct 18, 1901   NOTICE OF DEPARTMENTAL

14   For children of No.1 see NB (x) ACTION MARKED APPLICANT. Apr. 26 06 F # 1260

15 No1 denied by C.C. C.C. Case #36 March 9 04   MAY 18 1907

16

17   Dec 14/99

Choctaw By Blood Enrollment Cards 1898-1914

RESIDENCE: Atoka County
POST OFFICE: Coalgate I.T.

Choctaw **Nation** Choctaw **Roll**

CARD NO. 5112
FIELD NO.

Dawes' Roll No.	NAME	Relationship to Person First Named	AGE	SEX	BLOOD	TRIBAL ENROLLMENT		
						Year	County	No.
1	Bailey Mary	First Named	40	F				
2	" Emanuel W	Son	18	M				
3	" William A	Son	13	M				
4	" Minnie B	Dau	11	F				
5	" Mary A	Dau	9	F				
6	" Homer Belton	Son of No 2	7mo	M				
7								
8								
9								
10								
11								
12								
13								
14								
15								
16								
17								

TRIBAL ENROLLMENT OF PARENTS

	Name of Father	Year	County	Name of Mother	Year	County
1	W.R. Sessums		Non Citz	Liza A Sessums		Non Citz
2	W L Bailey		" "	No 1		
3	" " "		" "	No 1		
4	" " "		" "	No 1		
5	" " "		" "	No 1		
6	No2			Ever Bailey		non citizen
7	Nos 1 to 5 denied by Com in 1896 case # 452					
8	No2 is now husband of Ever Bailey a noncitizen; evidence of marriage					
9						
10	No6 Born April 21, 1902; enrolled Nov 21, 1902					
11	"Emanuel W" admitted as "Emanuel"					
12						
13	Admitted by U.S. Court at South Mᶜ Allester[sic]					
14	Court Case 10					
15						
16	Nos 1 to 5 incl denied by C.C.C.C. Case #36 March 9 '04					

For child of No2 see (Act Apr 26'06) NB #1047

Choctaw By Blood Enrollment Cards 1898-1914

RESIDENCE:	Chickasaw Natn							
POST OFFICE:	Earl I.T.							

Choctaw **Nation**   Choctaw **Roll**

CARD NO. 5113
FIELD NO.

Dawes' Roll No.	NAME	Relationship to Person First Named	AGE	SEX	BLOOD	TRIBAL ENROLLMENT		
						Year	County	No.
1	Hill Maud	Named	19	F				
2	" Rosie L G	Dau	6wks	"				
3	" Joseph Frances	Son	9mo	M				
4								
5								
6								
7								
8								
9	MAX 1904							
10								
11								
12								
13								
14								
15								
16								
17								

TRIBAL ENROLLMENT OF PARENTS

	Name of Father	Year	County	Name of Mother	Year	County
1	J F Sessums		Non Citz	Lizzie Sessums		Non Citz
2	J. W. Hill		" "	No 1		
3	" " "		" "	No 1		
4						
5						
6						
7						
8						
9	No.1 denied in 1896, case # 452					
10	Admitted by U.S. Court at South McAllester[sic] Jan 20th 1898					
11	Court Case 10					
12						
13	Maud Hill was married to William Hill Dec 16th 1897					
14	Maud Hill wad admitted as Maud Sessums					
15	No.3 Born Jan 28, 1901: Enrolled Nov 7, 1901					
16				Date for	9-22-98	
17				No2 enrolled Dec 20/99		

DENIED CITIZENSHIP BY THE CHOCTAW AND CHICKASAW CITIZENSHIP COURT

Choctaw By Blood Enrollment Cards 1898-1914

RESIDENCE: Atoka County
POST OFFICE: Coalgate I.T.

Choctaw **Nation**   Choctaw **Roll**

CARD NO. 5114
FIELD NO.

Dawes' Roll No.	NAME	Relationship to Person First Named	AGE	SEX	BLOOD	TRIBAL ENROLLMENT		
						Year	County	No.
1	Sessums W.R.		66	M				
2	" R R	Son	16	M				
3								
4								
5								
6								
7								
8								
9								
10								
11								
12								
13								
14								
15								
16								
17								

TRIBAL ENROLLMENT OF PARENTS

	Name of Father	Year	County	Name of Mother	Year	County
1	Reding Sessums	Dead	Non Citz	Mary A Sessums	Dead	Non Citz
1	No 1			Eliza A Sessums		" "
3						
4						
5						
6						
7	Nos 1&2 denied in 1896, case # 452					
8	Admitted by U.S. Court South McAllester[sic] Jan					
9						
10						
11						
12						
13	For child of No2 see NB (Apr 26'06) #1268					
14						
15						
16						9-22-98
17						Date of Application for Enrollment.

14

Choctaw By Blood Enrollment Cards 1898-1914

RESIDENCE: Chickasaw Natn
POST OFFICE: Healdton   I.T.

Choctaw **Nation**   Choctaw **Roll**

CARD NO. **5115**
FIELD NO.

Dawes' Roll No.	NAME	Relationship to Person First Named	AGE	SEX	BLOOD	TRIBAL ENROLLMENT		
						Year	County	No.
✓✓*	1 Sessums Henry D	Named	23	M				
✓✓	2 " Pearley Eliza Ellen	Dau	4mo	F				
	3							
	4							
	5							
	6							
	7							
	8							
	9		P.O. address Maxwell, I.T.					
	10							
	11							
	12							
	13							
	14							
	15							
	16							
	17							

TRIBAL ENROLLMENT OF PARENTS

	Name of Father	Year	County	Name of Mother	Year	County
1	W. R. Sessums		Non Citz	Eliza A Sessums		Non Citz
2	No1			Sarrah J Sessums		" "
3						

DENIED CITIZENSHIP BY THE CHOCTAW AND
CHICKASAW CITIZENSHIP COURT

9 No1 denied in 1896, case # 452

10 Admitted by U.S. Court South McAllester[sic] Jany 20 1898 Court Case 10

11 No.1 is the husband of Sarrah J Sessums a non citizen. Evidence of

12   marriage filed Nov   190

13 No.2 Born July 5, 1901 Enrolled Nov. 2 1901

Date of Application for Enrollment

For child of No1 see NB (Apr 26 '06) #1269

15

Choctaw By Blood Enrollment Cards 1898-1914

| RESIDENCE: | Chickasaw Natn | | | | | CARD NO. | 5116 |
| POST OFFICE: | Wilson   I.T. | Choctaw **Nation** | Choctaw **Roll** | | | FIELD NO. | 161 |

Dawes' Roll No.	NAME	Relationship to Person First Named	AGE	SEX	BLOOD	TRIBAL ENROLLMENT		
						Year	County	No.
1	Williams Laura		27	F				
2	" Nevel	Son	5	M				
3	" Vera	Dau	1½	F				
4								
5	DISMISSED							
6	#3							
7	JAN 2							
8								
9								
10								
11								
12								
13								
14								
15								
16								
17								

TRIBAL ENROLLMENT OF PARENTS

	Name of Father	Year	County	Name of Mother	Year	County
1	Bert Wainscott		Non Citz	Mary Wainscott	Dead	Non Citz
2	Geo Williams		" "	No2		
3	" "		" "	No2		
4	DENIED CITIZENSHIP BY THE CHOCTAW AND					
5	CHICKASAW CITIZENSHIP COURT					
6						
7						
8	Nos 1&2 denied in 1896, case # 18					
9	"Vera" was born Apr 18th 1897					
10						
11	Admitted by U.S. Court Ardmore I.T. Dec 22 1897					
12	Court Case 88					
13						
14						
15						
16					Date of Application	
17						

16

Choctaw By Blood Enrollment Cards 1898-1914

RESIDENCE:	Chickasaw Natn								
POST OFFICE:	Ardmore I.T.	Choctaw **Nation**				Choctaw **Roll**	CARD No. **5117**		
							FIELD No.		

Dawes' Roll No.	NAME	Relationship to Person First Named	AGE	SEX	BLOOD	TRIBAL ENROLLMENT		
						Year	County	No.
1	Gamel George	Named	25	M				
2	" Alice	Wife	24	F				
3	" George Jr	Son	1½yr	M				
4	" Henry	"	6mo	"				
5	" Izetta	Dau	4mo	F				
6								
7								
8								
9								
10								
11								
12								
13								
14								
15								
16								
17								

Nos 3-4 & 5 _OF 102_

TRIBAL ENROLLMENT OF PARENTS

	Name of Father	Year	County	Name of Mother	Year	County
1	Geo Gamel	Dead	Non Citz	Kate Gamel		Non Citz
2	J.J. Rotenberry	" "		Rotenberry		" "
3	No 1			No 2		
4	No 1			No 2		
5	No.1			No.2		
6						
7	Nos 1&2 denied in 1896, case # 24					
8	No3 was born Apr 31-1897					
9	"George Gamel" admitted as "George Gammell"					
10						
11	Admitted by U.S. Court Ardmore I.T. Dec 21-1898 Court Case 109					
12	No.5 Born Nov. 20, 1901; enrolled April 11, 1902					
13						
14						
15						
16						
17						

DENIED CITIZENSHIP BY THE CHOCTAW AND CHICKASAW CITIZENSHIP COURT

No4 enrolled Nov 1/99

Date of Application for Enrollment.

17

RESIDENCE: Chickasaw Natn
POST OFFICE: I.T.

Choctaw **Nation**   Choctaw **Roll**

CARD NO. 5118
FIELD NO.

Dawes' Roll No.	NAME	Relationship to Person First Named	AGE	SEX	BLOOD	TRIBAL ENROLLMENT		
						Year	County	No.
1	Reynolds Daisy ²¹		17	F				
DP 2	" John M	Son	2mo	M				
3	" Rollo Marion	Son	7mo	M				
4	" Ella Francis	Dau	1mo	F				
5								
6								
7								
8								
9								
10								
11								
12								
13								
14								
15								
16								
17								

Nos 2-3&4 DISMISSED SEP 15 1904

TRIBAL ENROLLMENT OF PARENTS

	Name of Father	Year	County	Name of Mother	Year	County
1	Geo Gamel	Dead	Non Citz	Kate Gamel		Non Citz
2	Ben L Reynolds		" "	No i		
3	" " "		" "	No. i		
4	" " "		" "	No. i		
5						
6	No.1 denied in 1896, case # 24					
7	No1 admitted as "Daisy Gamble"					
8	No2 was born July 29th 1898					
9	Admitted by U.S. Court Ardmore Dec 21					
10	No.3 Enrolled December 7th, 1900					
11	No.4 born Jany 8th, 1902: Enrolled Feby 31, 1902					
12						
13						
14						
15						
16						
17						

DENIED CITIZENSHIP BY THE CHOCTAW AND CHICKASAW CITIZENSHIP COURT

9-22-98   /24
Date of Application for Enrollment.

Choctaw By Blood Enrollment Cards 1898-1914

RESIDENCE: Chickasaw Natn
POST OFFICE: Authur[sic] I.T.

Choctaw **Nation**   Choctaw **Roll**

CARD No. **5119**
FIELD No. C 164

Dawes' Roll No.	NAME	Relationship to Person First Named	AGE	SEX	BLOOD	TRIBAL ENROLLMENT Year	County	No.
1	Graham Tommie		31	M				
2	" Jala	Wife	27	F				
3	" Freda √	Dau	4	F				
4								
5			1907					
6								
7	CE OF RD NTAL N							
8	S FOR NS		APR 3- 1907					
9								
10	NT							
11			APR 3- 1907					
12	DEPARTMEN							
13	MAILED A		- 1907					
14								
15								
16	Record							
17								

TRIBAL ENROLLMENT OF PARENTS

	Name of Father	Year	County	Name of Mother	Year	County
1	C. G. Graham		Non Citz	Mary Graham		Non Citz
2	L. L. Blake		Intermarried	Thedoa Blake		" "
3	No 1			No 2		
4						
5						
6						
7						
8	Nos 1,2&3 denied in 1896, case # 902					
9	Admitted by U.S. Court Ardmore Dec 21st 1897 Court Case 122					
10						
11						
12						
13						
14						
15						
16				Date of Application for Enrollment	9-22-98	
17	For child of Nos 1&2 see NB (Apr 26-'06) #1144					

19

Choctaw By Blood Enrollment Cards 1898-1914

RESIDENCE: Chickasaw Natn　　　　　　Choctaw **Nation**　　Choctaw **Roll**　　CARD NO. **5120**
POST OFFICE: Pauls Valley, Ind Terr　　　　　　　　　　　　　　　　　FIELD NO.

Dawes' Roll No.	NAME	Relationship to Person First Named	AGE	SEX	BLOOD	TRIBAL ENROLLMENT		
						Year	County	No.
1	Hiegel Annie 27	First Named	23	F				
2	" Leo	Son	6	M				
3	" Dora	Dau	3	F				
4	" Frank	Son	2 wks	M				
5								
6								
7								
8								
9								
10								
11								
12								
13								
14								
15								
16								
17								

TRIBAL ENROLLMENT OF PARENTS

	Name of Father	Year	County	Name of Mother	Year	County
1	John Bolt		Non Citz	Sallie Bolt		Non Citz
2	Lee Hiegel		" "	No 1		
3	" "		" "	No 1		
4	" "		" "	No 1		
5						
6						
7	Nos 1,2&3 denied in 1896, case # 24					
8						
9						
10						
11						
12	Marriage evidence filed July 7, 1900					
13	No.1 is the wife of Lee C Heigel[sic] on Choctaw card #D					
14						
15						
16					9-22-98	
17						

20

Choctaw By Blood Enrollment Cards 1898-1914

| RESIDENCE: | Chickasaw Natn |
| POST OFFICE: | Ardmore   I.T. |

Choctaw **Nation**   Choctaw **Roll**

CARD NO. **5121**
FIELD NO. C 166

Dawes' Roll No.	NAME	Relationship to Person First Named	AGE	SEX	BLOOD	TRIBAL ENROLLMENT Year	County	No.
1	Coleman T. N. ✓	Named	30	M				
2	" Tommye ✓	Wife	24	F				
3	" Geraidine ✓	Dau	2	F				
4	" Nelse N[illegible]✓	"	1mo	"				
5								
6	#4 DISMISSED							
7	JAN 1905							
	ACTION APPROVED BY SECRETARY OF INTERIOR.							
9								
	NOTICE OF DEPARTMENTAL ACTION FORWARDED ATTORNEYS FOR CHOCTAW AND CHICKASAW NATIONS APR 3- 1907							
12	NOTICE OF DEPARTMENTAL ACTION NEY ANT.							
13					APR 3- 1907			
	NOTICE OF DEPARTMENTAL ACTION MAILED APPLICANT. APR 3- 1907							
15								
16	See Petition #C 55							
17	Record in Choctaw #5091							

TRIBAL ENROLLMENT OF PARENTS

Name of Father	Year	County	Name of Mother	Year	County
1 N. T. Coleman	Dead	Non Citz	Sophia Coleman		Non Citz
2 L. L. Blake	" "		Thedia Blake		" "
3 No1			No2		
4 1,2,3 No1			No2		
5					
6					
7					
8 Nos 1,2&3 denied in 1896, case # 902					
9 Admitted by U.S. Court Ardmore I.T. Dec 21st 1898 Court Case 122					
10					
11					
12					
13					
14					
15					
16					
17					No4 enrolled Oct 30/99

DENIED CITIZENSHIP BY THE CHOCTAW AND CHICKASAW CITIZENSHIP COURT

DECISION RENDERED Nov 22 190

RESIDENCE:	Chickasaw Natn								
POST OFFICE:	Powell, I.T.								

Choctaw **Nation** Choctaw **Roll**

CARD NO. **5122**
FIELD NO.

Dawes' Roll No.	NAME	Relationship to Person First Named	AGE	SEX	BLOOD	TRIBAL ENROLLMENT		
						Year	County	No.
1	Brewer, Mary C		30	F				
2	" Emma	Dau	5	"				
3	" Elmer	Son	3	M				
4	" Mary B	Dau	11 mo	F				
5								
6	#4							
7								
8								
9								
10								
11								
12								
13								
14								
15								
16								
17								

TRIBAL ENROLLMENT OF PARENTS

	Name of Father	Year	County	Name of Mother	Year	County
1	M W Askew		Non Citz	Rebecca Askew		Non Citz
2	G. F. Brewer		" "	No 1		
3	" "		" "	No 1		
4	" "		" "	No 1		
5	Nos 1,2&3 denied in 1896, case # 2					
6	Admitted by the U.S. Court Ardmore, I.T. Dec 21, 1897 Court Case No 72					
7						
8	No4 enrolled Dec 18/99. Affidavit irregular and					
9	returned for correction					
10						
11						
12	DENIED CITIZENSHIP BY THE CHOCTAW AND					
13	CHICKASAW CITIZENSHIP COURT					
14						
15	No.1 denied by C.C.C.C. as Mary Catherine Brewer or May Catherine Brewer					
16	For child of No1 see N.B. #1070					
17						

22

Choctaw By Blood Enrollment Cards 1898-1914

RESIDENCE:	Chickasaw Natn		Choctaw **Nation**		Choctaw **Roll**	CARD NO.	**5123**
POST OFFICE:	Lebanon I.T.					FIELD NO.	C 168

Dawes' Roll No.	NAME	Relationship to Person First Named	AGE	SEX	BLOOD	TRIBAL ENROLLMENT		
						Year	County	No.
✓ ✓ 1	Turner, Martha E 28		24	F				
2								
3								
4								
5								
6								
7								
8								
9								
10								
11								
12								
13								
14								
15								
16								
17								

DISMISSED DEC 3 1904

TRIBAL ENROLLMENT OF PARENTS

Name of Father	Year	County	Name of Mother	Year	County
1 M. W. Askew		Non Citz	Rebecca Askew		Non Citz
2					
3					
4					
5					
6					
7 No.1 denied in 1896, case # 2					
8 Admitted by the U.S. Court Ardmore, I.T. Dec 21, 1897 Court Case No 72					
9					
10		DECISION RENDERED.			
11					
12					
13					
14					
15					
16					3/34
17				Date of Application for Enrollment	9-23-98

DISMISSED

RECORD FORWARDED DEPARTMENT

23

Choctaw By Blood Enrollment Cards 1898-1914

RESIDENCE:	Chickasaw Natn							
POST OFFICE:	Ardmore, I.T.	Choctaw **Nation**			Choctaw **Roll**	CARD NO. 5124		
						FIELD NO. C 169		

Dawes' Roll No.	NAME	Relationship to Person First Named	AGE	SEX	BLOOD	TRIBAL ENROLLMENT		
						Year	County	No.
✓ 1	Zumwalt, Emily C		46	F				
2								
3								
4								
5								
6								
7								
8								
9								
10								
11								
12								
13								
14								
15								
16								
17								

TRIBAL ENROLLMENT OF PARENTS

	Name of Father	Year	County	Name of Mother	Year	County
1	Bill Whitney	Dead	Non Citz	Polly Whitney	Dead	Non Citz
2						
3						
4						
5						
6	No. 1 admitted in 1896 case # 1164					
7	Admitted by the U.S. Court, South McAlester, I.T.					
8	Case No.					
9						
10						
11						
12						
13						
14						
15						
16						1/39
17						9-23-98

Choctaw By Blood Enrollment Cards 1898-1914

| RESIDENCE: | Chickasaw Natn | Choctaw **Nation** Choctaw **Roll** | CARD NO. **5125** |
| POST OFFICE: | Center, I.T. | | FIELD NO. (170 |

Dawes' Roll No.	NAME	Relationship to Person First Named	AGE	SEX	BLOOD	TRIBAL ENROLLMENT		
						Year	County	No.
1	Whitney, James H		49	M				
2								
3								
4								
5								
6								
7								
8								
9								
10								
11								
12								
13								
14								
15								
16								
17								

TRIBAL ENROLLMENT OF PARENTS

	Name of Father	Year	County	Name of Mother	Year	County
1	Bill Whitney	Dead	Non Citz	Polly Whitney	Dead	Non Citz
2						
3						
4						
5						
6	No.1 admitted in 1896 case #1164					
7	Admitted by the U.S. Court South McAlester					
8	Court Case No 202					
9						
10						
11	No 1 denied by C C C [remainder illegible]					
12						
13	Daughter Dora J Whitney on Choctaw R. 580					
14						
15						
16						3/40
17						

Choctaw By Blood Enrollment Cards 1898-1914

RESIDENCE: Chickasaw Natn
POST OFFICE: Mill Creek, I.T.

Choctaw **Nation** Choctaw **Roll**

CARD NO. 5126
FIELD NO.

Dawes' Roll No.	NAME	Relationship to Person First Named	AGE	SEX	BLOOD	TRIBAL ENROLLMENT		
						Year	County	No.
1	Hunter, James		21	M				
2	" R. M	brother	15	"				
3								
4								
5								
6								
7								
8								
9								
10								
11								
12								
13								
14								
15								
16								
17								

TRIBAL ENROLLMENT OF PARENTS

	Name of Father	Year	County	Name of Mother	Year	County
1	J. F. Hunter	Dead	Non Citz	Hannah C Hunter	Dead	Non Citz
2	" "	"	" "	"	"	" "
3						
4						
5	No 1 Denied in 1896, case # 1334					
6	Admitted by the U S Court, Ardmore, I T Jany 17, 1898 Court Case No 73					
7						
8						
9	Removed from Texas to the Territory in August					
10						
11						
12						
13						
14						
15						
16						
17						

Choctaw By Blood Enrollment Cards 1898-1914

| RESIDENCE: | Chickasaw Natn | | | | | CARD NO. **5127** |
| POST OFFICE: | Purcell, I.T. | Choctaw **Nation** Choctaw **Roll** | | | | FIELD NO. C 172 |

Dawes' Roll No.	NAME	Relationship to Person First Named	AGE	SEX	BLOOD	TRIBAL ENROLLMENT		
						Year	County	No.
✓ 1	May Mary	Named	26	F				
✓ 2	" Annie E	Dau	6	"				
3	" Ora Amanda	"	1mo	"				
4	" Emma Lora	Dau	6mo	F				
5								
6								
7								
Nos 8	DISMISSED							
3&4 9	SEP 15 1904							
10								
11								
12								
13								
14								
15								
16								
17								

TRIBAL ENROLLMENT OF PARENTS

	Name of Father	Year	County	Name of Mother	Year	County
1	G. T. Hunter	Dead	Non Citz	Manda Hunter		Non Citz
2	Luther May	" "		No 1		
3	" "	" "		No 1		
4	" "	" "		No 1		
5						
6	No.1 denied in 1896, case # 1334					
7	Admitted by the U.S. Court Ardmore, I.T. Jany 17, 1898 Court Case No 73					
8						
9						
10	Removed from Oklahoma to the Territory in August					
11						
12	No2 was admitted as "Elvin					
13	No4 Born Oct 31, 1901; enrolled April 20, 1902					
14	DENIED CITIZENSHIP BY THE CHOCTAW AND					
15	CHICKASAW CITIZENSHIP COURT					
16						54
17				Date of Application		9-23-98

27

Choctaw By Blood Enrollment Cards 1898-1914

						TRIBAL ENROLLMENT		
Dawes' Roll No.	NAME	Relationship to Person First Named	AGE	SEX	BLOOD	Year	County	No.
✓	1 Hunter, John		41	M				
✓	2 " Kate	Wife	30	F				
	3 " Mary M	Dau	13	"				
	4 " Mattie C	"	11	"				
	5 " George W	Son	9	M				
	6 " Jesse J	"	4	"				
	7 " Isaac R	"	8mo	"				
	8 " Ernest Cecil	Son	1mo	M				

RESIDENCE: Chickasaw Natn
POST OFFICE: Dougherty, I.T.
Choctaw Nation   Choctaw Roll
CARD NO. 5128
FIELD NO. C 173

No 7 & 8 DISMISSED SEP 15 1904

TRIBAL ENROLLMENT OF PARENTS

Name of Father	Year	County	Name of Mother	Year	County
1 J S Hunter		Non Citz	Sarah Hunter	Dead	Non Citz
2 Tom Dixon		" "	Sarah Dixon		" "
3 No1			No2		
4 No1			No2		
5 No1			No2		
6 No1			No2		
7 No1			No2		
8 No1			No2		

9 Nos 1 to 6 denied in 1896, case # 1334
10 Admitted by the U.S. Court Ardmore, I.T. Jan 17 1898 Court Case No 73
12 No7 was born Dec 16,
13 No.8 Enrolled May 21, 1901

DENIED CITIZENSHIP BY THE CHOCTAW AND CHICKASAW CITIZENSHIP COURT

Date of Application for Enrollment. 9-23-98

28

Choctaw By Blood Enrollment Cards 1898-1914

Dawes' Roll No.	NAME	Relationship to Person First Named	AGE	SEX	BLOOD	TRIBAL ENROLLMENT Year	County	No.
1	Hunter, Clinton A 40	First Named	36	M				
2	" Mary 26	Wife	32	F	IW			
3	" Moses S	Son	13	M				
4	" Lillie M	Dau	11	F				
5	" Charles R	Son	9	M				
6	" Lottie L 10	Dau	6	F				
7	" Aleck E 5	Son	1	M				
8	" Dewey	"	1mo	"				
9	" Lonie 2	Son	2mo	M				
10								
11								
13								
14								
15								
16								
17								

DISMISSED

SEP 15 1904

TRIBAL ENROLLMENT OF PARENTS

	Name of Father	Year	County	Name of Mother	Year	County
1	J.S. Hunter		Non Citz	Sarah Hunter	Dead	Non Citz
2	Joe Cunningham		" "	Matilda Cunningham	Dead	" "
3	No 1			No 2		
4	No 1			No 2		
5	No 1			No 2		
6	No 1			No 2		
7	No 1			No 2		
8	No 1			No 2		
9	No.1			No.2		
10	Nos 1 to 6 inclusive denied in 1896, case # 1334					
11	Admitted by the U.S. Court Ardmore, I.T. Jany 7, 1898 Court Case No 73					
12						
13	No7 was born July 4, 1898					
14						
15	No.9 Enrolled December 3rd 1900			No8 Apr 13/99		
16						
17						

DENIED CITIZENSHIP BY THE CHOCTAW AND
CHICKASAW CITIZENSHIP COURT

Date of Application for Enrollment 9-23-98

	RESIDENCE: Chickasaw Natn							CARD No. 5130
	POST OFFICE: Dougherty, I.T.	Choctaw **Nation**		Choctaw **Roll**				FIELD No. C 175

Dawes' Roll No.	NAME		Relationship to Person First Named	AGE	SEX	BLOOD	TRIBAL ENROLLMENT		
							Year	County	No.
✓	1 Hunter, James	33		29	M				
✓	2 " Lula	25	Wife	21	F	IW			
	3 " Roy L		Son	15mo	M				
	4 " Manta Irvin		"	5mo	"				
	5 " Beulah		Dau	3mo	F				
	6								
	7								
	8								
	9								
	10								
	11								
	12								
	13								
	14								
	15								
	16								
	17								

DISMISSED SEP 15 1904

TRIBAL ENROLLMENT OF PARENTS

	Name of Father	Year	County	Name of Mother	Year	County
1	J.S. Hunter		Non Citz	Sarah Hunter	Dead	Non Citz
2	Wm Oats			[Illegible] Oats		
3	No 1			No 2		
4	No 1			No 2		
5	No 1			No 2		
6	Nos 1 & 2 denied in 1896, case # 1334					
7						
8						
9						
10						
11						
12						
13						
14						
15						
16						
17						

DENIED CITIZENSHIP BY THE CHOCTAW AND CHICKASAW CITIZENSHIP COURT

Date of Application

Choctaw By Blood Enrollment Cards 1898-1914

| RESIDENCE: | Chickasaw Natn | | | | | | | CARD NO. | 5131 |

RESIDENCE: Chickasaw Natn
POST OFFICE: Dougherty, I.T.

Choctaw **Nation**   Choctaw **Roll**

CARD NO. 5131
FIELD NO. C 176

Dawes' Roll No.	NAME	Relationship to Person First Named	AGE	SEX	BLOOD	TRIBAL ENROLLMENT		
						Year	County	No.
✓ 1	Cunningham Jas H		14	M				
✓ 2	" William A	brother	13	"				
✓ 3	" Gertrude	sister	11	F				
✓ 4	" Georgia	"	9	"				
✓ 5	" Mabel F	"	7	"				
✓ 6	" Joseph E	brother	5	M				
7								
8								
9								
10								
11								
12								
13								
14								
15								
16								
17								

TRIBAL ENROLLMENT OF PARENTS

	Name of Father	Year	County	Name of Mother	Year	County
1	W.D. Cunningham		Non Citz	Mary [?] Cunningham	Dead	Non Citz
2	" "		" "	" "	" "	" "
3	" "		" "	" "	" "	" "
4	" "		" "	" "	" "	" "
5	" "		" "	" "	" "	" "
6	" "		" "	" "	" "	" "
7						
8						
9						
10						
11						
12						
13						
14						
15						
16						
17						

Choctaw By Blood Enrollment Cards 1898-1914

RESIDENCE: Chickasaw Natn
POST OFFICE: Purcell, I.T.

Choctaw **Nation**   Choctaw **Roll**

CARD NO. **5132**
FIELD NO.

Dawes' Roll No.	NAME	Relationship to Person First Named	AGE	SEX	BLOOD	TRIBAL ENROLLMENT		
						Year	County	No.
1	Isgrigg, James	35	31	M				
2								
3								
4								
5								
6								
7								
8								
9								
10								
11								
12								
13								
14								
15								
16								
17								

DENIED CITIZENSHIP BY THE CHOCTAW AND CHICKASAW CITIZENSHIP COURT

TRIBAL ENROLLMENT OF PARENTS

	Name of Father	Year	County	Name of Mother	Year	County
1	Wm Isgrigg		Non Citz	Manda Isgrigg	Dead	Non Citz
2						
3						
4						
5	No 1 denied in 1896, case # 1334					
6						
7						
8						
9						
10						
11						
12						
13						
14						
15						
16						
17						

Choctaw By Blood Enrollment Cards 1898-1914

| RESIDENCE: | Chickasaw Natn | | | | | CARD NO. 5133 |
| POST OFFICE: | Lone Grove, I.T. | Choctaw **Nation** | Choctaw **Roll** | | | FIELD NO. C 178 |

Dawes' Roll No.	NAME	Relationship to Person First Named	AGE	SEX	BLOOD	TRIBAL ENROLLMENT		
						Year	County	No.
1	Gilliland, Effie May ²¹	Named	47	F				
2	" John E ⁴	Son	1mo	M				
3	" Dean Olander ²	Son	5mo	M				
4								
5								
6								
7	DISMISSED							
8	SEP 15 1904							
9								
10								
11								
12								
13								
14								
15								
16								
17								

TRIBAL ENROLLMENT OF PARENTS

	Name of Father	Year	County	Name of Mother	Year	County
1	John F Hunter		Non Citz	Kate Hunter	Dead	Non Citz
2	J.D. Gilliland		" "	No 1		
3	" " "		" "	No.1		
4						
5	No1 not in original application in 1896 case #1384					
6	....itted by the U.S. Court, Ardmore, I.T. Ja....... Court Case					
7						
8	No2 was born Aug 24, 1898					
9						
10	.....from Texas to the Territory in					
11						
12	DENIED CITIZENSHIP BY THE CHOCTAW AND					
13						
14	CHICKASAW CITIZENSHIP COURT					
15	No3 Enrolled May 24, 1900					
16						1/65
17	P.O. is now Dibble I.T.				Date of Application for Enrollment	9-23-98

| RESIDENCE: | Chickasaw Natn | Choctaw **Nation** | Choctaw **Roll** | | CARD NO. **5134** |
| POST OFFICE: | Kingston, I.T. | | | | FIELD NO. C 179 |

Dawes' Roll No.	NAME	Relationship to Person First Named	AGE	SEX	BLOOD	TRIBAL ENROLLMENT		
						Year	County	No.
1	Bounds, James H		44	M	IW	1896	Chick Dist	14364
2	" Fannie	Wife	33	F				
3	" Young W	Son	22	M	1/16	1896	Chick Dist	2038
4	" James Jr	"	20	"	1/16	1896	" "	2016
5	" Overton M	"	4	"				
6	" Frank	"	3	"				
7								
8	Oct 25/99 Nos 1-3-4							
9	were admitted by Dawes							
10	Com Case No 863. No3 as							
11	Young Walker Bounds No4							
12	as James Bounds Dawes Com							
13	Citz Record 1896 shows case							
14	as appealed to So Dist Court							
15	also that said Court admitted							
16	only Nos 2-5-6							
17	See Petition No 2068							

See Petition No 17

TRIBAL ENROLLMENT OF PARENTS

	Name of Father	Year	County	Name of Mother	Year	County
1	O. Bounds		Non Citz	Parthenia Bounds		Non Citz
2	Martin		" "			" "
3	No 1			Joanna Bounds	Dead	Choc Ind
4	No 1			" "	"	" "
5	No 1			No 2		
6	No 1			No 2		
7	Admitted by the U S Court Ardmore, I.T. Dec 21, 1897 Court Case No 155					
8						
9	James H Bounds married to Choctaw Indian by whom he					
10	had the children Young W Bounds and James Bounds Jr.					
11	After the death of his first wife he married a white woman					
12	by whom he has two children, Overton M Bounds and					
13	Frank Bounds					
14	No1 on 1896 roll as J H Bond					
15	No3 " 1896 " " Y W Bonds			Oct 25/99 Nos 3-4 also appear		
16	No4 " 1896 " " James Bond			on regular Choctaw Card No 271		
17						

Choctaw By Blood Enrollment Cards 1898-1914

RESIDENCE: Chickasaw Natn
POST OFFICE: Fleetwood, I.T.

Choctaw **Nation**   Choctaw **Roll**

CARD NO. **5135**
FIELD NO. C 180

Dawes' Roll No.	NAME	Relationship to Person First Named	AGE	SEX	BLOOD	TRIBAL ENROLLMENT		
						Year	County	No.
1	Vernon, M J	First Named	46	F	IW			
2	" Geo W	Son	21	M				
3	" Robert E L	"	16	"				
4	" Francis M	"	14	"				
5	" Maudie A	Dau	12	F				
6	" Samuel H	Son		M				
7	" Oscar Lee	G Son	1mo	M				
8								
#1-2-3-4-5-6-7- DISMISSED								
10								
11								
12								
13								
14								
15								
16								
17								

TRIBAL ENROLLMENT OF PARENTS

	Name of Father	Year	County	Name of Mother	Year	County
1	Chesley Slobaugh	Dead	Non Citz	Mary Slobaugh		Non Citz
2	Jackson Taylor	Dead	" "	No 1		
3	" "	"	" "	No 1		
4	" "	"	" "	No 1		
5	" "	"	" "	No 1		
6	" "	"	" "	No 1		
7	No 2			Callie P Vernon		noncitizen
8						
9	No 1 to 6 incl denied in 96, Case # 250					
10	Admitted by the U.S. Court South McAlester I.T. Aug 26, 1897					
11	Court Case No 98					
12	No 2 is now the husband of Callie P Vernon a non citizen. Evidence of marriage					
13	filed Sept 20, 1901. No 7 enrolled Sept. 20, 1901					
14						
15						
16	Sept 14.					7134
17	1901 PO Lonegrove IT					9-23-98

35

Choctaw By Blood Enrollment Cards 1898-1914

RESIDENCE: Chickasaw Natn
POST OFFICE: Terral, I.T.

Choctaw **Nation**   Choctaw **Roll**

CARD NO. **5136**
FIELD NO.

Dawes' Roll No.	NAME	Relationship to Person First Named	AGE	SEX	BLOOD	TRIBAL ENROLLMENT		
						Year	County	No.
✓ 1	Howard, Theodosha E	First Named	19	F	1/8			
2	" Robert L	Son	1½	M	1/16			
3	" Charley F	"	1	"	1/16			
4	" Mattie Belle	Dau	1 mo	F	1/16			
5								
6								
7								
8								
9								
10								
11								
12								
13								
14	#1-2-3-4- DISMISSED							
15								
16								
17								

TRIBAL ENROLLMENT OF PARENTS

	Name of Father	Year	County	Name of Mother	Year	County
1	Jackson Taylor	Dead	Non Citz	Martha J Vernon		Non Citz
2	U. P. Howard		" "	No1		
3	" " "		" "	No1		
4	" " "		" "	No.1		
5						
6	No1 denied in 96, Case # 250					
7	Admitted by the U.S. Court South McAlester I.T. Aug 26, 1898					
8						
9						
10	No1 was admitted as "Theodosha E Vernon"					
11						
12	No2 was born April 10, 1898					
13	No4 Enrolled Feby 8th 1901					
14						
15	Child Annie May Howard on Choctaw R. 577			No3 enrolled Jany 17, 1900		
16						
17						

36

Choctaw By Blood Enrollment Cards 1898-1914

RESIDENCE: Chickasaw Natn
POST OFFICE: Ryan, I.T.

Choctaw **Nation**   Choctaw **Roll**

CARD NO. 5137
FIELD NO. C 182

Dawes' Roll No.	NAME	Relationship to Person First Named	AGE	SEX	BLOOD	TRIBAL ENROLLMENT		
						Year	County	No.
✓✓ 1	Vernon D B		47	M	1/8			
✓ 2	" John H	Son	24	"	1/16			
✓ 3	" Chesley T	"	23	"	1/16			
✓ 4	" Sophia F	Dau	15	F	1/16			
✓ 5	" James W	Son	14	M	1/16			
✓ 6	" Caswell B	"	11	"	1/16			
✓ 7	" Clydie B	"	10	"	1/16			
✓ 8	" Iver L	Dau	8	F	1/16			
✓ 9	" Ida B	"	4	"	1/16			
10	" Pearl Magnolia	G Dau	3mo	F	1/32			
11								
13								
14								
15								
17								

#2-3-4-5-6-7-8-9-10 } DISMISSED DEC __ 1906

Sept 1901 Longrove IT

TRIBAL ENROLLMENT OF PARENTS

	Name of Father	Year	County	Name of Mother	Year	County
1	S. H. Vernon	Dead	Non Citz	Elizabeth Vernon	Dead	Non Citz
2	No 1			Margaret Vernon		" "
3	No 1			" "		" "
4	No 1			" "		" "
5	No 1			" "		" "
6	No 1			" "		" "
7	No 1			" "		" "
8	No 1			" "		" "
9	No 1			" "		" "
10	No 2			Minnie M Vernon		" "

DENIED CITIZENSHIP BY THE CHOCTAW AND CHICKASAW CITIZENSHIP COURT

11 Nos1 to 9 incl denied in 96, Case # 250
12 Admitted by the U.S. Court South McAlester I.T. Aug 21, 1897
13 Court Case No 98
14 Judgement of U.S. Ct admitting No1 to 9 incl vacated
15 No9 was admitted as "Ida Vernon"
16 No.2 is now the husband of Minnie M Vernon a noncitizen. Evidence of marriage filed Sept 20 1901
17 No10 Enrolled Sept 20, 1901

Date of Application 9-23-98

No1 No appeal to C.C.C.C. Case #81   No1 Denied by C.C.C.C. March 21 '04

Choctaw By Blood Enrollment Cards 1898-1914

RESIDENCE: Pickens County
POST OFFICE: Loco, I.T.

Choctaw **Nation**   Choctaw **Roll**

CARD NO. 5138
FIELD NO. C

Dawes' Roll No.	NAME	Relationship to Person First Named	AGE	SEX	BLOOD	TRIBAL ENROLLMENT Year	County	No.
✓✓	1 Reed, Serena	Named	42	F	1/2			
✓	2 " Thomas L	Son	25	M	1/4			
✓✓	3 " Eva	Dau	20	F	1/4			
✓	4 " Olive	"	18	"	1/4			
✓	5 " Carol	"	15	"	1/4			
✓	6 " Rutha	"	13	"	1/4			
✓	7 " Mabel	"	11	"	1/4			
✓	8 " Jesse	Son	8	M	1/4			
✓	9 " Josie	Dau	6	F	1/4			
✓	10 " Theron P	Son	8mo	M	1/4			
✓	11 " Zada Pearl	GrandDau	1mo	F	1/4			
✓	12 Calloway, Charles F	GrandSon	2mo	M	1/8			
	13				For child of No5 see NB (Act Apr 26-06) #951			
Not in original application in			"	"	" No3 "	"	"	" 1074
1896, see case # 969			"	children " No2 "	"	"	" 1081
	16 No12 Born Feby 2, 1902. Enrolled April 4, 1902							
No.5 is the wife of C.D. Bynum on Choctaw Card D #690								

TRIBAL ENROLLMENT OF PARENTS

	Name of Father	Year	County	Name of Mother	Year	County
1	Thos Barron	Dead	Non Citz	Mary Barron	Dead	Non Citz
2	W. J Reed	"	"	No1		
3	" "	"	"	No1		
4	" "	"	"	No1		
5	" "	"	"	No1		
6	" "	"	"	No1		
7	" "	"	"	No1		
8	" "	"	"	No1		
9	" "	"	"	No1		
10	" "	"	"	No1		
11	No2			Lizzie Reed		non citz
12	James T Calloway		non citizen	No.3		
13				For child of No5 see NB (Apr 26 1906) #951		

14 Admitted by the U.S. Court South McAlester, I.T Jan 27, 1898   Judgment vacated by Decree of C.C.C.C. Dec 17/02

15 Court Case No 105 No3 is now the wife of J.T. Calloway noncitizen. Evidence of marriage filed April 4, 1902

16 No10 was born Jan 27, 1898   For children of No4 see NB 947 (Act Apr 26-06)

17 No11 Born Sept 10, 1901 and enrolled Oct 16, 1901

145

Date of Application for Enrollment 9-23-98

No2 is now married to Lizzie Reed a noncitizen. Evidence of marriage filed Oct 18, 1901

Choctaw By Blood Enrollment Cards 1898-1914

RESIDENCE: Chickasaw Natn
POST OFFICE: Grady, I.T.

Choctaw **Nation** Choctaw **Roll**

CARD NO. **5139**
FIELD NO. C 184

Dawes' Roll No.		NAME	Relationship to Person First Named	AGE	SEX	BLOOD	TRIBAL ENROLLMENT		
							Year	County	No.
✓ ✓	1	Sharp, Viola	Named	36	F	1/2			
✓	2	" Robert E	Son	16	M				
✓	3	" Martin L	"	14	"				
✓	4	" John T	"	11	"				
✓	5	" J B	"	8	"				
✓	6	" Willie B	"	5	"				
✓	7	" Josephine	Dau	3	F				
✓	8	" Marie	"	1	"				
✓	9	" Samuel Hudson	Son	1mo	M				
	10								
	11								
	12								
	13								
	14	DISMISSED							
	15	MAY 27 1904							
	16								
	17								

TRIBAL ENROLLMENT OF PARENTS

	Name of Father	Year	County	Name of Mother	Year	County
1	Thomas Barron	Dead	Non Citz	Mary Barron	Dead	Non Citz
2	J. W. Sharp	"	" "	No1		
3	" "		" "	No1		
4	" "		" "	No1		
5	" "		" "	No1		
6	" "		" "	No1		
7	" "		" "	No1		
8	" "		" "	No1		
9	" "		" "	No1		
10	Not in original application in 896 case #969					
11	Admitted by the U.S. Court South M°Alester. I.T. Aug 25, 1897					
12	Court Case No 105					
13						
14	No8 was born July 3 1897					
15	No9 Enrolled December 14 1900					
16						
17						Date of Application for Enrollment 9-23-98

DENIED CITIZENSHIP BY THE CHOCTAW AND CHICKASAW CITIZENSHIP COURT

Choctaw By Blood Enrollment Cards 1898-1914

RESIDENCE:	Chickasaw Natn	P.O. Grady I.T.				CARD NO. **5140**
POST OFFICE:	Loco, I.T.	Choctaw **Nation**	Choctaw **Roll**			FIELD NO.

Dawes' Roll No.	NAME	Relationship to Person First Named	AGE	SEX	BLOOD	TRIBAL ENROLLMENT Year	County	No.
✓	1 Porter, Lou		37	F	1/4			
✓	2 " Archibald W	Son	19	M				
✓	3 " Due	"	17	"				
✓	4 " Lycurgus	"	15	"				
✓	5 " Thomas H	"	12	"				
✓	6 " Hugh	"	8	"				
✓	7 " Viola	Dau	6	F				
✓	8 " Henry W	Son	4	M				
✓	9 " Newman	"	2mo	"				
	10							
	11							
	12							
	13							
	14							
	15							
	16							
	17							

DISMISSED
MAY -- 1904

TRIBAL ENROLLMENT OF PARENTS

	Name of Father	Year	County	Name of Mother	Year	County
1	Thos Barron	Dead	Non Citz	Mary Barron	Dead	Non Citz
2	A. R. Porter		" "	No 1		
3	" "		" "	No 1		
4	" "		" "	No 1		
5	" "		" "	No 1		
6	" "		" "	No 1		
7	" "		" "	No 1		
8	" "		" "	No 1		
9	" "		" "	No 1		
10	Not in original application in case #969 of 1896					
11	Admitted by the U.S. Court South McAlester, I. T. Aug 25, 1897					
12	Court Case No 105					
13						
14	No9 was born July 20, 1898					
15						
16						
17						9-23-

DENIED CITIZENSHIP BY THE CHOCTAW AND CHICKASAW CITIZENSHIP COURT

40

Choctaw By Blood Enrollment Cards 1898-1914

RESIDENCE: **Chickasaw Natn**
POST OFFICE: **Ardmore, I.T.**

Choctaw Nation Choctaw **Roll**

CARD NO. **5141**
FIELD NO. C 186

Dawes' Roll No.	NAME	Relationship to Person First Named	AGE	SEX	BLOOD	TRIBAL ENROLLMENT		
						Year	County	No.
DEAD. 1	Boyd, John T	Named	60	M	I.W.	1896	Atoka	14350
2	" John T	Son	23	"	1/16	1896	"	2001
3	" Louis H	"	17	"	1/16	1896	"	2002
4								
5								
6								
7								
8								
9								
10								
11								
12								
13								
14								
15								
16								
17								

TRIBAL ENROLLMENT OF PARENTS

	Name of Father	Year	County	Name of Mother	Year	County
1	John Boyd	Dead	Non Citz	Susan Boyd	Dead	Non Citz
2	No 1			Annie Boyd	"	Choc Ind
3	No 1			" "	"	" "
4						
5						
6	Nos 1,2 & 3 transferred to No. 4 Card # 265					
7	Admitted by the U.S. Court, Ardmore I.T. Dec 2 1897					
8						
9	No 3 was admitted as "Lewis"					
10						
11	No 1 on 1896 roll as John Boyd					
12						
13						
14						
15	No 1 Died June 4, 1901 proof of death filed Oct 24, 1902					
16						3/152
17	Nos 2 & 3 transferred to Choctaw [remainder illegible]					9-23-98

41

Choctaw By Blood Enrollment Cards 1898-1914

RESIDENCE: Chickasaw Natn   Choctaw **Nation**   Choctaw **Roll**   CARD NO. **5142**
POST OFFICE: Overbrook, I.T.   FIELD NO.

Dawes' Roll No.	NAME	Relationship to Person First Named	AGE	SEX	BLOOD	TRIBAL ENROLLMENT Year	County	No.
1	Forbes, J A	First Named	57	M	1/4			
2	" Mary S	Wife	53	F				
3	" Sarah A	Dau	32	"				
4	" Edwin A	G. Son	7	M				
5								
6								
7								
8								
9								
10								
11								
12								
13								
14								
15								
16								
17								

TRIBAL ENROLLMENT OF PARENTS

	Name of Father	Year	County	Name of Mother	Year	County
1	W M Forbes	Dead	Non Citz	Rebecca Forbes	Dead	Non Citz
2	James Murphy		" "	Sarah Murphy		
3	No1			No2		
4	John Wilson		No Citz	No3		
5						
6						
7						
8	Nos 1 to 4 denied in 1896. Case # 447					
9	Admitted by the U.S. Court Ardmore I.T. Dec 22, 1897 Court Case No 111					
10						
11	No4 is an illegitimate child					
12						
13						
14						
15						
16						
17						

Choctaw By Blood Enrollment Cards 1898-1914

RESIDENCE: Chickasaw Natn   Addington I.T.   Choctaw **Nation**   Choctaw **Roll**   CARD NO. **5143**

POST OFFICE: ~~Orr, I.T.~~   FIELD NO.

Dawes' Roll No.	NAME	Relationship to Person First Named	AGE	SEX	BLOOD	TRIBAL ENROLLMENT		
						Year	County	No.
1	Addington, William		23	M	1/32			
2	" Clyde	Son	9mo	"	1/64			
3	" Chester	"	2mo	"	1/64			
4	" Otis Preston	"	7wks	"	1/64			
5								
6								
7								
8								
9	#2-3&4 DISMISSED							
10								
11								
12								
13								
14								
15								
16								
17								

TRIBAL ENROLLMENT OF PARENTS

	Name of Father	Year	County	Name of Mother	Year	County
1	Col Addington	Dead	Non Citz	Belle Addington	Dead	Non Citz
2	No 1			Betty Addington		" "
3	No 1			" "		" "
4	No 1			" "		" "
5	No.1 denied in 1896, case # 1282					
6	Admitted by the U.S. Court, South McAlester, I.T. Aug. 27-1897					
7	Court Case No [?]					
8						
9	No2 was born Nov 9, 1899					
10						
11	No3 enrolled Oct 30/99, subject to receipt of evidence of marriage of					
12	parents. Letter requesting such, this day: Received and filed, March 30th, 1900					
13	No.4 born Oct. 5, 1901: Enrolled Dec. 26, 1901					
14	DENIED CITIZENSHIP BY THE CHOCTAW AND					
15	CHICKASAW CITIZENSHIP COURT					
16						
17	For child of No1 see NB 940 (Act Apr 26-1906)					

43

Choctaw By Blood Enrollment Cards 1898-1914

RESIDENCE: Chickasaw Natn
POST OFFICE: Ardmore, I.T.

Choctaw **Nation**   Choctaw **Roll**

CARD NO. 5144
FIELD NO.

Dawes' Roll No.	NAME	Relationship to Person First Named	AGE	SEX	BLOOD	TRIBAL ENROLLMENT		
						Year	County	No.
1	Bottoms, William M		28	M	1/8			
2	" Ethel	Wife	24	F	IW			
3	" Allie A	Son	3	M	1/16			
4	" Bertha Ann	Dau	1	F	1/16			
5	" Clemmie Hugh	Son	3mo	M	1/16			
6	" Ruth	Dau	2wk	F	1/16			
7								
#5-6 8								
9								
#2 10								
11								
12								
13	No.4 was stricken from judgment as not being included							
14	in original application: was born March 21, 1897, subse-							
15	quent to date of filing of original application, and							
16	on submission of proper affidavits as to her birth							
17	is this day listed for enrollment: July 2, 1901							

TRIBAL ENROLLMENT OF PARENTS

	Name of Father	Year	County	Name of Mother	Year	County
1	Aleck Bottoms	Dead	Non Citz	Mary C Bottoms		Non Citz
2	B F McKilvy		" "	Cynthia M Kilvy		" "
3	No 1			No 2		
4	No 1			No 2		
5	No. 1			No. 2		
6	No. 1			No. 2		
7	Admitted by the U.S. Court, Ardmore, I.T. Dec 29, 1897					
8						
9	No 3 was admitted as "Allia A"					
10						
11	No.4 was born March 21 1897					
12	Nos 1,2 & 3 denied in 1896 case # 1896 case #8					
13	Nos 1-2 were remarried under Chickasaw law July 4, [illegible]					
14	No6 born Feby 8, 1902. Enrolled Feby 10, 1902					
15	No 5 enrolled May 24, 1906					
16	Evidence of birth of No6 filed July 2, 1902			3153		
17	2-67-1902 PO Roll, IT					

For children of Nos 1&2 see NB #1039- (Act Apr 26 '06)

44

Choctaw By Blood Enrollment Cards 1898-1914

RESIDENCE:	Chickasaw Natn
POST OFFICE:	Fox, I.T.

Choctaw **Nation**   Choctaw **Roll**

CARD NO. **5145**
FIELD NO. C 190

Dawes' Roll No.	NAME	Relationship to Person First Named	AGE	SEX	BLOOD	TRIBAL ENROLLMENT		
						Year	County	No.
1	Smith, Melissa J	Named	31	F	1/8			
2	" Ruby[sic] L M	Son	10	M				
3	" Martin E	"	9	"				
4	" Mauton[sic] L	"	6	"				
5	" Guy	"	4	"				
6	" Amos	"	2	"				
7	" Virgie	Dau	2mo	F				
8	" Vivian Grace	Dau	1mo	F				
9								
10	Not Enrolled [Remainder illegible]							
11								
12								
13	#7-8 DISM							
14	JAN .190							
15								
16								
17								

TRIBAL ENROLLMENT OF PARENTS

	Name of Father	Year	County	Name of Mother	Year	County
1	Amos Morris	Dead	Non Citz	Betty Morris	Dead	Non Citz
2	[Illegible] Smith	" "	No 1			
3	" "	" "	No 1			
4	" "	" "	No 1			
5	" "	" "	No 1			
6	" "	" "	No 1			
7	" "	" "	No 1			
8	" "	" "	No.1			
9	Nos 1 to 6 denied in 1896, case # 839					
10	Admitted by the U.S. Court, Ardmore, I.T. Dec 21, 1897, Court Case No 124					
11						
12	No7 was born July 15, 1898					
13	No.8 Enrolled July 6, 1901					
14						
15		NSHIP BY THE CHOTLAW AND				
16						
17						9-23-98

Choctaw By Blood Enrollment Cards 1898-1914

Dawes' Roll No.	NAME	Relationship to Person First Named	AGE	SEX	BLOOD	TRIBAL ENROLLMENT		
						Year	County	No.
1	Hignight, W. H.		74	M	I.W.			
2	" Elizabeth	Wife	45	F				
3	" Joseph	Son	18	M				
4	" Bula	Grand dau	6mo	F				
5								
6								
7								
8								
9								
10								
11								
12								
13								
14								
15								
16								
17								

No 4

TRIBAL ENROLLMENT OF PARENTS

	Name of Father	Year	County	Name of Mother	Year	County
1	[Illegible] Hignight	Dead	Non Citz	Drusilla Hignight	Dead	Non Citz
2	Thos Power	"	" "	Patsy Power		" "
	No 1			No 2		
4	No.5			Mattie Hignight		non-citizen
5	Nos 1,2&3 denied in 1896, case # 426					
6	Admitted by the U.S. Court, Ardmore, I.T. March 10, 1898, Court Case No 145					
7						
8	No.3 was on July 29, 1900 married to Mattie Vance, a non-citizen					
9	white woman					
10	No 4 born May 19th, 1901, Enrolled Nov. 13th [illegible]					
11						
12						
13						
14						
15						
16						
17						

Choctaw By Blood Enrollment Cards 1898-1914

RESIDENCE: Chickasaw Natn							CARD NO. 5147	
POST OFFICE: Ardmore, I.T.		Choctaw **Nation**		Choctaw **Roll**			FIELD NO.	

Dawes' Roll No.	NAME	Relationship to Person First Named	AGE	SEX	BLOOD	TRIBAL ENROLLMENT		
						Year	County	No.
1	Hignight J H	Named	34	M	1/16			
2	" Willie	Son	13	"	1/32			
3	" Lillie	Dau	11	F	1/32			
4	" Sarah	"	5	"	1/32			
5	" Lottie	"	3	"	1/32			
6	" Nevada	"	2mo	"	1/32			
7	" James Bryan	Son	2mo	M	1/32			
8	" Charles R	Son	2 wks	M	1/32			
9								
10	Nos 6-18&8 DISMISSED							
11								
12	SEPT 10 1904							
13								
14								
15								
16								
17								

TRIBAL ENROLLMENT OF PARENTS

	Name of Father	Year	County	Name of Mother	Year	County
1	W H Hignight		Non Citz	Elizabeth Hignight		Non Citz
2	No 1			Annie Hignight		" "
3	No 1			" "		" "
4	No 1			" "		" "
5	No 1			" "		" "
6	No 1			" "		" "
7	No 1			" "		" "
8	No 1			" "		" "
9	Nos 1 to 5 inclusive denied in 1896, case # 126					
10	Admitted by the U.S. Court Ardmore I.T. March 10, 1898, Court Case No 111					
11						
12	No 6 was born July 25 1901					
13						
14	No 7 Enrolled Oct 29th 1900					
15	No 8 Born Sept 13 1902 Enrolled Sept 25 1902					
16	DENIED CITIZENSHIP BY THE CHOCTAW AND					2165
17	CHICKASAW CITIZENSHIP COURT			Date of Application for Enrollment 9-23-98		

47

Choctaw By Blood Enrollment Cards 1898-1914

RESIDENCE: Chickasaw Natn
POST OFFICE: Davis, I.T.

Choctaw **Nation**   Choctaw **Roll**

CARD NO. **5148**
FIELD NO. C 193

Dawes' Roll No.	NAME	Relationship to Person First Named	AGE	SEX	BLOOD	TRIBAL ENROLLMENT Year	County	No.
1	Goins, James		65	M	1/2			
2	" Randolph	Son	21	"	1/4			
3	Padier, Lizzie	Dau	17	F	1/4			
4	Padier, Ira	Son of No3	10m	M	1/8			
5								
6								
7								
8								
9								
10								
11								
12								
13								
14								
15								
16								
17								

TRIBAL ENROLLMENT OF PARENTS

	Name of Father	Year	County	Name of Mother	Year	County
1	Jeremiah Goins	Dead	Non Citz	Sharaphine[sic] Goins	Dead	Non Citz
2	No 1			Adeline Goins		" "
3	No 1			"		" "
4	Seaborn Padier		noncitizen	N°3		
5						
6						
7	Nos 1,2&3 denied in 1896, case # 55					
8	Admitted by the U.S. Court, Ardmore, I.T. Dec. 21, 1897, Court Case No 127					
9						
10						
11						
12						
13	N°3 is now the wife of Seaborn Padier-non-citizen Evidence of marriage					
14	filed Oct. 6, 1902					
15	N°4 Born Dec 11, 1901, Enrolled Oct 6, 1902					
16						
17						

Choctaw By Blood Enrollment Cards 1898-1914

RESIDENCE:	Chickasaw Natn								CARD NO.	5149
POST OFFICE:	Davis, I.T.	Choctaw **Nation**		Choctaw **Roll**					FIELD NO.	194

Dawes' Roll No.	NAME	Relationship to Person First Named	AGE	SEX	BLOOD	TRIBAL ENROLLMENT		
						Year	County	No.
1	Goins, James		24	M	1/4			
2								
3								
4								
5								
6								
7								
8								
9								
10								
11								
12								
13								
14	#4-3- DISMISSED							
15	MAY 27 1905							
16								
17								

TRIBAL ENROLLMENT OF PARENTS

	Name of Father	Year	County	Name of Mother	Year	County
1	James Goins		Non Citz	Adeline Goins		Non Citz
2						
3						
4						
5						
6						
7	Not denied in 1896 case # 55					
8	Admitted by the U.S. Court, Ardmore, I.T. Dec. 21, 1897, Court Case No. 125					
9						
10						
11						
12						
13						
14						
15						
16					7168	
17					9-23-98	

Choctaw By Blood Enrollment Cards 1898-1914

					CARD NO. 5150
RESIDENCE: Chickasaw Natn		Choctaw **Nation**		Choctaw **Roll**	
POST OFFICE: Naples, I.T.					FIELD NO.

Dawes' Roll No.	NAME	Relationship to Person First Named	AGE	SEX	BLOOD	TRIBAL ENROLLMENT Year	County	No.
1	Goins, William		38	M				
2	" Clarence E	Son	9mo	"	1/4			
3	" Allie May	Dau	4mo	F	1/4			
4								
5								
6								
7								
8								
9								
10								
11								
12								
13								
14								
15								
16								
17								

TRIBAL ENROLLMENT OF PARENTS

	Name of Father	Year	County	Name of Mother	Year	County
1	Henry Goins	Dead	Non Citz	Sarah Goins		Non Citz
2	No1			Lizzie Goins		" "
3	No1			" "		" "
4						
5						
6	No1 denied in 1896, case # 55					
7	Admitted by the U.S. Court, Ardmore, I.T. Dec. 21, 1897, Court Case No 127					
8						
9	No2 was born Dec 13, 1897					
10						
11	No1 was admitted as William Henry Goins					
12						
13	Present P.O. address is [Illegible], Ind. Ter.					
14						
15	No1 Father of children on Choctaw R 483					
16	No3 Enrolled Sept 10th, 1900					
17						

50

Choctaw By Blood Enrollment Cards 1898-1914

RESIDENCE: Chickasaw Natn
POST OFFICE: Ardmore, I.T.

Choctaw **Nation**   Choctaw **Roll**

CARD NO. **5151**
FIELD NO. 196

Dawes' Roll No.	NAME	Relationship to Person First Named	AGE	SEX	BLOOD	TRIBAL ENROLLMENT		
						Year	County	No.
1	Paddieo, Eveline	Named	78	F				
2	" Tasso	Son	43	M				
3	" Reuben	"	23	"				
4								
5								
6								
7								
8								
9								
10								
11								
12								
13								
14	#1-3- DISMISSED							
15	MAY 27 190							
16								
17								

TRIBAL ENROLLMENT OF PARENTS

	Name of Father	Year	County	Name of Mother	Year	County
1	Jeremiah Goins	Dead	Non Citz	Sharaphine Goins	Dead	Non Citz
2	Antone Paddieo	"	" "	No 1		
3	" "	"	" "	No 1		
4						
5						
6						
7						
8	Nos 1, 2 & 3 denied in 1896, case # 55					
9	Admitted by the U.S. Court, Ardmore, I.T. Dec 21, 1897, Court Case No 12[?]					
10						
11						
12						
13						
14						
15						
16						
17						

Choctaw By Blood Enrollment Cards 1898-1914

Dawes' Roll No.	NAME	Relationship to Person First Named	AGE	SEX	BLOOD	TRIBAL ENROLLMENT		
						Year	County	No.
1	Paddieo, John	Named	51	M	1/4			
2	" James I	Son	9mo	"				
3	" Eugene	Son	1½	M				
4								
5								
6								
7								
8								
9								
10								
11								
12								
13								
14								
15								
16								
17								

TRIBAL ENROLLMENT OF PARENTS

	Name of Father	Year	County	Name of Mother	Year	County
1	Antone Paddico	Dead	Non Citz	Eveline Paddico		Non Citz
2	No 1			Melvey Paddieo		" "
3	No 1			" "		" "
4						
5						
6						
7	Nos[six] denied in 1896, case # 55					
8	Admitted by the U.S. Court, Ardmore, I.T. Dec 21, 1897, Court Case No 127					
9						
10	No2 was born Jany 22, 1898					
11						
12	No.1 - Evidence of marriage filed Sept 18, 1901					
13	No3 Enrolled Sept 27, 1901					
14						
15						
16						
17						

Choctaw By Blood Enrollment Cards 1898-1914

RESIDENCE: Chickasaw Natn
POST OFFICE: Ardmore, I.T.

Choctaw **Nation**   Choctaw **Roll**

CARD NO. **5153**
FIELD NO.

Dawes' Roll No.	NAME	Relationship to Person First Named	AGE	SEX	BLOOD	TRIBAL ENROLLMENT		
						Year	County	No.
1	Cox, Martha	Named	42	F	1/4			
2	" John L S	Son	1	M				
3								
4								
5								
6								
No2 7								
8								
9								
10								
11								
12								
13								
14								
15								
16								
17								

TRIBAL ENROLLMENT OF PARENTS

	Name of Father	Year	County	Name of Mother	Year	County
1	Antone Paddico	Dead	Non Citz	Eveline Paddico		Non Citz
2	Milton Cox	"	" "	No1		
3	DENIED CITIZENSHIP BY THE CHOCTAW AND					
4	CHICKASAW CITIZENSHIP COURT					
5						
6	No1 was denied in 1896, case # 55					
7	Admitted by the U.S. Court, Ardmore, I.T. Dec 21, 1897, Court Case No 127					
8						
9	No2 was born May 23, 1897					
10						
11	No1 was admitted as "Martha Paddico"					
12						
13						
14						
15						
16						
17					Date of Application for Enrollment	9-23-98

53

Choctaw By Blood Enrollment Cards 1898-1914

RESIDENCE: Chickasaw Natn
POST OFFICE: Ardmore, I.T.

Choctaw **Nation**   Choctaw **Roll**

CARD NO. 5154
FIELD NO.

Dawes' Roll No.	NAME	Relationship to Person First Named	AGE	SEX	BLOOD	TRIBAL ENROLLMENT		
						Year	County	No.
1	Paddico, James		37	M	1/4			
2	" Eva	Dau	9mo	F	1/8			
3	" Josie	"	8mo	"	1/8			
4								
5								
6								
7								
8								
9								
10								
11								
12								
13								
14								
15								
16								
17								

TRIBAL ENROLLMENT OF PARENTS

	Name of Father	Year	County	Name of Mother	Year	County
1	Antone Paddico	Dead	Non Citz	Eveline Paddico		Non Citz
2	No 1			Martha Paddico		" "
3	No 1			" "		" "
4						
5						
6						
7	No. 1 denied in 1896, case # 55					
8	Admitted by the U.S. Court, Ardmore, I.T. Dec. 21, 1897, Court Case No					
9	127					
10						
11	No2 was born Jan 15, 1898					
12						
13	No3 enrolled Nov 1/99, subject to receipt of evidence of marriage of					
14	parents Letter requesting same, this day.					
15						
16						
17						

Choctaw By Blood Enrollment Cards 1898-1914

RESIDENCE: Chickasaw Natn
POST OFFICE: Center, I.T.

Choctaw **Nation**   Choctaw **Roll**

CARD NO. **5155**
FIELD NO. C 290

Dawes' Roll No.	NAME	Relationship to Person First Named	AGE	SEX	BLOOD	TRIBAL ENROLLMENT		
						Year	County	No.
1	Jones, Frank C		32	M	IW			
2	" Sarah J	Wife	30	F	1/4			
3	" Jessie M	Dau	7	"	1/8			
4	" Gypsy	"	4	"	1/8			
5	" Bessie M	"	1½	"	1/8			
6	" James	Son	6	M	1/8			
7	" Flora Leona	Dau	8mo	F	1/8			
8								
9	" Buel[sic] Bradford	Son	5wks	M	1/8			
10	DENIED CITIZENSHIP BY THE CHOCTAW AND							
11	CHICKASAW CITIZENSHIP COURT							
12								
13	Nos DISMISSED							
14	7 & 9							
15	SEP 10 1904							
16	Nos 1 to [blank] denied in 1896, case # 55							
17	For child of Nos 1&2 see NB 96 - (Act Apr 26 - 06)							

TRIBAL ENROLLMENT OF PARENTS

	Name of Father	Year	County	Name of Mother	Year	County
1	Covington Jones	Dead	Non Citz	Rebecca H Jones	Dead	Non Citz
2	Spencer Morris	"	" "	Caroline Morris		
3	No 1			No 2		
4	No 1			No 2		
5	No 1			No 2		
6	No 1			No 2		
7	No 1			No 2		
8	Admitted by the U.S. Court, Ardmore, I.T. Dec. 21, 1897. Court Case No 127					
9	Nº 1			Nº 2		
10	No 3 was admitted as "James Jessie"					
11	No 4 " " "Ismaunde illegible)					
12	No 5 was born Feby 9, 1897					
13	Evidence of birth of No 5 received and filed Aug. 22d 1900					
14	No 7 Enrolled Aug. 22d, 1900					
15	No 9 Born Aug. 14, 1902; enrolled Sep 22, 1902					
16						7160
17					Date of Application for Enrollment	9-26-98

55

Choctaw By Blood Enrollment Cards 1898-1914

RESIDENCE: Chickasaw Natn   Choctaw **Nation**   Choctaw **Roll**   CARD No. **5156**

POST OFFICE: Center, I.T.   FIELD No.

Dawes' Roll No.	NAME	Relationship to Person First Named	AGE	SEX	BLOOD	TRIBAL ENROLLMENT		
						Year	County	No.
1	Morris, Kansas		22	F				
2	Hinkle, General Jackson	Son	1mo	M	1/16			
3								
4								
5								
6								
7								
8								
9								
10								
11								
12								
13								
14								
15								
16								
17								

No 2

TRIBAL ENROLLMENT OF PARENTS

	Name of Father	Year	County	Name of Mother	Year	County
1	Spencer Morris	Dead	Non Citz	Caroline Morris	Dead	Non Citz
2	Geo W Hinkle				Noi	
3						
4						
5						
6	No.1 denied in 1896, case # 55					
7	Admitted by the U.S. Court, Ardmore, I.T. Dec. 21, 1897, Court Case No 127					
8						
9						
10	No1 is now the wife of George W Hinkle					
11	on Choctaw					
12	No2 Enrolled July 2, 1901					
13	Full given name of No1 is Kansas E. See letter of George W. Hinkle					
14	filed July 25, 1901.					
15						
16						
17						

DENIED CITIZENSHIP BY THE CHOCTAW AND CHICKASAW CITIZENSHIP COURT

56

Choctaw By Blood Enrollment Cards 1898-1914

RESIDENCE: Atoka County								
POST OFFICE: Lehigh, I.T.	Choctaw **Nation** Choctaw **Roll**				CARD NO. **5157** FIELD NO.			

Dawes' Roll No.	NAME	Relationship to Person First Named	AGE	SEX	BLOOD	TRIBAL ENROLLMENT		
						Year	County	No.
1	Wheat, Margaret		15	F				
2								
3								
4								
5								
6								
7								
8								
9								
10								
11								
12								
13								
14								
15								
16								

DENIED CITIZENSHIP BY THE CHOCTAW AND CHICKASAW CITIZENSHIP COURT

TRIBAL ENROLLMENT OF PARENTS

	Name of Father	Year	County	Name of Mother	Year	County
1	J M Gardner		Non Citz	Sally Gardner	Dead	Non Citz
2						
3						
4						
5	No.1 denied in 1896, case # 55					
6	Admitted by the U.S. Court, Ardmore, I.T. Dec. 21, 1897, Court Case No 127					
7						
8						
9	Margaret L Wheat, was married June 1st, 1898, to Victor Wheat under license					
10	issued by the U.S. Court at Atoka, I.T. She was admitted as "Margaret					
11	Lugenia[sic] Os[illegible]					
12						
13						
14						
15						
16					Date of Application for Enrollment	186
17						9-23-98

Choctaw By Blood Enrollment Cards 1898-1914

RESIDENCE: Chickasaw Natn

POST OFFICE: Davis, I.T.

Choctaw **Nation**   Choctaw **Roll**

CARD NO. **5158**

FIELD NO.

Dawes' Roll No.	NAME	Relationship to Person First Named	AGE	SEX	BLOOD	TRIBAL ENROLLMENT Year	County	No.
1	Parks, K. C.		49	M	1/4			
2	" Nancy	Wife	44	F				
3	" Perry	Son	21	M				
4	" George W	"	17	"				
5	" Relbu[sic]	Dau	13	F				
6	" Spencer L	Son	11	M				
7	" Joe	"	8	"				
8								
9								
10								
11								
12								
13								
14								
15								
16								
17								

TRIBAL ENROLLMENT OF PARENTS

	Name of Father	Year	County	Name of Mother	Year	County
1	Wm Parks	Dead	Non Citz	Rebecca Parks	Dead	Non Citz
2	Pat McGonagill	" "	Emila McGonagill	" "
3	No 1			No 2		
4	No 1			No 2		
5	No 1			No 2		
6	No 1			No 2		
7	No 1			No 2		
8						
9	Denied in 1896, case # 552					
10	Admitted by the U.S. Court, Ardmore, I.T. Jan 20, 1899, Court Case No 133					
11						
12						
13						
14						
15		For children of No4 see NB #1012 (Act Apr 26-06)				
16		" " " No3 " " 1013 " " "				
17						

Choctaw By Blood Enrollment Cards 1898-1914

Dawes' Roll No.	NAME	Relationship to Person First Named	AGE	SEX	BLOOD	TRIBAL ENROLLMENT Year	County	No.
Refused	1 Parks, James A	Named	36	M	1/4			
Refused	2 " William R	Son	2	"	1/8	DEP		
Refused	3 " Luther T	"	3mo	"	1/8	COMMISS		
Refused	4 " James W.	Son	2mo	M	1/8	JUD		
	5							
	6	REFUSED JAN 19 1905						
	7	DECISION RENDERED.						
	8	COPY OF DECISION FORWARDED						
	9	ATTORNEYS FOR CHOCTAW AND CHICKASAW NATIONS. JAN 19 1905						
	10	NOTICE OF DECISION FORWARDED						
	11	ATTORNEY FOR APPLICANT						
	12	JAN 19 1905						
	13	COPY OF DECISION FORWARDED						
	14	APPLICANT JAN 19 1905						
	15							
	16	RECORD FORWARDED DEPARTMENT.						
	17	JAN 19 1905						

TRIBAL ENROLLMENT OF PARENTS

	Name of Father	Year	County	Name of Mother	Year	County
1	Wm Parks	Dead	Non Citz	Rebecca Parks	Dead	Non Citz
2	No 1			Mattie Parks		" "
3	No 1			" "	ACTION APPROVED BY	
4	No 1			" "	SECRETARY OF INTERIOR.	
5					MAR 30 1905	
6	Admitted by the U.S. Court, Ardmore, I.T. Jan. 20, 1898, Court Case No 133					
7				NOTICE OF DEPARTMENTAL ACTION		
8	No2 was born Jan 6, 1897			FORWARDED ATTORNEYS FOR CHOCTAW		
9	No3 " " June 15, 1898			AND CHICKASAW NATIONS. APR 1		
10				NOTICE OF DEPARTMENTAL ACTION		
11				FORWARDED ATTORNEY FOR APPLICANT.		
12				APR 1 NOTICE OF DEPARTMENTAL ACTION MAILED PARTIES HEREIN.		
13	"James H Parks, Sr" stricken from original judgment by nunc pro tunc order					905
14	of January 20, 1898. See testimony James A Parks taken at Colbert June 8, 1900 as					
15	to identity of James A Parks and "James H Parks Sr". No.1 was not a party					
16	to original application in 1896					3/190
17	No.1 is father of Nos 1,2 and 3 on Choctaw rejected card #730.					9-23-98

Date of Application for Enrollment.

59

RESIDENCE:	Chickasaw Natn							CARD No.	**5160**
POST OFFICE:	Ardmore, I.T.	Choctaw **Nation**			Choctaw **Roll**			FIELD No.	

Dawes' Roll No.	NAME	Relationship to Person	AGE	SEX	BLOOD	TRIBAL ENROLLMENT		
						Year	County	No.
1	Stout, Mary	First Named	39	F	1/4			
2								
3	REFUSED							
4	JAN 19 1905							
5	DECISION RENDERED.							
	COPY OF DECISION FORWARDED ATTORNEYS FOR CHOCTAW AND CHICKASAW NATIONS							
8	JAN 19 1905							
9	COPY OF DECISION FORWARDED							
10	APPLICANT JAN 19 1905							
11								
12	RECORD FORWARDED DEPARTMENT.							
13								
14	JAN 19 1905							
15								
16								
17								

TRIBAL ENROLLMENT OF PARENTS

	Name of Father	Year	County	Name of Mother	Year	County
1	Wm Parks	Dead	Non Citz	Rebecca Parks	Dead	Non Citz
2						
3						
4	Admitted by the U.S. Court, Ardmore, I.T. Jan 20, 1898, Court Case No 133					
5				ACTION APPROVED BY		
6				SECRETARY OF INTERIOR.		
7				APR 13 1905		
8						
9				NOTICE OF DEPARTMENTAL ACTION		
10				FORWARDED ATTORNEYS FOR CHOCTAW AND CHICKASAW NATIONS. APR 13 1905		
11						
12				NOTICE OF DEPARTMENTAL ACTION		
13				MAILED PARTIES HEREIN. MAR 31 1905		
14						
15						
16						
17						

Choctaw By Blood Enrollment Cards 1898-1914

RESIDENCE:	Chickasaw Natn						CARD No. 5161
POST OFFICE:	Davis, I.T.	Choctaw **Nation**		Choctaw **Roll**			FIELD No.

Dawes' Roll No.	NAME	Relationship to Person First Named	AGE	SEX	BLOOD	TRIBAL ENROLLMENT Year	County	No.
1	Harbolt, Maggie		26	F	1/8			
2	" Harvey	Son	6	M				
3	" Edgar	"	5	"				
4	" Deola	Dau	3	F				
5	" Obie	"	5mo	"				
6								
7								
8								
9								
10								
11								
12								
13								
14								
15								
16								
17								

TRIBAL ENROLLMENT OF PARENTS

	Name of Father	Year	County	Name of Mother	Year	County
1	K. C. Parks		Non Citz	Nancy Parks		Non Citz
2	Wilson Harbolt		" "	No1		
3	" "		" "	No1		
4	" "		" "	No1		
5	" "		" "	No1		
6						
7						
8	Nos 1 to 4 denied in 1896, case # 552					
9	Admitted by the U.S. Court, Ardmore, I.T. Jan 20, 1898, Court Case No 133					
10						
11						
12	No5 was born April 23, 1898					
13	DENIED CITIZENSHIP BY THE CHOCTAW AND					
14	CHICKASAW CITIZENSHIP COURT					
15						
16	For children of No1 see NB #986 (Act Apr 26-06)					
17						

61

Choctaw By Blood Enrollment Cards 1898-1914

RESIDENCE: Chickasaw Natn
POST OFFICE: Elk, I.T.

Choctaw **Nation**   Choctaw **Roll**

CARD NO. **5162**
FIELD NO.

Dawes' Roll No.	NAME	Relationship to Person First Named	AGE	SEX	BLOOD	TRIBAL ENROLLMENT		
						Year	County	No.
1	Gardner, J M		43	M	IW			
2	" James M	Son	18	"				
3	" Maudie E	Dau	12	F				
4	" Cora L	"	10	"				
5								
6								
7								
8								
9								
10								
11								
12								
13								
14								
15								
16								
17								

TRIBAL ENROLLMENT OF PARENTS

	Name of Father	Year	County	Name of Mother	Year	County
1	J C Gardner		Non Citz	Lucinda Gardner		Non Citz
2	No 1			Sally Gardner	Dead	" "
3	No 1			" "	"	" "
4	No 1			" "	"	" "
5						
6						
7	Nos 1 to 4 denied in 1896, case # 55					
8	Admitted by the U.S. Court, Ardmore, I.T. Dec. 21. 1897, Court Case No 127					
9						
10	No3 was admitted as "Manda Eldora Gardner"					
11						
12						
13						
14						
15						
16						
17						

Choctaw By Blood Enrollment Cards 1898-1914

RESIDENCE:	Chickasaw Natn		CARD NO.	**5163**
POST OFFICE:	Naples, I.T.	Choctaw **Nation** Choctaw **Roll**	FIELD NO.	C 208

Dawes' Roll No.	NAME	Relationship to Person First Named	AGE	SEX	BLOOD	TRIBAL ENROLLMENT		
						Year	County	No.
1	Southward, W C	Named	49	M	IW			
2	" Mary	Wife	49	F				
3	" Mary E	Dau	19	"				
4	" John F	Son	17	M				
5	" James M	"	14	"				
6	" Jessie M	Dau	12	F				
7	" Maggie M	"	8	"				
8	Ramsey, William Adolphus	Son of No 3	7mo	M				
9								
10								
11	No8 DISMISSED							
12	SEP 10 1902							
13								
14								
15	DENIED CITIZENSHIP BY THE CHOCTAW AND							
16	CHICKASAW CITIZENSHIP COURT							
17								

TRIBAL ENROLLMENT OF PARENTS

	Name of Father	Year	County	Name of Mother	Year	County
1	J F Southward	Dead	Non Citz	Mary P Southward		Non Citz
2	Jerry Goins	"	" "	Sharaphine Goins	Dead	" "
3	No1			No2		
4	No1			No2		
5	No1			No2		
6	No1			No2		
7	No1			No2		
8	William W Ramsey		Non Citizen	No3		
9	Nos 1 to 7 denied in 1896, case # 55					
10	Admitted by the U.S. Court, Ardmore, I.T. Dec 21, 1898, Court Case No 127					
11						
12	No3 was admitted as "Elizabeth Southward"					
13	No3 now the wife of William W Ramsey, Non Citizen, June 23rd 1902 Evidence of marriage					
14	filed Aug 5, 1902					
15	No8 Born Nov 29th 1901: Enrolled June 23rd 1902					
16					Date of Application for Enrollment	9-23-98
17						

63

Choctaw By Blood Enrollment Cards 1898-1914

RESIDENCE: Chickasaw Natn   Choctaw **Nation**   Choctaw **Roll**   CARD NO. **5164**
POST OFFICE: Naples, I.T.   FIELD NO.

Dawes' Roll No.	NAME	Relationship to Person First Named	AGE	SEX	BLOOD	TRIBAL ENROLLMENT Year	County	No.
1	Goins, Jeremiah Jr		32	M				
2	" Monroe	Son	23	"				
3	" William	"	18	"				
4	" Frank	"	16	"				
5	" Leonard	"	11	"				
6								
7								
8								
9								
10								
11								
12								
13								
14								
15								
16								
17	For child of No3 see NB #990 - (Act Apr 26-06)							

TRIBAL ENROLLMENT OF PARENTS

	Name of Father	Year	County	Name of Mother	Year	County
1	Jeremiah Goins	Dead	Non Citz	Sharaphine Goins	Dead	Non Citz
2	No 1			Alice Goins		" "
3	No 1			" "		" "
4	No 1			" "		" "
5	No 1			" "		" "
6						
7	Nos 1 to 5 denied in 1896, case # 55					
8	Admitted by the U.S. Court, Ardmore, I.T. Dec 21, 1898, Court Case No 12					
9						
10	Evidence of Marriage filed July 12, 1900					
11						
12						
13						
14						
15						
16						
17						

Choctaw By Blood Enrollment Cards 1898-1914

RESIDENCE: Chickasaw Natn
POST OFFICE: Purcell, I.T.

Choctaw **Nation** Choctaw **Roll**

CARD No. **5165**
FIELD No.

Dawes' Roll No.	NAME	Relationship to Person First Named	AGE	SEX	BLOOD	TRIBAL ENROLLMENT Year	County	No.
1	Goins, Reuben	Named	57	M				
2	" Mary	Dau	26	F				
3	" Cora	"	23	"				
4								
5								
6								
7								
8								
9								
10								
11								
12								
13								
14								
15								
16								
17								

TRIBAL ENROLLMENT OF PARENTS

	Name of Father	Year	County	Name of Mother	Year	County
1	Jeremiah Goins	Dead	Non Citz	Sharaphine Goins	Dead	Non Citz
2	No 1			Matilda Goins	"	" " "
3	No 1			" "	"	" " "
4						
5	Nos 1 to 3 denied in 1896, case # 55					
6	Admitted by the U.S. Court, Ardmore, I.T. Dec 21, 1897, Court Case No 127					
7						
8	The family of Reuben Goins have not removed to the Territory					
9						
10	As to residence of Nos 1 and 3 see testimony of No1					
11	No1 also appears on 1897 Chickasaw roll as Rube Goins					
12	a Chickasaw by intermarriage					
13	No2 is a resident of Austin, Texas: see testimony of No.1					
14	No2 is now the wife of Washington Lynch: a non citizen: July 6, 1901. Evidence					
15	of marriage to her former husband and also to Washington Lynch filed Aug 6, 1901. See					
16	also letter of No2 filed Aug 6, 1901					
17	Copy of bill of divorce from first husband filed Aug 24, 1901					

65

Choctaw By Blood Enrollment Cards 1898-1914

RESIDENCE: Chickasaw Natn

POST OFFICE: Naples, I.T.

Choctaw **Nation**   Choctaw **Roll**

CARD No. **5166**

FIELD No.

Dawes' Roll No.	NAME	Relationship to Person First Named	AGE	SEX	BLOOD	TRIBAL ENROLLMENT		
						Year	County	No.
1	Perice, Emily		56	F				
2								
3								
4								
5								
6								
7								
8								
9								
10								
11								
12								
13								
14								
15								
16								
17								

TRIBAL ENROLLMENT OF PARENTS

	Name of Father	Year	County	Name of Mother	Year	County
1	Jeremiah Goins	Dead	Non Citz	Sharaphine Goins	Dead	Non Citz
2						
3						
4						
5						
6	No.1 denied in 1896, case # 55					
7	Admitted by the U.S. Court, Ardmore, I.T. Dec 21, 1897, Court Case No 127					
8						
9						
10						
11						
12						
13						
14						
15						
16						
17						

Choctaw By Blood Enrollment Cards 1898-1914

| RESIDENCE: | Chickasaw Natn | | | | Choctaw **Nation** | Choctaw **Roll** | CARD NO. **5167** |
| POST OFFICE: | Ardmore, I.T. | | | | | | FIELD NO. C 212 |

Dawes' Roll No.	NAME	Relationship to Person First Named	AGE	SEX	BLOOD	TRIBAL ENROLLMENT		
						Year	County	No.
1	Malore[sic], Susan C		56	F	1/4			
2								
3								
4								
5								
6								
7								
8								
9								
10								
11								
12								
13								
14								
15								
16								
17								

TRIBAL ENROLLMENT OF PARENTS

	Name of Father	Year	County	Name of Mother	Year	County
1	Buckner Smith	Dead	Non Citz	Susan J Smith	Dead	Non Citz
2						
3	No1 denied in 1896, case # 1316					
4	Admitted by the U.S. Court, Ardmore, I.T. Dec 21, 1897, Court Case No 136					
5						
6	Removed from Texas to the Territory in [illegible]					
7						
8						
9						
10						
11						
12	December 15th 1898: This name is very likely "Malone". See testimony.					
13						
14						
15						
16						
17						

Date of Application for Enrollment 9-24-98

DENIED CITIZENSHIP BY THE CHOCTAW AND CHICKASAW CITIZENSHIP COURT

Choctaw By Blood Enrollment Cards 1898-1914

RESIDENCE: Chickasaw Natn
POST OFFICE: Ardmore, I.T.

Choctaw **Nation**   Choctaw **Roll**

CARD NO. **5168**
FIELD NO.

Dawes' Roll No.	NAME	Relationship to Person First Named	AGE	SEX	BLOOD	TRIBAL ENROLLMENT		
						Year	County	No.
1	Cartwright, Susan M		25	F	1/8			
2	" James D	Son	8	M				
3	" Alonzo A	"	5	"				
4	" Willie L		6mo	"				
5	" Winnie L	Dau		F				
6								
7								
8								
9								
10								
11								
12								
13								
14								
15								
16								
17								

TRIBAL ENROLLMENT OF PARENTS

	Name of Father	Year	County	Name of Mother	Year	County
1	J M Malore[sic]		Non Citz	Susan C Malore[sic]		Non Citz
2	James Cartwright		" "	No 1		
3	" "		" "	No 1		
4	" "		" "	No 1		
5	" "		" "	No 1		
6	Nos 1,2&3 denied in 1896, case # 740					
7	Admitted by the U S Court, Ardmore, I.T. Dec 31, 1898[ser. Court Case No 136]					
8						
9	Removed from Texas to the Territory Aug 10, 1898					
10						
11	Nos 4&5 are twins - born March 2, 18[illegible]					
12						
13	No4 died in April, 189[?]					
14						
15						
16						
17						

DENIED CITIZENSHIP BY THE CHOCTAW AND CHICKASAW CITIZENSHIP COURT

68

Choctaw By Blood Enrollment Cards 1898-1914

RESIDENCE:	Chickasaw Natn								
POST OFFICE:	Ardmore, I.T.								

Choctaw **Nation** Choctaw **Roll**

CARD NO. **5169**
FIELD NO. 214

Dawes' Roll No.	NAME	Relationship to Person First Named	AGE	SEX	BLOOD	TRIBAL ENROLLMENT		
						Year	County	No.
1	Thomas, William L	Named	30	M	1/8			
2	" Jesse T	Son	6	"				
3								
4								
5								
6								
7								
8								
9								
10								
11								
12								
13								
14								
15								
16								
17								

TRIBAL ENROLLMENT OF PARENTS

	Name of Father	Year	County	Name of Mother	Year	County
1	W. L. Thomas	Dead	Non Citz	Susan M Thomas		Non Citz
2	No 1			Mary E Thomas		" "
3						
4						
5						
6	Nos 1 & 2 denied in 1896 case # 1399					
7	Admitted by the U.S. Court, Ardmore, I.T. Dec 21, 1897, Court Case No 136					
8						
9	Removed from Texas to the Territory Aug. [illegible]					
10						
11						
12						
13						
14						
15						
16						
17						

Date of Application for Enrollment 9-21-98

69

Choctaw By Blood Enrollment Cards 1898-1914

RESIDENCE: Chickasaw Natn

POST OFFICE: Marlow   I.T.

Choctaw **Nation**   Choctaw **Roll**

CARD NO. 5170

FIELD NO.

Dawes' Roll No.	NAME	Relationship to Person First Named	AGE	SEX	BLOOD	TRIBAL ENROLLMENT Year	County	No.
1	Hill, J H	Named	33	M				
2	" Caroline	Wife	55	F				
3	" J T	Son		M				
4	" Emma	Dau	18	F				
5								
6								
7								
8								
9								
10								
11								
12								
13								
14								
15								
16								
17								

TRIBAL ENROLLMENT OF PARENTS

	Name of Father	Year	County	Name of Mother	Year	County
1	Hiram Hill		Non Citz	Matilda Hill	Dead	Non Citz
2	[illegible]			[Blank]		
3	No 1			No2		
4	No 1			No2		
5						
6						
7						
8	Nos 1 to 4 denied in 1896, case # 1375					
9	Admitted by the U.S. Court, Ardmore, I.T. Dec. 22, 1897, Court Case No 147					
10						
11	No 1 denied by C.C.C.C. as J H Hill or J W Hill					
12						
13						
14						
15						
16						
17						

Choctaw By Blood Enrollment Cards 1898-1914

RESIDENCE:	Chickasaw Natn		Choctaw **Nation**			Choctaw **Roll**	CARD NO.	**5171**
POST OFFICE:	Marlow I.T.						FIELD NO.	C 216

Dawes' Roll No.	NAME	Relationship to Person First Named	AGE	SEX	BLOOD	TRIBAL ENROLLMENT		
						Year	County	No.
1	Stover, P O	Named	46	M				
2	" Annie	Wife	43	F				
3	" Luther	Son	20	M				
4	" Lula	Dau	20	F				
5	" Alice	"	18	"				
6	" Orion	Son	13	M				
7	" Hubert	"	9	"				
8	" Maggie	Dau	7	"				
9	" Lillie	"						
10								
11								
12								
13								
14								
15								
16								
17								

TRIBAL ENROLLMENT OF PARENTS

	Name of Father	Year	County	Name of Mother	Year	County
1	L D Stover	Dead	Non Citz	Ann Stover	Dead	Non Citz
2	Hiram Hill	"	" "	Matilda Hill	Dead	" "
3	No1			No2		
4	No1			No2		
5	No1			No2		
6	No1			No2		
7	No1			No2		
8	No1			No2		
9	No1			No2		
10	Nos 1 to 9 denied in 1896, case # 1373					
11	Admitted by the U.S. Court, Ardmore, I.T. Dec 22, 1897, Court Case No 35					
12	No3 is the husband of Lanice Stover on Choctaw card #D699, Feby 3d, 1902					
13	No2 was admitted as " Annie "	No2 denied by C.C.C.C. as Anna B Stover				
14	No5 " " " Allie "	No4 " " " " Lulu Stover or Lula Stover				
15	No6 " " " "Olian"	No5 " " " " Ollie "				
16	No7 " " " "Herbert"	No6 " " " " Olian " or Olion Stover				
17		No7 " " " " Herbert " Date of Application for Enrollment 9-24-98				

RESIDENCE:	Chickasaw Natn					CARD NO. **5172**
POST OFFICE:	Marlow I.T.	Choctaw **Nation**	Choctaw **Roll**			FIELD NO.

Dawes' Roll No.	NAME	Relationship to Person First Named	AGE	SEX	BLOOD	TRIBAL ENROLLMENT		
						Year	County	No.
1	Stover, Theodore		22	M	1/16			
2								
3								
4								
5								
6								
7								
8								
9								
10								
11								
12								
13								
14								
15								
16								
17	For children of No1 see NB #1032 (Act Apr 26 '06)							

TRIBAL ENROLLMENT OF PARENTS

	Name of Father	Year	County	Name of Mother	Year	County
1	P. O. Stover		Non Citz	Annie Stover		Non Citz
2						
3						
4						
5						
6						
7						
8						
9						
10						
11						
12						
13						
14						
15						
16						
17						

72

Choctaw By Blood Enrollment Cards 1898-1914

RESIDENCE: Chickasaw Natn			Choctaw **Nation** Choctaw **Roll**			CARD No. **5173**	
POST OFFICE: Keller, I.T.						FIELD No.	

Dawes' Roll No.	NAME	Relationship to Person First Named	AGE	SEX	BLOOD	TRIBAL ENROLLMENT Year	County	No.
✓ 1	Hill, B. C.		46	M	1/8			
2	" Adelia	Wife	36	F	IW			
✓ 3	" Leona	Dau	12	"				
4	" Albert	Son	10	M				
✓ 5	" Ray	"	7	"				
✓ 6	" Bertha	Dau	5	F				
7	" Mada	"	1½	F				
8	" Emmet	Son	5mo	M				
9								
10								
11								
12								
13	No appeal to C.C.C.C.							
14	#1-2-3-4-5-6-7-8- DISMISSED							
15								
16								
17								

TRIBAL ENROLLMENT OF PARENTS

	Name of Father	Year	County	Name of Mother	Year	County
1	Hiram Hill	Dead	Non Citz	Matilda Hill	Dead	Non Citz
2	Wm McKinney	" "		Caroline McKinney	" "	
3	No1			No2		
4	No1			No2		
5	No1			No2		
6	No1			No2		
7	No1			No2		
8	No.1			No.2		
9	Nos 1,2,3,4,5&6 denied in 1896 case # 1365 No4 denied in 1896 as Wm A Hill					
10	Admitted by the U.S. Court, Ardmore, I.T. March 8 [illegible] Court Case					
11						
12	[illeg. illegible]					
13						
14						
15						
16	No8 enrolled May 24, 1900 7194					
17	1900 PO Woodford IT Date of Application for Enrollment 9-24-98					

73

Choctaw By Blood Enrollment Cards 1898-1914

RESIDENCE: Chickasaw Natn
POST OFFICE: Keller, I.T.

Choctaw **Nation**   Choctaw **Roll**

CARD NO. **5174**
FIELD NO.

Dawes' Roll No.	NAME		Relationship to Person First Named	AGE	SEX	BLOOD	TRIBAL ENROLLMENT		
							Year	County	No.
1	Hill, J M	55	First Named	51	M	1/8			
2	" Amanda		Wife	46	F	IW			
3	" Carrie		Dau	15	"				
4	" Grover		Son	13	M				
5	" Surany[sic]		Dau	11	F				
6	" Myrtie		"	9	"				
7	" Philip		Son	7	M				
8	" Jewell		Dau	5	F				
9	Jackson, Pearl		Grandau[sic]	4mo	F				
10									
11									
12									
13									
14									
15									
16									
17									

TRIBAL ENROLLMENT OF PARENTS

	Name of Father	Year	County	Name of Mother	Year	County
1	Hiram Hill	Dead	Non Citz	Matilda Hill	Dead	Non Citz
2	Jas Jomer		" "	Lucy Jomer		
3	No 1			No 2		
4	No 1			No 2		
5	No 1			No 2		
6	No 1			No 2		
7	No 1			No 2		
8	No 1			No 2		
9	Geoge[sic] Jackson		Non Citz	No 3		
10	Nos 1 to 8 denied in 1896, case # 1365					
11						
12	Admitted by the U.S. Court, Ardmore, I.T. March 8, 1898. Court Case No 149					
13						
14	No 9 Enrolled May 24. [illegible]					
15						
16	No. 8 is now the wife of George Jackson [remainder illegible]				7/194	
17	For child of No3 see NB 985 (Act Apr 26-1906)					

Choctaw By Blood Enrollment Cards 1898-1914

RESIDENCE: **Chickasaw Natn**			Choctaw **Nation**			Choctaw **Roll**	CARD NO. **5175**	
POST OFFICE: **Keller, I.T.**							FIELD NO. 220	

Dawes' Roll No.	NAME	Relationship to Person First Named	AGE	SEX	BLOOD	TRIBAL ENROLLMENT		
						Year	County	No.
✓	1 Bickham, Ada J	Named	23	F				
	2 " Culley	Son	2	M				
	3 Buchanan, Ada Edna	Dau	2mo	F				
	4							
	5							
#1-2-3	6 DISMISSED							
	7 DEC 12 1901							
	8							
	9							
	10							
	11							
	12							
	13							
	14							
	15							
	16							
	17							

TRIBAL ENROLLMENT OF PARENTS

Name of Father	Year	County	Name of Mother	Year	County
1 J M Hill		Non Citz	Amanda Hill		Non Citz
2 Culley Bickham	Dead	" "	No 1		
3 A M Buchanan		" "	No. 1		
4					
5 No 1 denied in 1896 case # 1365					
6					
7 Admitted by the U.S. Court, Ardmore, I.T. March 8, 1898, Court Case No 149					
8					
9 No. 1 is now the wife of A.M. Buchanan					
10			November 19th, [illegible]		
11 Evidence of marriage filed January 5, 1901					
12 Is not No. 1 now a resident of Texas? Jany 8th, 1901					
13 No.3 Enrolled January 29, 1901					
14					
15 1901- PO Dallas Tx					
16					1901
17			Date of Application for Enrollment		9-24-98

75

Choctaw By Blood Enrollment Cards 1898-1914

RESIDENCE: Chickasaw Natn
POST OFFICE: Keller, I.T.

Choctaw **Nation** Choctaw **Roll**

CARD NO. 5176
FIELD NO.

Dawes' Roll No.	NAME	Relationship to Person First Named	AGE	SEX	BLOOD	TRIBAL ENROLLMENT Year	TRIBAL ENROLLMENT County	TRIBAL ENROLLMENT No.
✓	1 Hill, Willie	First Named	27	M	1/16			
	2 " [illegible]	Son	2	"	1/32			
	3 " Clarice	Dau	4mo	F	1/32			
	4 " Olen	Son	1mo	M	1/32			
	5							
	6							
	7							
	8							
	9							
	10							
	11							
	12							
	13							
	14							
	15							
	16							
	17							

TRIBAL ENROLLMENT OF PARENTS

	Name of Father	Year	County	Name of Mother	Year	County
1	J M Hill		Non Citz	Amanda Hill		Non Citz
2	No 1			Lillie Hill		" "
3	No 1			" "		" "
4	No 1			" "		" "
5						
6						
7	No 1 denied in 1896 case # 1365					
8						
9	Admitted by the U.S. Court, Ardmore, I.T. March 8, 1898. Court Case No 149					
10						
11						
12						
13						
14						
15						
16						
17						

Choctaw By Blood Enrollment Cards 1898-1914

RESIDENCE:	Chickasaw Natn
POST OFFICE:	Keller, I.T.

Choctaw **Nation**   Choctaw **Roll**

CARD NO. **5177**
FIELD NO. C 222

Dawes' Roll No.	NAME	Relationship to Person First Named	AGE	SEX	BLOOD	TRIBAL ENROLLMENT		
						Year	County	No.
1	Simpson, Fannie	First Named	25	F	1/16			
2	" Clyde	Son	5	M	1/32			
3	" John	"	4	"	1/32			
4	" Grady	"	2	"	1/32			
5	" Mattie E	Dau	3mo	F	1/32			
6								
7								
8								
9								
10								
11								
12								
13								
14								
15								
16								
17	For child of No1 see NB #1033 (Act Apr 26 06)							

#1-2-3-4-5 DISMISSED DEC

TRIBAL ENROLLMENT OF PARENTS

	Name of Father	Year	County	Name of Mother	Year	County
1	J M Hill		Non Citz	Amanda Hill		Non Citz
2	V. Simpson		" "	No1		
3	" "		" "	No1		
4	" "		" "	No1		
5	" "		" "	No1		
6						
7	No.1 denied in 1896, case # 1365					
8						
9	Admitted by the U.S. Court, Ardmore, I.T. March 8, 1898, Court Case No 149					
10					PO address is now	
11						
12	Removed from Texas to the Territory Aug 16 [illegible]			Rush Springs, I.T.		
13						
14	Nos 2 and 3 not enrolled. No.4 enrolled, birth					
15	certificate to be supplied.			No5 enrolled Nov 1/99		
16						195
17					Date of Application for Enrollment	9-24-98

77

Choctaw By Blood Enrollment Cards 1898-1914

RESIDENCE: Chickasaw Natn   Choctaw **Nation**   Choctaw **Roll**   CARD NO. **5178**
POST OFFICE: Marlow, I.T.   FIELD NO.

Dawes' Roll No.	NAME	Relationship to Person First Named	AGE	SEX	BLOOD	TRIBAL ENROLLMENT		
						Year	County	No.
1	Miles, Laura	First Named	20	F	1/16			
2	" Mabel	Dau	2	"				
3	" Oma V	"	4mo	"				
4	" Lydia	"	5mo	"				
5	" Johnie Eveline	Dau	1mo	F				
6								
7								
8								
9								
10								
11								
12								
13								
14								
15								
16								
17								

TRIBAL ENROLLMENT OF PARENTS

	Name of Father	Year	County	Name of Mother	Year	County
1	J M Hill		Non Citz	Amanda Hill		Non Citz
2	Van Miles		" "	No 1		
3	" "		" "	No 1		
4	C. E. Miles		" "	No 1		
5	" "		" "	No 1		
6	Admitted by the U.S. Court, Ardmore, I.T. March 8, 1898, Court Case No 149					
7						
8						
9	No.1 denied in 1896, case # 1365					
10	Van (or C.E.) Miles, father of Nos 2,3,4 & 5 denied in 1896, case # 1365					
11						
12						
13						
14	No.4 Enrolled May 24, 1912					
15	No.5 Born March 28, 1901, enrolled April 25, 1902					
16						
17						

Choctaw By Blood Enrollment Cards 1898-1914

RESIDENCE: Chickasaw Natn   **Choctaw Nation**   Choctaw **Roll**   CARD No. **5179**
POST OFFICE: McGee, I.T.   FIELD No. 224

Dawes' Roll No.	NAME	Relationship to Person First Named	AGE	SEX	BLOOD	TRIBAL ENROLLMENT Year	County	No.
✓ 1	Hyden, D M		42	M	1/8			
2	" Sallie V	Dau	15	F	1/16			
✓ 3	" Pearl M	"	13	"	1/16			
✓ 4	" Samuel M	Son	12	M	1/16			
✓ 5	" Garnett M	Dau	7	F	1/16			
6	Wilcoxson, Claud Ray	G.Son	2wks	M	1/32			
7								
8								
#6 9								
10	JAN 24 1905							
11								
12								
13								
14								
15								
16								
17								

TRIBAL ENROLLMENT OF PARENTS

	Name of Father	Year	County	Name of Mother	Year	County
1	Sam'l Hyden	Dead	Non Citz	Nancy Hyden		Non Citzd
2	No 1			Dicey J Hyden	Dead	" "
3	No 1		" "	" "	" "	" "
4	No 1		" "	" "	" "	" "
5	No 1		" "	" "	" "	" "
6	William Wilcoxson		noncitizen	No3		
7	Nos 1 to 5 denied in 1896, case # 1344					
8	Admitted by the U.S. Court, Ardmore, I.T. Dec. 22, 1897, Court Case No 12					
9						
10	No2 admitted as "Sallie"					
11	No3 " " "Pearl "No4 " " "Sam"			Oct 20.99. No2 placed on		
12	No5 " " "Garnett"			Card No 4848 with husband.		
13	No2 on 1896 roll as "Sallie Hyden"			No3 is now the wife of Willie Wilcoxson		
14	No3 " 1896 " " "Pearl	" "		Evidence of marriage filed Aug. 17, 1901		
15	No4 " 1896 " " "Sam	" "		No.6 Enrolled Aug. 17, 1902		
16	No5 " 1896 " " "Garnett	" "				
17				Date of Application for Enrollment 9-24-98		

DENIED CITIZENSHIP BY THE CHOCTAW AND CHICKASAW CITIZENSHIP COURT

79

RESIDENCE:	Chickasaw Natn								
POST OFFICE:	McGee, I.T.								

RESIDENCE: Chickasaw Natn
POST OFFICE: McGee, I.T.
Choctaw **Nation** Choctaw **Roll**
CARD No. **5180**
FIELD No.

Dawes' Roll No.	NAME	Relationship to Person	AGE	SEX	BLOOD	TRIBAL ENROLLMENT		
						Year	County	No.
1	Hyden, Nancy D	First Named	82	IW				
2								
3								
4								
5								
6								
7								
8								
9								
10								
11								
12								
13								
14								
15								
16								
17								

TRIBAL ENROLLMENT OF PARENTS

	Name of Father	Year	County	Name of Mother	Year	County
1	Lockhart	Dead	Non Citz	[Illegible]	Dead	Non Citz
2						
3						
4						
5						
6	No 1 denied in 1896, case # 344					
7	Admitted by the U.S. Court, Ardmore, I.T. Dec. 22, 1897, Court Case No 114					
8						
9						
10						
11						
12						
13						
14						
15						
16						
17						

Choctaw By Blood Enrollment Cards 1898-1914

RESIDENCE:	Chickasaw Natn							CARD NO.	**5181**
POST OFFICE:	M°Gee, I.T.		Choctaw **Nation**		Choctaw **Roll**			FIELD NO.	C 226

Dawes' Roll No.	NAME	Relationship to Person First Named	AGE	SEX	BLOOD	TRIBAL ENROLLMENT		
						Year	County	No.
✓	1 Hood, Nancy J	Named	55	F	1/8	1896	Chick Dist	6172
✓	2 " Edward	Son	20	M	1/16			
✓	3 Mapes, Willie	G.Son	11	"	1/32	1896	Chick Dist	8936
	4							
	5							
	6							
	7							
	8							
No1 Denied by CCCC as "M J Hood"								
" 2	10 " " " " "Edward Hood"							
"	11 " " " " "Elwood Hood"							
" 3	12 " " " " "Willie Mopes"							
"	13 " " " " "Willie Mapes"							
	14							
	15							
	16							
	17							

TRIBAL ENROLLMENT OF PARENTS

	Name of Father	Year	County	Name of Mother	Year	County
1	Sam'l Hyden	Dead	Non Citz	Nancy D Hyden		Non Citz
2	J. T. Hood			No1		
3	W M Mapes			Lenora Mapes	Dead	Non Citz
4						
5						
6	Denied in 1896 case # 1341					
7	Admitted by the U.S. Court, Ardmore, I.T. Dec. 22, 1897 Court Case No 141					
8						
9						
10	No1 admitted ad "M.J"					
11						
12	No1 on 1896 roll as N. J. Hood					
13	No3 " 1896 " " William Mapes					
14						
15						
16						195
17					Date of Application for Enrollment	9-24-98

See C-112

81

Choctaw By Blood Enrollment Cards 1898-1914

RESIDENCE: Chickasaw Natn   Choctaw **Nation**   Choctaw **Roll**   CARD NO. **5182**
POST OFFICE: McGee,   I.T.   FIELD NO.

Dawes' Roll No.	NAME	Relationship to Person First Named	AGE	SEX	BLOOD	TRIBAL ENROLLMENT		
						Year	County	No.
1	Hyden, Martha		47	F	IW	1896	Chickasaw Dist	14665
2								
3								
4								
5								
6								
7								
8								
9								
10								
11								
12								
13								
14								
15								
16								
17								

TRIBAL ENROLLMENT OF PARENTS

	Name of Father	Year	County	Name of Mother	Year	County
1	[Illegible]	Dead	Non Citz		Dead	Non Citz
2						
3						
4	No 1 born in 1847; dist # 1341					
5	Admitted by the U.S. Court, Ardmore, I.T. Dec. 22, 1897 (court case No. 111)					
6						
7	No 1 is wife of Wm W Hyden on Choctaw card [illegible]					
8						
9	GRANTED OCT 1906					
10						
11						
12	COPY OF DECISION FORWARDED					
13	CHICKASAW NATIONS					
14						
15	RECORD FORWARDED DEPARTMENT					
16						
17						

Choctaw By Blood Enrollment Cards 1898-1914

RESIDENCE: Chickasaw Natn
POST OFFICE: McGee, I.T.

Choctaw **Nation**   Choctaw **Roll**

CARD NO. **5183**
FIELD NO. C 228

Dawes' Roll No.	NAME	Relationship to Person First Named	AGE	SEX	BLOOD	TRIBAL ENROLLMENT Year	County	No.
✓	1 Jackson, A M	Named	50	M	IW	1896	Chick Dist	14714
✓	2 " Sallie	Wife	48	F	1/8	1896	" "	7410
✓	3 " Oscar	Son	18	M	1/16	1896	" "	7412
✓	4 " Willie	"	15	"	1/16	1896	" "	7413
✓	5 " Albert	"	13	"	1/16	1896	" "	7414
✓	6 " Bessie	Dau	13	F	1/16	1896	" "	7415
	7 " Eddrie[sic] Beryl	Grand Dau	10	F	1/32	1896	" "	7415
	8							
	9							
	10							
	11							
	12							
	13							
	14							
	15							
	16							
	17							

#7 DISMISSED JAN 24 1905

TRIBAL ENROLLMENT OF PARENTS

	Name of Father	Year	County	Name of Mother	Year	County
1	Branch Jackson	Dead	Non Citz	Flavory Jackson	Dead	Non Citz
2	Saml Hyden		" "	Nancy Hyden		" "
3	No1			No2		
4	No1			No2		
5	No1			No2		
6	No1			No2		
7	No.3			Georgia Belle Jackson		non-citizen
8	Nos 1 to 6 denied in 1896, case # 1344					
9	Admitted by the U.S. Court, Ardmore, I.T. Dec. 22, 1897, Court Case No 141					
10						
11	No2 on 1896 roll as Sally Jackson					
12	No.3 is now the husband of Georgia Belle Jackson a non citizen. Evidence					
13	of marriage filed May 23, 1901					
14	No.7 Enrolled May 23, 1901					
15	DENIED CITIZENSHIP BY THE CHOCTAW AND					
16	CHICKASAW CITIZENSHIP COURT					
17						

83

RESIDENCE:	Chickasaw Natn							CARD NO. 5184
POST OFFICE:	McGee, I.T.		Choctaw **Nation**	Choctaw **Roll**				FIELD NO.

Dawes' Roll No.	NAME	Relationship to Person First Named	AGE	SEX	BLOOD	TRIBAL ENROLLMENT		
						Year	County	No.
✓ 1	Hyden, J M		46	M	1/8	1896	Chick Dist	6187
✓ 2	" Mollie	Wife	36	F	IW	1896	" "	14675
3	" George	Son	16	M	1/16	1896	" "	6188
✓ 4	" Cleveland	"	14	"	1/16	1896	" "	6191
✓ 5	" Maud	Dau	9	F	1/16	1896	" "	6190
✓ 6	" Mollie	"	5	"	1/16	1896	" "	6189
7	" Nancy [Illegible]	"	4mo	F	1/16			
8								
9								
10	No2 denied by C.C.C.C. as "Mrs Mollie Hyden"							
11								
12								
13								
14								
15	#3 DISMISSED							
16	FEB -9 1905							
17								

	TRIBAL ENROLLMENT OF PARENTS						
	Name of Father	Year	County	Name of Mother	Year	County	
1	Saml Hyden	Dead	Non Citz	Nancy Hyden		Non Citz	
2	G.W. Featherston	" "		Mary Featherston	Dead	" "	
3	No1			No2			
4	No1			No2			
5	No1			No2			
6	No1			No2			
7	No1			No2			
8							
9	Nos 1 to 6 denied in 1896, case # 1344						
10	Admitted by the U.S. Court, Ardmore, I.T. Dec. 22, 1897, Court Case No 141						
11							
12							
13	No5 on 1896 roll a Maggie Hyden						
14	No.7 Enrolled January 19, 1901						
15							
16							
17							

DENIED CITIZENSHIP BY THE CHOCTAW AND CHICKASAW CITIZENSHIP COURT

Choctaw By Blood Enrollment Cards 1898-1914

RESIDENCE:	Chickasaw Natn						CARD No. 5185
POST OFFICE:	McGee, I.T.	Choctaw **Nation**	Choctaw **Roll**				FIELD No. (230)

Dawes' Roll No.	NAME	Relationship to Person First Named	AGE	SEX	BLOOD	TRIBAL ENROLLMENT		
						Year	County	No.
1	Smith, Cecil		24	M	IW	1896	Chick Dist	15084
2	" Maud	Wife	21	F	1/16	1896	" "	7411
3	" Mumford M	Son	8mo	M	1/32			
4	" Cecil Jackson	Son	2mo	M	1/32			
5								
6								
#3-4	7							
8								
9								
10								
11								
12								
13								
14								
15								
16								
17								

#3-4 DISMISSED

TRIBAL ENROLLMENT OF PARENTS

	Name of Father	Year	County	Name of Mother	Year	County
1	Mumford Smith		Non Citz	Annie Smith		Non Citz
2	A M Jackson		" "	Sally Jackson		" "
3	No1			No2		
4	No1			No2		
5	Nos 1&2 denied in 1896, case # 1344					
6	Admitted by the U.S. Court, Ardmore, I.T. Dec. 22, 1897, Court Case No 141					
7						
8	No3 was born Jan 13, 1898					
9						
10	No1 on 1896 roll as Sesel Smith					
11	No2 " 1896 " " Maud Jackson					
12	No4 enrolled November 14th 1900					
13						
14						
15						
16						
17						

DENIED CITIZENSHIP BY THE CHOCTAW AND CHICKASAW CITIZENSHIP COURT

Date of Application for Enrollment 9-24-98

85

Choctaw By Blood Enrollment Cards 1898-1914

RESIDENCE: Chickasaw Natn   Choctaw **Nation**   Choctaw **Roll**   CARD NO. **5186**
POST OFFICE: FIELD NO.

Dawes' Roll No.	NAME	Relationship to Person	AGE	SEX	BLOOD	TRIBAL ENROLLMENT		
						Year	County	No.
1	Connely [sic], James H	First Named	35	M	IW			
2	" Alberta E	Wife	21	F	1/16			
3	" Willaim W	Son	2½	M				
4	" Virginia C	Dau	4mo	F				
5	" Lawrence H	Son	4mo	M		New born		
6								
7								
8								
9								
10								
11								
12								
13								
14								
15								
16								
17								

TRIBAL ENROLLMENT OF PARENTS

	Name of Father	Year	County	Name of Mother	Year	County
1	R M Connely		Non Citz	Catherine Connely	Dead	Non Citz
2	Shepherd Evans		" "	Virginia Evans	"	" "
3	No 1			No 2		
4	No 1			No 2		
5	No. 1			No. 2		
6	Nos 1,2&3 denied in 1896, case # 1344					
7	Admitted by the U.S. Court, Ardmore, I.T. Dec. 22, 1897, Court Case No 141					
8	Judgement of [remainder illegible]					
9	Admitted under name of Conley					
10						
11	No2 admitted as Albert Evans					
12						
13	No.5 Enrolled June 8, 1900					
14						
15						
16						
17						

Choctaw By Blood Enrollment Cards 1898-1914

RESIDENCE: Chickasaw Natn	POST OFFICE: Ardmore, I.T.		Choctaw **Nation**			Choctaw **Roll**	CARD NO. **5187**	FIELD NO. 232

Dawes' Roll No.	NAME	Relationship to Person First Named	AGE	SEX	BLOOD	TRIBAL ENROLLMENT		
						Year	County	No.
✓ 1	Pruitt, Henry	Named	31	M	IW	1896	Chick Dist	14952
✓ 2	" Nancy	Wife	26	F	1/16	1896	" "	10618
✓ 3	" John H	Son	10	M	1/32	1896	" "	10620
✓ 4	" Ernest A	"	8	"	1/32	1896	" "	10623
✓ 5	" Lula T	Dau	7	F	1/32	1896	" "	10624
6								
7								
8								
9								
10								
11								
12								
13								
14								
15								
16								
17								

TRIBAL ENROLLMENT OF PARENTS

	Name of Father	Year	County	Name of Mother	Year	County
1	T J Pruitt	Dead	Non Citz	Oriulha[sic] Pruitt		Non Citz
2	A M Jackson			Sally Jackson		" "
3	No1			No2		
4	No1			No2		
5	No1			No2		

6 Nos 1 to 5 denied in 1896, case # 1344

7 Admitted by the U.S. Court, Ardmore, I.T. Dec. 22, 1897, Court Case No 141

8

9

10 No4 admitted as "Evans C"

11   Dec 6/99 Examine record of 1896

12 No1 on 1896 roll as Henry Pruitt   and see if original application was

13 No2 " 1896 " " Nancy "   made to Commission

14 No3 " 1896 " " John "

15 No4 " 1896 " " Ernest A "

16 No5 " 1896 " " Urie[sic] "

17

Date of Application for Enrollment 9-24-98

87

Choctaw By Blood Enrollment Cards 1898-1914

RESIDENCE: Chickasaw Natn
POST OFFICE: Province, I.T.

Choctaw **Nation** Choctaw **Roll**

CARD NO. 5188
FIELD NO.

Dawes' Roll No.	NAME	Relationship to Person First Named	AGE	SEX	BLOOD	TRIBAL ENROLLMENT Year	County	No.
1 ✓ *	Shockley Chas L	First Named	31	M	1/16			
2 ✓ *	" Callie	Wife	20	F	1W			
3 ✓ *	" Albert	Son	3	M	1/32			
4 ✓	" ✓ Hurman	"	1½	"	1/32			
5 ✓	" ✓ Mamie	Dau	2mo	F	1/32			
6								
7								
8								
9								
10								
11								
12								
13								
14								
15								
16								
17								

DENIED CITIZENSHIP BY THE CHOCTAW AND
CHICKASAW CITIZENSHIP COURT

TRIBAL ENROLLMENT OF PARENTS

	Name of Father	Year	County	Name of Mother	Year	County
1	John Shockley		Non Citz	Fatina Shockley	Dead	Non Citz
2	Young Mitchussen[sic]			Fanny Mitchussen		" "
3	No 1			No 2		
4	No 1			No 2		
5	No 1			No 2		
6						
7	Nos 1,2&3 admitted in 1896 case #955					
8	Admitted by the U.S. Court, Ardmore, I.T. Dec. 22, 1897, Court Case No 226					
9						
10						
11						
12						
13						
14						
15						
16						
17						

88

Choctaw By Blood Enrollment Cards 1898-1914

RESIDENCE: State of Arkansas POST OFFICE: Cecil Ark.		Choctaw **Nation** Choctaw **Roll**				CARD NO. **5189** FIELD NO. C 234		

Dawes' Roll No.	NAME	Relationship to Person	AGE	SEX	BLOOD	TRIBAL ENROLLMENT		
						Year	County	No.
✓ * 1	Shockley Elzora	First Named	32	F				
✓ * 2	" Ethel	Dau	7	"				
3								
4								
5								
6		DECISION RENDERED. MAR 19 1906						
7		REFUSED						
8								
9								
10								
11								
12								
13								
14								
15								
16								
17								

TRIBAL ENROLLMENT OF PARENTS

	Name of Father	Year	County	Name of Mother	Year	County
1	John Gage		Non Citz			Non Citz
2	Willie Shockley	Dead	Choc Citz	No 1		
3						
4						
5						
6	Nos 1&2 admitted in 1896 case #955					
7	Admitted by the U.S. Court, South McAlester, I.T. Aug 30, 189[?], Court Case No 226					
8						
9						
10						
11						
12						
13						
14						
15						
16				Date of Application		1196
17						9-24-98

DENIED CITIZENSHIP BY THE CHOCTAW AND CHICKASAW CITIZENSHIP COURT

89

RESIDENCE:	Chickasaw Natn							
POST OFFICE:	Durwood, I.T.			Choctaw **Nation**		Choctaw **Roll**	CARD NO. **5190**	FIELD NO.

Dawes' Roll No.	NAME	Relationship to Person First Named	AGE	SEX	BLOOD	TRIBAL ENROLLMENT		
						Year	County	No.
1	Parker, Nora		26	F	1/16			
2	" Trever M	Dau	1½	"	1/32			
3	" Ludie F	Son	3mo	M	1/32			
4	" William Leslie	Son	2wks	M	1/32			
5								
6								
7								
8								
9								
10								
11								
12								
13								
14								
15								
16								
17								

2-3-4

TRIBAL ENROLLMENT OF PARENTS

	Name of Father	Year	County	Name of Mother	Year	County
1	Willie Shockley	Dead	Choc Citz	Betty Shockley	Dead	Non Citz
2	W. T. Parker		Non Citz	No 1		
3	" " "		" "	No 1		
4	" " "		" "	No 1		
5	No1 admitted in 1896 case #955					
6	Admitted by the U S Court, South [remainder illegible]					
7	Court Case No 226					
8						
9	No2 was born Feby 26 [illegible]					
10						
11	No1 was admitted as Nora Shockley					
12	No4 Born April 14, 1902 enrolled April 29 1902					
13						
14	DENIED CITIZENSHIP BY THE CHOCTAW AND					
15	CHICKASAW CITIZENSHIP COURT					
16						
17	For child of No1 see NB #1018 (Act Apr 26 '06)					

Choctaw By Blood Enrollment Cards 1898-1914

RESIDENCE: Chickasaw Natn   Choctaw **Nation**   Choctaw **Roll**   undetermined   CARD NO. **5191**
POST OFFICE: Durwood, I.T.   FIELD NO. 236

Dawes' Roll No.	NAME	Relationship to Person First Named	AGE	SEX	BLOOD	TRIBAL ENROLLMENT		
						Year	County	No.
1	West, Lula		25	F	1/16			
2	" Roy	Son	8	M	1/32			
3	" Marie	Dau	3	F	1/32			
4	" Corine	"	1mo	"	1/32			
5	" F. K.							
6								
7								
8								
9								
10								
11								
12								
13								
14								
15								
16								
17								

DISMISSED MAY 27 1904

DECISION RENDERED MAR 19 1906

No.1,2,3&4 GRANTED

No.5 REFUSED

NOTICE OF DECISION FORWARDED APPLICANT

RECORD FORWARDED DEPARTMENT

TRIBAL ENROLLMENT OF PARENTS

	Name of Father	Year	County	Name of Mother	Year	County
1	John Shockley	Dead	Non Citz	Fatima Shockley	Dead	Non Citz
2	F. K. West		" "	No1		
3	" " "		" "	No1		
4	" " "		" "	No1		
5	Nos 1,2&3 admitted in 1896 case 955					
6	Admitted by the U.S. Court Sou in M Alester I.T., Aug 25, 1897					
7	Court Case No[illegible]					
8	No4 was born Aug 25, 1898					
9						
10						
11						
12						
13						
14						
15						
16						
17						

No.1,2,3&4

DENIED CITIZENSHIP BY THE CHOCTAW AND CHICKASAW CITIZENSHIP COURT

Date of Application for Enrollment 9-24-98

Choctaw By Blood Enrollment Cards 1898-1914

RESIDENCE: Chickasaw Natn
POST OFFICE: Ardmore, I.T.

Choctaw **Nation**   Choctaw **Roll**

CARD NO. 5192
FIELD NO.

Dawes' Roll No.	NAME	Relationship to Person First Named	AGE	SEX	BLOOD	TRIBAL ENROLLMENT		
						Year	County	No.
1	Gamel, Henry		23	M	1/8			
2	" Lula	Wife	16	F	IW			
3								
4								
5								
6								
7								
8								
9								
10								
11								
12								
13								
14								
15								
16								
17								

TRIBAL ENROLLMENT OF PARENTS

	Name of Father	Year	County	Name of Mother	Year	County
1	Geo Gamel	Dead	Non Citz	Kate Gamel		Non Citz
2	Caldwell Brooks			Margaret Brooks		
3						
4						
5						
6						
7						
8						
9						
10						
11						
12						
13						
14						
15						
16						
17						

Choctaw By Blood Enrollment Cards 1898-1914

RESIDENCE: Chickasaw Natn

POST OFFICE: Durwood, I.T.

Choctaw **Nation**   Choctaw **Roll**

CARD NO. **5193**

FIELD NO. C 238

Dawes' Roll No.	NAME	Relationship to Person First Named	AGE	SEX	BLOOD	TRIBAL ENROLLMENT		
						Year	County	No.
1	Shockley Albert R	First Named	18	M	1/32			
2								
3	DECISION RENDERED MAR 19 1906							
4	GRANTED							
	NOTICE OF DECISION FORWARDED APPLICANT							
	COPY OF DECISION FORWARDED ATTORNEY FOR APPLICANT.							
8	COPY OF DECISION FORWARDED ATTORNEYS FOR CHOCTAW AND							
9	CHICKASAW NATIONS.							
	RECORD FORWARDED DEPARTMENT							
11								
12								
13								
14								
15								
16								
17								

TRIBAL ENROLLMENT OF PARENTS

	Name of Father	Year	County	Name of Mother	Year	County
1	Wallie Shockley		Choc Citz	Betta Shockley	Dead	Non Citz
2						
3						
4						
5	No. 1 admitted in 1896, case					
6	Admitted by the U.S. Court South McAlester, I.T. Aug. 30, 1897					
7	Court Case No. 2					
8						
9						
10						
11						
12						
13	[Written on back] Mar. 19, 1906, Commissioner renders decision in accordance with the					
14	opinions of the Assistant Atty General of Feby. 10, 1905 (I.T.D. 10353-1904) and Dec. 8, 1905 (I. T. D. 3693-1905) in the case of Lula West enrolling No. 1 as a citizen by blood of					
15	the Choctaw Nation.					
16						
17						Date of Application for Enrollment 9-24-98

93

Choctaw By Blood Enrollment Cards 1898-1914

RESIDENCE: Chickasaw Natn

POST OFFICE REFUSED Grady, I.T.

Choctaw **Nation** Choctaw **Roll**

CARD NO. 5194

FIELD NO.

Dawes' Roll No.	NAME	Relationship to Person First Named	AGE	SEX	BLOOD	TRIBAL ENROLLMENT		
						Year	County	No.
1	Gann, William Newton		42	M	IW			
REFUSED 2	" Nancy R	Dau	1	F				
3								
4								
5								
6								
7								
8								
9	Admitted by the U.S. Court, South McAlester, I.T. Sept 11, 1897							
10	Court Case (No. [illegible])							
11								
12								
13								
14								
15								
16								
17								

TRIBAL ENROLLMENT OF PARENTS

	Name of Father	Year	County	Name of Mother	Year	County
1	Sam Gann	Dead	Non Citz	Nancy Gann	Dead	Non Citz
2	No 1			Minnie Gann	"	" "
3						
4						
5						
6	N° 1 GRANTED		W N. Gann married a Choctaw Indian from whom he was divorced.			
7			He afterward married a white woman by whom he has one child,			
8			Nancy.			
9			No 1 admitted in 1896, case #1010			
10			No2 was born June 3, 1897, while No1 was not admitted until			
11			Sept. 11, 1897			
12	No2 refused: see					
13	Choctaw card #101		Aug 17/99. As to marriage, remarriage and birth of children,			
14			see testimony of No. 1			
15						
16						
17	Ryan I.T. April 13, 04					

Choctaw By Blood Enrollment Cards 1898-1914

RESIDENCE: Chickasaw Natn   Choctaw **Nation**   Choctaw **Roll**   CARD NO. **5195**
POST OFFICE: Overbrook   I.T.   FIELD NO. C 240

Dawes' Roll No.	NAME	Relationship to Person	AGE	SEX	BLOOD	TRIBAL ENROLLMENT		
						Year	County	No.
✓	1 Cross, William R	First Named	48	M	IW		[Information illegible]	
✓	2 " Mary M	Dau	5mos	F			[Information illegible]	
	3							
	4							
	5							
	6							
	7							
#2	8							
	9							
	10							
	11							
	12							
	13							
	14							
	15							
	16							
	17							

DENIED CITIZENSHIP BY THE CHOCTAW AND CHICKASAW CITIZENSHIP COURT

DISMISSED

TRIBAL ENROLLMENT OF PARENTS

	Name of Father	Year	County	Name of Mother	Year	County
1	Wᵐ Cross	Dead	Non Citz	Malinda Cross	Dead	Non Citz
2	No 1			Mary Cross		
3						
4	No. 1 denied in 1896, case #761					
5	Admitted by the U.S. Court, South McAlester, I.T. Aug 25, 1897					
6	Court Case No. 18?					
7	William R Cross, married a Choctaw Indian who dies. He then married a white woman by					
8	whom he has the child, Mary M					
9						
10	No1 denied by C.C.C.C. Feb 29-04 Case #52					
11						
12						
13						
14						
15						
16						
17			Date of Application for Enrollment			9-24-98

Choctaw By Blood Enrollment Cards 1898-1914

RESIDENCE: Chickasaw Natn
POST OFFICE: I.T.

Choctaw **Nation**   Choctaw **Roll**

CARD NO. **5196**
FIELD NO.

Dawes' Roll No.	NAME	Relationship to Person	AGE	SEX	BLOOD	TRIBAL ENROLLMENT		
						Year	County	No.
✓	1 Jackson, Mary E	First Named	30	F			D	
✓	2 " Taylor F	Son	9	M			D	
✓ ✓	3 " Alma	Dau	7	F			D	
✓ ✓	4 " Charley	Son	5	M			D	
✓ ✓	5 " Roscoe	Son	3	M			D	
✓	6 " Ethel	Dau	1	F			D	
	7							
	8							
	9							
	10 No6 was born Dec 5th 1896							
	11 Nos 1 to 5 denied in 1896, case #2.							
	12 Admitted by U.S. Court, Ardmore Dec 21st 1899 Court Case [?]							
	13							
	14							
	15							
	16							
	17							

TRIBAL ENROLLMENT OF PARENTS

	Name of Father	Year	County	Name of Mother	Year	County
1	Newt Askew		Non Citz	Nancy M Askew		Non Citz
2	Tom Jackson		" "	No. 1		
3	" "		" "	No. 1		
4	" "		" "	No. 1		
5	" "		" "	No. 1		
6	" "		" "	No. 1		
7				DECISION RENDERED		
8				OCT 23 1906		
9						
10				RECORD FORWARDED DEPARTMENT.		
11						
12						
13						
14	No1 denied by C.C.C.C. as Mary Ellen Jackson					
15	No2 " " " " Taylor Franklin "					
16	No4 " " " " Charlie "					
17						

Choctaw By Blood Enrollment Cards 1898-1914

RESIDENCE: Chickasaw Natn				Choctaw **Nation**	Choctaw **Roll**		CARD No. **5197**	
POST OFFICE: Powell Ind. Ter.							FIELD No.	

Dawes' Roll No.	NAME	Relationship to Person First Named	AGE	SEX	BLOOD	TRIBAL ENROLLMENT		
						Year	County	No.
✓ ✓ 1 Askew, Rebecca			62	F				
2								
3								
4								
5						DECISION RENDERED		
6						DISMISSED		
7								
8								
9								
10								
11								
12								
13								
14								
15								
16								
17								

TRIBAL ENROLLMENT OF PARENTS

	Name of Father	Year	County	Name of Mother	Year	County
1	Nicholas Wright	Dead	Non-Citz	Barbara Wright	Dead	Non Citz
2						
3						
4						
5						
6	No. 1 denied in 1896, case #2.					
7	Admitted by U.S. Court, Ardmore I.T. Dec. 21st 1897 Court Case 72					
8						
9						
10						
11						
12						
13						
14						
15				Date of Application for Enrollment.	9-23-08	738
16						
17						

Choctaw By Blood Enrollment Cards 1898-1914

RESIDENCE: Chickasaw Natn
POST OFFICE: [Illegible]   I.T.

Choctaw **Nation**   Choctaw **Roll**

CARD NO. **5198**
FIELD NO. C 243

Dawes' Roll No.	NAME	Relationship to Person First Named	AGE	SEX	BLOOD	TRIBAL ENROLLMENT Year	County	No.
1	Davis, David		44	M				
2	" Mary	Wife	28	F	I.W.			
3	" William	Son	16	M				
4	" Joseph	Son	14	M				
5	" Lucy	Dau	12					
6	" Mary	Dau						
7	" Noah	Son		M				
8	" Eddie	Son		M				
9								
10								
11								
13								
14								
15								
16								
17								

(watermark: DENIED CITIZENSHIP BY THE CHOCTAW AND CHICKASAW CITIZENSHIP COURT)

TRIBAL ENROLLMENT OF PARENTS

	Name of Father	Year	County	Name of Mother	Year	County
1	Caloway Davis	Dead	Non Citz	Rachel Davis	Dead	Non Citz
2	Albert Burch	Dead	" "	Burch	Dead	" "
3	No 1			No 2		
4	No 1			No 2		
5	No 1			No 2		
6	No 1			No 2		
7	No 1			No 2		
8	No 1			No 2		
9						
10	Denied in 1896, case #320					
11	No 2 admitted as "Mary Burch"					
12	No 8 " " Edith "					
13	Admitted by U. S. Court Ardmore Jan 17th 1898 Court Case 77					
14						
15					Date of Application	
16						
17						

Choctaw By Blood Enrollment Cards 1898-1914

RESIDENCE: Chickasaw Natn
POST OFFICE: Daugherty   I.T.   Choctaw **Nation**   Choctaw **Roll**   CARD NO. **5199**   FIELD NO. C 244

Dawes' Roll No.	NAME	Relationship to Person First Named	AGE	SEX	BLOOD	TRIBAL ENROLLMENT		
						Year	County	No.
1	Hunter, Joseph S		73	M				
2								
3								
4								
5								
6								
7								
8								
9								
10								
11								
12								
13								
14								
15								
16								
17								

TRIBAL ENROLLMENT OF PARENTS

	Name of Father	Year	County	Name of Mother	Year	County
1	Wm Hunter	Dead	Non Citz	Minerva Hunter	Dead	Non Citz
2						
3						
4						
5						
6						
7	No1 denied in 1896, case #1334					
8	Admitted by U.S. Court Ardmore, Jan. 17th 1898 Court Case 73					
9						
10						
11						
12						
13						
14						
15						
16						
17						

RESIDENCE: Chickasaw Natn   Choctaw **Nation**   Choctaw **Roll**   CARD No. **5200**
POST OFFICE: Willis   I.T.   FIELD No. C 245

Dawes' Roll No.		NAME	Relationship to Person	AGE	SEX	BLOOD	TRIBAL ENROLLMENT		
							Year	County	No.
✓	✓	1 Askew, Newt	First Named	53	M			D	
✓	✓	2 " Nancy M	Wife	49	F			D	
✓	✓	3 " William H	Son	31	M			D	
✓	✓	4 " Henry E	Son	25	M			D	
✓	✓	5 " Elizabeth V	Dau	25	F			D	
✓	✓	6 " Dallas A	Son	19	M			D	
✓	✓	7 " Roxy C	Dau	15	F			D	
✓		8 Hefner, Alpha Marie	grand dau	13	F				
✓		9 Askew, Julius Edward	Gr Son	2mo	M				
✓		10 Hefner, Nancy Ann	Gr Dau	19mo	F				

DISMISSED
NOV 27 1904

11
No.2 denied by C.C.C.C. as Nancy Malinda Askew
No.3 denied by C.C.C.C. as William Howard Askew
12 Nos. 1 to 7 denied in 1896; case #2 / Admitted by U.S. Court Ardmore Dec. 21st 1896
13 Court Case 72 / No 10 Born Aug 25. 1901; enrolled April 25, 1902.
14 No. 5 is now the wife of Joe Hefner, April 10, 1900 / No. 7 denied by C.C.C.C. as Roxie
Cordelia Carter (nee Askew) or Roxie Cordelia Askew /
15 No. 4 denied by C.C.C.C. as Henry Edward Askew / No 6 Enrolled May 24, 1900 /
16 No. 3 is now the husband of Tavia Askew, a non-citizen. Evidence of marriage filed
17 Apr 11, 1902.

TRIBAL ENROLLMENT OF PARENTS

	Name of Father	Year	County	Name of Mother	Year	County
1	Tom Askew	Dead	Non Citz	Elizabeth Askew	Dead	Non Citz
2	Sam Bassham	"	"	Elizabeth Bassham	"	"
3	No 1			No 2		
4	No 1			No 2		
5	No 1			No 2		
6	No 1			No 2		
7	No 1			No 2		
8	Joe Hefner		non citizen			No. 5
9	No 3			Tavia Askew		non citizen
10	Joe Hefner		non citizen			No. 5
11						

ACTION APPROVED BY
SECRETARY OF INTERIOR. MAR 4 - 1907

NOTICE OF DEPARTMENTAL ACTION
FORWARDED ATTORNEYS FOR CHOCTAW APR. 22 1907
AND CHICKASAW NATIONS.

NOTICE OF DEPARTMENTAL ACTION
FORWARDED ATTORNEY FOR APPLICANT APR 22 1907

11
No6 denied by C.C.C.C. as Dallas Alexander Askew Born March 2, 1902 Enrolled April 11, 1902
12 No5 denied by C.C.C.C. as Elizabeth Viola Hefner (nee Askew) or Elizabeth Viola Askew

NOTICE OF DEPARTMENTAL
ACTION MAILED APPLICANT. APR 22 1907

13
14 [On Back]
15 For children of No6 see N.B. 967 - (see Act Apr 26 '06)
16 " child " No3 " 968 - " " "
17

Choctaw By Blood Enrollment Cards 1898-1914

| RESIDENCE: Chickasaw Natn | | | | | | CARD NO. 5201 |
| POST OFFICE: Powell I.T. | | Choctaw **Nation** | Choctaw **Roll** | | | FIELD NO. C 246 |

Dawes' Roll No.	NAME	Relationship to Person	AGE	SEX	BLOOD	TRIBAL ENROLLMENT		
						Year	County	No.
✓ ✓	1 Askew, John	First Named	22	M				
	2							
	3							
	4 DECISION RENDERED							
	5 DISMISSED							
	6							
	7							
	8 RECORD FORWARDED DEPARTMENT.							
	9							
	10							
	11							
	12 Decision in [illegible]							
	13 See Petition [illegible]							
	14							
	15							
	16							
	17							

TRIBAL ENROLLMENT OF PARENTS

	Name of Father	Year	County	Name of Mother	Year	County
1	M W Askew	Dead	Non Citz	Rebecca Askew		Non Citz
2						
3						
4						
5						
6						
7	No. 1 denied in 1896, case #2.					
8	Admitted by U.S. Court Ardmore Dec. 21st 1897 Court Case 72					
9						
10	No. 1 denied by C.C.C.C. as Jonnie Askew or John Askew.					
11						
12						
13						
14						
15						
16						
17						

DENIED CITIZENSHIP BY THE CHOCTAW AND CHICKASAW CITIZENSHIP COURT

Date of Enrollment for Enrollment 9-23-98

Choctaw By Blood Enrollment Cards 1898-1914

RESIDENCE:	Chickasaw Natn					
POST OFFICE:	Ardmore	Choctaw **Nation**	Choctaw **Roll**	CARD NO. **5202**	
				FIELD NO. C 247	

Dawes' Roll No.	NAME	Relationship to Person First Named	AGE	SEX	BLOOD	TRIBAL ENROLLMENT		
						Year	County	No.
✓ *	1 Zumwalt, Amanda A		13	F				
	2							
	3							
	4							
	5							
	6							
	7							
	8							
	9							
	10							
	11							
	12							
	13							
	14							
	15							
	16							
	17							

TRIBAL ENROLLMENT OF PARENTS

Name of Father	Year	County	Name of Mother	Year	County
1 Frank Zumwalt		Non Citz	Amanda A. Zumwalt	Dead	Non Citz
2					
3					
4					
5					
6					
7 No.1 admitted in 1896 case #1164.					
8 Admitted by U.S Court at South McAlester Aug 25th 1897 Court Case 233					
9 No. 1 is now the wife of Blummer Anderson on Choctaw card #5052					
10					
11					
12 No 1 Denied by C.C.C.C. June 21st 04					
13					
14					
15					
16					
17					

Choctaw By Blood Enrollment Cards 1898-1914

RESIDENCE: Chickasaw Natn		Choctaw **Nation** Choctaw **Roll**			CARD No. **5203**	
POST OFFICE: Ardmore I.T.					FIELD No. C 248	

Dawes' Roll No.	NAME	Relationship to Person First Named	AGE	SEX	BLOOD	TRIBAL ENROLLMENT Year	County	No.
1	Ford, Adeline	Named	32	F	1/16			
2	" William	Son	14	M				
3	" Bruce	Son	12	M				
4	" Eva	Dau	10	F				
5	" Henry J.	Son	9	M				
6	" Fred	Son	8	M				
7	" Sydney E	Son	7	M				
8	" Joseph	Son	6	M				
9	" Samuel	Son	4	M				
10	" Luther	Son	3	M				
DP 11	" Andrew Cavitt	"	8mo	M				
DP 12	" Thomas Needles	Son	1 wk	M				
DP 13	" Fannie Ellen	Son[sic]	3mo	F				
#11-12&13 14	DISMISSED				"Henry J" admitted as "Henry"			
15	SEPT 15 1904							
16								
17	DENIED CITIZENSHIP BY THE CHOCTAW AND CHICKASAW CITIZENSHIP COURT							

TRIBAL ENROLLMENT OF PARENTS

	Name of Father	Year	County	Name of Mother	Year	County
1	Felix Roberts		Non Citz	Rachel Roberts	Dead	Non Citz
2	Sidney Ford		" "	No. 1		
3	" "		" "	No. 1		
4	" "		" "	No. 1		
5	" "		" "	No. 1		
6	" "		" "	No. 1		
7	" "		" "	No. 1		
8	" "		" "	No. 1		
9	" "		" "	No. 1		
10	" "		" "	No. 1		
11	" "		" "	No. 1		
12	" "		" "	No. 1		
13	" "		" "	No. 1		
14	Denied in 1896, case #320; Admitted by U.S. Court Ardmore I.T. Jan. 17th 1898 Court Case 74					
15	No. 12 Enrolled Sept. 10th, 1900					
16	No. 13 Enrolled June 17th 1902. Born March 12th 1902.			Date of Application for Enrollment. 9-23-98 3/63		
17	☞ Nos 1 to 10 inclusive in C.C.C.C. Case #501			No. 11 enrolled Jany 17, 1900		

RESIDENCE:	Chickasaw Natn				CARD NO.	**5204**
POST OFFICE:	Ardmore	Choctaw **Nation** Choctaw **Roll**			FIELD NO.	C 249

Dawes' Roll No.	NAME	Relationship to Person First Named	AGE	SEX	BLOOD	TRIBAL ENROLLMENT		
						Year	County	No.
1	Cotton, Bertie		37	F	I.W.			
2	" Jenny Lind	Dau	6	F				
3								
4								
5								
6								
7								
8								
9	Nos. 1&2, denied in 1896, case #930							
10								
11	Admitted by U.S. Court Ardmore I.T. Court Case 90 admitted Nov. 8th 1898							
12	C.C.C.C. Case #116T 3/16/03							
13								
14								
15								
16								
17								

TRIBAL ENROLLMENT OF PARENTS

	Name of Father	Year	County	Name of Mother	Year	County
1	Denton Nesmith		Non-Citz	Elizabeth J Nesmith	Dead	Non-Citz
2	D.B. Cotton	Dead	" "	No. 1		
3						
4						
5						
6						
7						
8						
9						
10						
11						
12						
13						
14						
15						
16						
17						

DENIED CITIZENSHIP BY THE CHOCTAW AND CHICKASAW CITIZENSHIP COURT

Choctaw By Blood Enrollment Cards 1898-1914

RESIDENCE:	Chickasaw Natn		CARD NO. **5205**
POST OFFICE:	Ryan I.T.	Choctaw **Nation** Choctaw **Roll**	FIELD NO. C 250

Dawes' Roll No.	NAME	Relationship to Person First Named	AGE	SEX	BLOOD	TRIBAL ENROLLMENT Year	County	No.
✓ *	1 Morgan, Amy P	Named	19	F	1/8			
✓ *	2 " Callie B	Dau	2	F				
✓ *	3 " Basil B	Dau	1	F				
✓ *	4 " Chesley A	Son	6mo	M				
✓	5 " James Cecil	Son	3mo	M				
	6							
	7	DENIED CITIZENSHIP BY THE CHOCTAW AND						
	8	CHICKASAW CITIZENSHIP COURT						
	9							
	10	2.3.4&5 DISMISSED						
	11							
	12	No. denied in 1896, case #250						
	13	No.1 admitted as "Amy Pearl Vernon"						
	14	No.2 was born Aug. 22nd 1896						
	15	No.3 " " Jan. 26th 1898						
	16							
	17							

TRIBAL ENROLLMENT OF PARENTS

	Name of Father	Year	County	Name of Mother	Year	County
1	D.B. Vernon		Non-Citz	Margaret T. Vernon		Non Citz
2	James C. Morgan		" "	No. 1		
3	" " "		" "	No. 1		
4	" " "		" "	No. 1		
5	" " "		" "	No. 1		
6	Admitted by U.S. Court South McAllester Aug 26-1897 Court Case 98					
7	No. 4 Enrolled June 30th, 1900					
8	N°5 Born Feby 26, 1902; enrolled June 9, 1902					
9	No.1 [illegible] C.C.C. Case #1					
10	No.1 denied by C.C.C. Case #81 [illegble]					
11	No. 2,3,4 dismissed " " "					
12						
13						
14	For child of No1 see N.B. (Mar 3-1905) #1536					
15						
16						
17					Date of Application for Enrollment.	9-23-98 7138

Choctaw By Blood Enrollment Cards 1898-1914

| RESIDENCE: | Chickasaw Natn | | | | | | | CARD No. | 5206 |

RESIDENCE: Chickasaw Natn
POST OFFICE: Ardmore I.T.

Choctaw **Nation**   Choctaw **Roll**

CARD No. 5206
FIELD No. C 251

Dawes' Roll No.	NAME	Relationship to Person First Named	AGE	SEX	BLOOD	TRIBAL ENROLLMENT		
						Year	County	No.
1	Turner, J. F.		42	M	1/8			
2								
3								
4								
5								
6								
7	DISMISSED							
8	SEP 20 1904							
9								
10								
11	No.1 admitted by Commission in 1896 case #295 as a [illegible]							
12								
13								
14								
15								
16								
17								

TRIBAL ENROLLMENT OF PARENTS

	Name of Father	Year	County	Name of Mother	Year	County
1	John Turner	Dead	Non Citz	Mary Turner	Dead	Non Citz
2						
3						
4						
5						
6						
7	Admitted by U.S. Court South McAllester Oct 8-1897					
8	Court Case 124					
9						
10	No.1 is the husband of Katie Turner on Choctaw card #273.					
11				Oct. 30, 1901.		
12						
13						
14						
15						
16				Date of Application for Enrollment.	9-23-98	3/160
17						

106

Choctaw By Blood Enrollment Cards 1898-1914

RESIDENCE: Chickasaw Natn		Choctaw **Nation** Choctaw **Roll**				CARD NO. **5207**	
POST OFFICE: I.T.						FIELD NO. C 252	

Dawes' Roll No.	NAME	Relationship to Person First Named	AGE	SEX	BLOOD	TRIBAL ENROLLMENT Year	County	No.
1	Burks, Burton S	Named	39	M	1/4			
2	" Callie	Wife	37	F				
3	" Ira	Dau	17	F				
4	" Nina	Dau	14	F				
5	" Orbie	Son	12	M				
6	" Charley	Son	10	M				
7	" Edgar	Son	7	M				
8	" Julia	Dau	5	M[sic]	#9	DISMISSED		
DP 9	" Burton S, Jr	Son	1	M		OCT 28 1904		
" 10	Davis, William Trenton	GSon	2wks	M				
" 11	" Ira May	GDau	3mo	F				
13	Nos 10 & 11 DISMISSED							
14	N°11 Born Sept 14, 1902							
15	Application made Oct 18, 1902.							
16	Nos 1 to 8 denied in '96: case #889							
17								

TRIBAL ENROLLMENT OF PARENTS

	Name of Father	Year	County	Name of Mother	Year	County
1	B.F. Burks	Dead	Non Citz	Emily Burks		Non Citz
2	B.B. Smith	"	" "	J.A. Smith	Dead	" "
3	No1			No2		
4	No1			No2		
5	No1			No2		
6	No1			No2		
7	No1			No2		
8	No1			No2		
9	No1			No2		
10	Charley W Davis		non-citizen	No3		
11	Charles W Davis		" "	No3		
12	Admitted by U.S. Court Ardmore Dec. 22nd 1897 Court Case 123					
13	No.3 is the wife of Charley W. Davis on Choctaw card #D.545: May 8, 1900					
14	Jany 23, 1900 No3 is now wife of C.W. Davis.					
15	Evidence of birth of No10 filed January 2, 1901					
16	Evidence of birth of No11 filed Feb 5, 1903.			Date of Application for Enrollment	9-23-98 3/157	
17						

RESIDENCE:	Chickasaw Natn							
POST OFFICE: Addington I.T.		Choctaw **Nation**			Choctaw **Roll**	CARD NO. **5208** FIELD NO. C 253		

Dawes' Roll No.	NAME	Relationship to Person First Named	AGE	SEX	BLOOD	TRIBAL ENROLLMENT		
						Year	County	No.
✓ *	1 Addington, Zachariah	Named	18	M	1/32			
✓ *	2 " Burrell	Brother	14	M				
✓	3 " Zackybelle	Dau	1mo	F	1/64			
✓	4 " Ruby Florence	Dau of N°2	4mo	F	1/64			
	5							
3&4	6							
	7							
	8							
	9							
	10							
	11							
	12							
	13							
	14							
	15							
	16							
	17							

DENIED CITIZENSHIP BY THE CHOCTAW AND CHICKASAW CITIZENSHIP COURT

TRIBAL ENROLLMENT OF PARENTS

	Name of Father	Year	County	Name of Mother	Year	County
1	Columbus Addington	Dead	Non Citz	Belle Addington	Dead	Non Citz
2	" "	"	" "	" "	"	" "
3	No 1			Gracie Addington		" "
4	N°2			Daisy Addington		" "
5						
6	Nos 1&2 denied in 1896, case #1282.					
7	Admitted by U.S. Court South McAllester Aug 25th 1899					
8	Court Case 121 [remainder illegible]					
9	No.2 is now the husband of Daisy Addington on Choctaw card #D.667			Oct 7, 1901.		
10	No.1 is the husband of Gracie Addington on Choctaw Card #D.639			June 20, 1901		
11	No.3 born Oct. 22, 1901: Enrolled Nov. 29, 1901					
12	N°4 Born May 20, 1902, enrolled Sept. 20, 1902					
13	Nos 1&2 now in C.C.C.C. Case #64					
14	Nos 1&2 denied by C.C.C.C. case #68 March 4-04					
15					Date of Application for Enrollment.	
16	For children of No2 see NB 948					
17	(Act Apr 25-06)					

Choctaw By Blood Enrollment Cards 1898-1914

						TRIBAL ENROLLMENT		
RESIDENCE: Chickasaw Natn					CARD NO. **5209**			
POST OFFICE: Marrietta I.T.	Choctaw **Nation**			Choctaw **Roll**	FIELD NO. C 254			

Dawes' Roll No.	NAME	Relationship to Person First Named	AGE	SEX	BLOOD	Year	County	No.
1	Pittman William H	Named	35	M	I.W.			
2	" Mollie E	Wife	30	F	1/8			
3	" Eddie N	Son	12	M	1/16			
4	" Myrtle M	Dau	10	F	1/16			
5	" Joseph H	Son	8	M	1/16			
6	" Alice M	Dau	5	F	1/16			
7	" Ruby E	Dau	3	F	1/16			
DP 8	" Hardy M	Son	1	M	1/16			
DP 9	" Nellie L	Dau	1mo	F	1/16			
10								
11	Nos 8&9 DISMISSED							
12								
13	DENIED CITIZENSHIP BY THE CHOCTAW AND							
14	CHICKASAW CITIZENSHIP COURT							
15								
16								
17								

TRIBAL ENROLLMENT OF PARENTS

	Name of Father	Year	County	Name of Mother	Year	County
1	Henry P. Pittman	Dead	Non Citz	Eliza Pittman		Non Citz
2	J. N. Forbes		" "	Sue Forbes		" "
3	No 1			No 2		
4	No 1			No 2		
5	No 1			No 2		
6	No 1			No 2		
7	No 1			No 2		
8	No 1			No 2		
9	No 1			No 2		
10	Nos 1 to 7, denied in 1896, case #447.					
11	Nellie L. Pittman on Card No D-[?]					
12	No.9 born December 12, 1899; transferred to this card May 24, 1902					
13	Admitted by U.S. Court Ardmore Dec 22nd 1897 Court Case 111.					
14						
15	Nos 1 to 7 incl now in C.C.C.C. Case #691			9-23-98 11:30		
16				Date of Application		
17				for Enrollment.		

Choctaw By Blood Enrollment Cards 1898-1914

RESIDENCE: Chickasaw Natn   Choctaw **Nation**   Choctaw **Roll**   CARD No. **5210**

POST OFFICE: Leon   I.T.   FIELD No. **C 255**

Dawes' Roll No.	NAME	Relationship to Person First Named	AGE	SEX	BLOOD	TRIBAL ENROLLMENT Year	County	No.
1	Johnson, Jeff C.		50	M	I.W.			
2	" Lydia M	Wife	45	F	I.W.			
3	" Burleigh	Son	18	M				
4	" Pearl	Dau	15	F				
5	" Burnice	Dau	10	F				

Transferred

ACTION APPROVED BY FEB 26 1907
SECRETARY OF INTERIOR.

NOTICE OF DEPARTMENTAL ACTION FORWARDED ATTORNEYS FOR CHOCTAW AND CHICKASAW NATIONS. APR 16 1907

NOTICE OF DEPARTMENTAL ACTION FORWARDED ATTORNEY FOR APPLICANT. APR 16 1907

NOTICE OF DEPARTMENTAL ACTION MAILED APPLICANT. APR 907

DENIED CITIZENSHIP BY THE CHOCTAW AND
CHICKASAW CITIZENSHIP COURT

TRIBAL ENROLLMENT OF PARENTS

	Name of Father	Year	County	Name of Mother	Year	County
1	L.F. Johnson	Dead	Non Citz	Ellen Johnson	Dead	Non-Citz
2	Starlon Evans	"	" "	Evans	"	" "
3	No 1			No 2		
4	No 1			No 2		
5	No 1			No 2		

DECISION RENDERED NOV 1906

COPY OF DECISION FORWARDED ATTORNEYS FOR CHOCTAW AND CHICKASAW NATIONS. NOV 23 1906

8   Nos 1 to 5 denied in 1896, case #1052

9   Admitted by U.S. Court Ardmore Dec 21st 1897 Court Case 107

11   No 2 transferred to 7-252

17   See Petition = [Illegible]

Choctaw By Blood Enrollment Cards 1898-1914

RESIDENCE:	Chickasaw Natn						CARD NO. **5211**
POST OFFICE:	Marsden I.T.	Choctaw **Nation** Choctaw **Roll**					FIELD NO. C 256

Dawes' Roll No.	NAME	Relationship to Person First Named	AGE	SEX	BLOOD	TRIBAL ENROLLMENT		
						Year	County	No.
1	Forbes H E	Named	37	F	IW			
2	" Eugene E	Son	18	M				
3	" Staniey M	Son	11	M				
4								
5								
6								
7								
8								
9								
10								
11								
12								
13								
14								
15								
16								
17								

DENIED CITIZENSHIP BY THE CHOCTAW AND CHICKASAW CITIZENSHIP COURT

TRIBAL ENROLLMENT OF PARENTS

	Name of Father	Year	County	Name of Mother	Year	County
1	J. Cushman		Non Citz	Mary Cushman		Non Citz
2	Eli H Forbes	Dead	" "	No 1		
3	" " "	"	" "	No 1		
4						
5						
6						
7	Nos 1, 2 & 3 denied Aug 1896, case #447					
8	Admitted by U.S. Court Ardmore Dec 22nd 1897 Court Case 111					
9						
10						
11						
12						
13						
14						
15						
16						
17						

Choctaw By Blood Enrollment Cards 1898-1914

RESIDENCE:	Chickasaw Natn					CARD NO. 5212
POST OFFICE:	Ryan I.T.	Choctaw **Nation** Choctaw **Roll**				FIELD NO. C 257

Dawes' Roll No.	NAME	Relationship to Person First Named	AGE	SEX	BLOOD	TRIBAL ENROLLMENT		
						Year	County	No.
✓ ✓	1 Barron, Lycurgus C		31	M	1/2			
✓ ✓	2 " Mattie	Wife	26	F	I.W.			
	3							
	4							
	5							
	6							
	7							
	8							
	9							
	10							
	11							
	12							
	13							
	14							
	15							
	16 See Petition #C-124							
	17 Duplicate record in Choctaw #352							

DENIED CITIZENSHIP BY THE CHOCTAW AND CHICKASAW CITIZENSHIP COURT

TRIBAL ENROLLMENT OF PARENTS

Name of Father	Year	County	Name of Mother	Year	County
1 Thos H. Barron	Dead	Non Citz	Mary Barron	Dead	Non Citz
2 J H Nealy	"	" "	M. J. Nealy		" "
3					
4					
5					
6 Not original applicants before Com. in 1896 in case #868					
7 Admitted by U.S. Court South McAllester Aug. 25th 1897 Court Case 105					
8					
9					
10					
11					
12					
13					
14					
15					
16					
17					

Choctaw By Blood Enrollment Cards 1898-1914

RESIDENCE:	Blue County		Choctaw **Nation**			Choctaw **Roll**	CARD NO.	**5213**
POST OFFICE:	Durant	I.T.					FIELD NO.	C 258

Dawes' Roll No.	NAME	Relationship to Person First Named	AGE	SEX	BLOOD	TRIBAL ENROLLMENT Year	County	No.
✓ DP 1	Berry, Lela	Named	22	F	1/4			
✓ DP 2	" Ethel C	Dau	8mo	F				
✓ DP 3	" Ruby Dale	Dau	2mo	F	1/8			
✓ DP 4	" Cyrel Claton	Son	2mo	M	1/8			
5								
6								
7								
8								
9								
10								
11								
12								
13								
14								
15								
16								
17								

DENIED CITIZENSHIP BY THE CHOCTAW AND CHICKASAW CITIZENSHIP COURT DISMISSED MAY 27 1904

TRIBAL ENROLLMENT OF PARENTS

	Name of Father	Year	County	Name of Mother	Year	County
1	Wm Reid		non Citz	Serena Reid		Non Citz
2	C.A. Berry		" "	No 1		
3	C.A. Berry		" "	No 1		
4	" " "		" "	No. 1		
5						
6	No.1 not an original applicant before Com in 1896 in case #969.					
7	No.1 was admitted as "Lela Reed"					
8	No2 was born Jan 29th 1898					
9	Admitted by U.S. Court South McAllester Aug. 25th 1897 Court Case 105					
10	N^o4 Born July 5, 1902. Enrolled Aug. 30, 1902					
11						
12						
13						
14						
15						
16					Date of Application for Enrollment	
17					No.3 Enrolled May 24, 1900	

113

Choctaw By Blood Enrollment Cards 1898-1914

RESIDENCE:	Chickasaw Natn			Choctaw **Nation**	Choctaw **Roll**	CARD NO. **5214**	
POST OFFICE:	Ada I.T.					FIELD NO. C 259	

Dawes' Roll No.	NAME	Relationship to Person First Named	AGE	SEX	BLOOD	TRIBAL ENROLLMENT		
						Year	County	No.
✓ ✓	1 Askew, Sam	First Named	24	M	1/16			
DP ✓	2 " Lena	Wife	15	F	I.W.			
DP ✓	3 " Frankie Beatrice	Dau	6mo	F				
DP ✓	4 " Leo	Son	2mo	M				
	5							
	6							
	7							
	8							
	9							
	10							
	11							
	12							
	13							
	14							
	15							
	16							
	17							

DENIED CITIZENSHIP BY THE CHOCTAW AND CHICKASAW CITIZENSHIP COURT

#2-3 DISMISSED

DISMISSED NOV 12 1904

DECISION RENDERED

DISMISSED OCT

RECORD FORWARDED DEPARTMENT.

TRIBAL ENROLLMENT OF PARENTS

	Name of Father	Year	County	Name of Mother	Year	County
1	Wm D. Askew		Non Citz	Martha Askew	Dead	Non Citz
2	Lancaster	Dead	" "	Mary Lancaster		" "
3	No. 1			No.2		
4	No. 1			No.2		
5						
6						
7						
8	No.1 denied in 1896, case #1.					
9	Married under license issued by United States Court at Ardmore Aug 19th 1898					
10	License & certificate exhibited					
11						
12	No.1 Admitted by U.S. Court Ardmore Dec. 21st 1897 Court Case 71					
13	Evidence of marriage of (Nos 1 and 2 filed April 2, 1901					
14	No.4 Enrolled April 2, 1901.					
15						
16					No.3 Enrolled May 24 1898	
17	P.O. seems to be Kemp I.T. April 2, 1901.					

114

Choctaw By Blood Enrollment Cards 1898-1914

RESIDENCE: Chickasaw Natn					CARD NO. **5215**
POST OFFICE: Leon I.T.	Choctaw **Nation** Choctaw **Roll**				FIELD NO. C 260

Dawes' Roll No.	NAME	Relationship to Person First Named	AGE	SEX	BLOOD	TRIBAL ENROLLMENT		
						Year	County	No.
1	Sorrells, H. J		59	M	I.W.			
2								
3								
4								
5								
6								
7								
8								
9								
10								
11								
12								
13								
14								
15								
16								
17								

TRIBAL ENROLLMENT OF PARENTS

	Name of Father	Year	County	Name of Mother	Year	County
1	Sorrells	Dead	Non Citz	Frances Sorrells	Dead	Non Citz
2						
3						
4						
5						
6						
7	No.1 denied in 1896, case #826.					
8	Admitted by U.S. Court Ardmore Dec. 21st 1897 Court Case 130					
9						
10						
11						
12						
13						
14						
15						
16						
17						

Choctaw By Blood Enrollment Cards 1898-1914

RESIDENCE: Chickasaw Natn   Choctaw **Nation**   Choctaw **Roll**   CARD NO. **5216**

POST OFFICE: Ardmore   I.T.   FIELD NO. C 261

Dawes' Roll No.	NAME	Relationship to Person First Named	AGE	SEX	BLOOD	TRIBAL ENROLLMENT		
						Year	County	No.
1	Hignight, G.T.		36	M	1/16			
2	" R Lette M	Dau	13	F				
3	" George W.	Son	5	N				
4								
5								
6								
7								
8								
9								
10								
11								
12								
13								
14								
15								
16								
17								

TRIBAL ENROLLMENT OF PARENTS

	Name of Father	Year	County	Name of Mother	Year	County
1	W. H. Hignight		Non Citz	Elizabeth Hignight		Non Citz
2	No. 1			Lula Hignight		" "
3	No 1			" "		" "
4						
5						
6						
7	Nos 1,2&3 denied in 1896, case #426					
8	Admitted by U.S. Court Ardmore Mch 10th 1898 Court Case 144					
9						
10	For child of No. 2; see NB # 1059 (Act Apr 26 '06)					
11						
12						
13						
14						
15						
16						
17						

Choctaw By Blood Enrollment Cards 1898-1914

| RESIDENCE: | Chickasaw Natn |
| POST OFFICE: | Naples   I.T. |

Choctaw **Nation**   Choctaw **Roll**

CARD NO. **5217**
FIELD NO. C 262

Dawes' Roll No.	NAME	Relationship to Person	AGE	SEX	BLOOD	TRIBAL ENROLLMENT		
						Year	County	No.
	1 Southward, William M	First Named	29	M	1/4			
DP	2 " Effie S	Dau	1 1/2	F	1/8			
DP	3 " Susan	"	1	"	1/8			
DP	4 " Edith	"	2mo	F	1/8			
	5							
	Nos DISMISSED 2-3 & 4 SEP							
	7							
	8							
	9							
	10 DENIED CITIZENSHIP BY THE CHOCTAW AND CHICKASAW CITIZENSHIP COURT							
	11							
	12							
	13							
	14							
	15							
	16							
	17							

TRIBAL ENROLLMENT OF PARENTS

Name of Father	Year	County	Name of Mother	Year	County
1 W.C. Southward		Non Citz	Mary Southward		Non Citz
2 No. 1			Haiia Southward		" "
3 No. 1			" "		" "
4 No. 1			" "		" "
5					
6					
7 No.1 denied in 1896, case #55					
8 No.2 was born Feb. 28-1897					
9					
10 Admitted by U.S. Court Ardmore Dec. 21st 1897 Court Case 127					
11 [Entry illegible]					
12 No.3 enrolled Oct 30/99, subject to receipt of evidence of marriage of parents					
13 Letter requesting same this day. Filed Nov 23/99					
14 No. 4 Enrolled Aug 27, 1901					
15					
16				Date of Application	
17					

117

Choctaw By Blood Enrollment Cards 1898-1914

RESIDENCE:								
POST OFFICE:		Choctaw **Nation**		Choctaw **Roll**		CARD NO. **5218**		
						FIELD NO. C 263		

Dawes' Roll No.	NAME	Relationship to Person First Named	AGE	SEX	BLOOD	TRIBAL ENROLLMENT		
						Year	County	No.
1	Morris, Spencer, Jr.		33	M	1/4			
2								
3								
4								
5								
6								
7								
8								
9								
10								
11								
12								
13								
14								
15								
16								
17								

DENIED CITIZENSHIP BY THE CHOCTAW AND CHICKASAW CITIZENSHIP COURT

TRIBAL ENROLLMENT OF PARENTS

	Name of Father	Year	County	Name of Mother	Year	County
1	Spencer Morris	Dead	Non Citz	Caroline Morris	Dead	Non Citz
2						
3						
4						
5						
6	No.1 denied in 1896, case #55.					
7	Admitted by U.S. Court Ardmore, I.T. Dec. 21st 1897, Court Case 127.					
8						
9	No.1 admitted as Spencer W. Morris, Jr.					
10						
11						
12						
13						
14						
15						
16						
17						

| RESIDENCE: | Chickasaw Natn |
| POST OFFICE: | Palmer   I.T. |

Choctaw **Nation**   Choctaw **Roll**

CARD NO. **5219**
FIELD NO. C 264

Dawes' Roll No.	NAME	Relationship to Person First Named	AGE	SEX	BLOOD	TRIBAL ENROLLMENT		
						Year	County	No.
1	Morris, G.W.		41	M	1/4			
2	" Wilmoth	Son	21	21				
3	" Nora L	Dau	14	14				
4	" Mollie	Dau	12	12				
5	" Cora M	Dau	5	5				
6	" Kansas V	Dau	3	3				
DP 7	" William W	Son	9mo	9mo				
DP 8	" Lula Mamie	Dau	1mo	1mo				
9								
10 No. 7&8	DISMISSED							
11	SEP 1904							
12	DENIED CITIZENSHIP BY THE CHOCTAW AND							
13	CHICKASAW CITIZENSHIP COURT							
14								
15								
16								
17								

TRIBAL ENROLLMENT OF PARENTS

	Name of Father	Year	County	Name of Mother	Year	County
1	Spencer Morris	Dead	Non Citz	Caroline Morris	Dead	Non Citz
2	No.1			Annie L. Morris	Dead	" "
3	No.1			" " "	"	" "
4	No.1			" " "	"	" "
5	No.1			Nancy E. Morris	"	" "
6	No.1			" " "	"	" "
7	No.1			" " "	"	" "
8	No.1			" " "	"	" "
9						
10		No. 7 was born Jan 13th 1898				
11		No 1 to 6 denied in 1896, case #55				
12		Admitted by U.S. Court Ardmore I.T. Dec. 21st 1897 Court Case 127				
13		No.8 born Nov. 2d, 1901; Enrolled Dec. 21st 1901.				
14	[Entries illegible]					
15						
16				Date of Application 9-23-98 478		
17						

| RESIDENCE: Chickasaw Natn | | | | | | CARD NO. **5220** | | |
| POST OFFICE: Purcell I.T. | | Choctaw **Nation** | | Choctaw **Roll** | | FIELD NO. C 265 | | |

Dawes' Roll No.	NAME	Relationship to Person First Named	AGE	SEX	BLOOD	TRIBAL ENROLLMENT		
						Year	County	No.
1	Morris, Jerry M		47	M	1/4			
2	" Ebenezer S	Son	20	M				
3	" Gertrude E	Dau	18	F				
4	" Joel W	Son	17	M				
5	" Jessie C	Son	14	M				
6	" Augustus B	Son	10	M				
7								
8								
9								
10								
11								
12								
13								
14								
15								
16								
17								

TRIBAL ENROLLMENT OF PARENTS

	Name of Father	Year	County	Name of Mother	Year	County
1	Spencer Morris	Dead	Non Citz	Caroline Morris	Dead	Non Citz
2	No.1			Kansas Morris	Dead	" "
3	No.1			" "	"	" "
4	No.1			" "	"	" "
5	No.1			" "	"	" "
6	No.1			" "	"	" "
7						
8	Nos. 1 to 6 denied in 1896, case #53					
9	Admitted by U.S. Court Ardmore, Dec. 21, 1897, Court Case 127					
10	No.8 is now the wife of C. A. Laxton a non citizen. Evidence of marriage					
11	filed Nov. 19, 1901.					
12	[Entry illegible]					
13	[Entry illegible]					
14	For child of No3 see NB #1058 - (Act Apr 26 '06)					
15						
16						
17						

120

Choctaw By Blood Enrollment Cards 1898-1914

RESIDENCE: Chickasaw Natn
POST OFFICE: Center I.T.

Choctaw **Nation** Choctaw **Roll**

CARD NO. **5221**
FIELD NO. C 266

Dawes' Roll No.	NAME	Relationship to Person First Named	AGE	SEX	BLOOD	TRIBAL ENROLLMENT		
						Year	County	No.
1	Dorn, Amanda		32	F	1/4			
DP 2	" Andrew J, Jr.	Son	9mo	M	1/8			
DP 3	" Tommy O	Dau	4	F	1/8			
DP 4	" Robert A	Son	2mo	M	1/8			
5								
6	Nos	DISMISSED						
7	2, 3 & 4	SEP 1904						
8								
9								
10								
11	DENIED CITIZENSHIP BY THE CHOCTAW AND							
12	CHICKASAW CITIZENSHIP COURT							
13								
14								
15								
16								
17								

TRIBAL ENROLLMENT OF PARENTS

	Name of Father	Year	County	Name of Mother	Year	County
1	Antonio Paddier	Dead	Non Citz	Evaline Paddier		Non Citz
2	T. J. Dorn		Non citizen	No 1		
3	" " "		" "	No 1		
4	" " "		" "	No 1		
5						
6						
7	No.1 denied in 1896, case #55.					
8	No.1 Admitted as Amanda "Paddieo"					
9	Admitted by U.S. Court Ardmore I.T. Dec. 21st 1897 Court Case 127					
10						
11	Nos. 3 and 4 Enrolled Aug 22d, 1900.					
12	No.3 was originally rejected by Dawes Commission in an application for enrollment					
13	in 1899; see Choctaw card #R.76; transferred to this card Aug. 22d, 1901 on					
14	presentation of proper birth affidavits.					
15						
16					Date of Application for Enrollment	9-23-98
17						

121

Choctaw By Blood Enrollment Cards 1898-1914

RESIDENCE: Chickasaw Natn
POST OFFICE: Naples   I.T.

Choctaw **Nation**   Choctaw **Roll**

CARD No. **5222**
FIELD No. C 267

Dawes' Roll No.	NAME	Relationship to Person First Named	AGE	SEX	BLOOD	TRIBAL ENROLLMENT Year	County	No.
1	Goins, Raborn		62	M	1/2			
2	" Thomas L	Son	35	M				
3	" William M	Son	31	M				
4	" Collin	Son	28	M				
5	" Eli	Son	25	M				
6	" Raborn Jr	Son	23	M				
7	" Campbell	Son	21	M				
8	" Martha M	Dau	19	F				
9	" Missouri E	Dau	16	F				
10	" Maudie M	Dau	14	F				
11	" Dinky	Dau	12	F				
12								
13								
14								
15								
16								
17								

DENIED CITIZENSHIP BY THE CHOCTAW AND CHICKASAW CITIZENSHIP COURT

TRIBAL ENROLLMENT OF PARENTS

	Name of Father	Year	County	Name of Mother	Year	County
1	J Goins	Dead	Non Citz	Sharaphine Goins	Dead	Non Citz
2	No 1			Caroline Goins		" "
	No 1			" "		" "
4	No 1			" "		" "
5	No 1			" "		" "
6	No 1			" "		" "
7	No 1			" "		" "
8	No 1			" "		" "
9	No 1			" "		" "
10	No 1			" "		" "
11	No 1			" "		" "
12	Nos 1 to 11 denied in 1896, case #55.					
13	No.10 Admitted as "Amanda May"					
14	Admitted by U.S. Court Ardmore, Dec 21st 1897 Court Case 127					
15						
16						
17						

122

Choctaw By Blood Enrollment Cards 1898-1914

RESIDENCE:	Chickasaw Natn		Choctaw **Nation** Choctaw **Roll**				CARD NO.	**5223**	
POST OFFICE:	Ardmore I.T.						FIELD NO.	C 268	

Dawes' Roll No.	NAME	Relationship to Person First Named	AGE	SEX	BLOOD	TRIBAL ENROLLMENT		
						Year	County	No.
1	Hignight, W.R.	Named	26	M	1/16			
2	" Nancy	Dau	2	F				
DP 3	" Earl	Son	5mo	M				
DP 4	" Ella May	Dau	5mo	F				
5								
6								
7	Nos DISMISSED 3&4							
8	SEP 10 1904							
9								
10								
11								
12								
13								
14	DENIED CITIZENSHIP BY THE CHOCTAW AND							
Nos 1,2 15	CHICKASAW CITIZENSHIP COURT							
16								
17								

TRIBAL ENROLLMENT OF PARENTS

	Name of Father	Year	County	Name of Mother	Year	County
1	W.H. Hignight		Non Citz	Elizabeth Hignight		non Citz
2	No 1			Ruth Hignight		" "
3	No 1			" "		" "
4	No 1			" "		" "
5						
6						
7	No.1 denied in 1896, case #426					
8	Admitted by U.S. Court Ardmore Mch 10 1898 Court Case 144					
9						
10	No.4 Enrolled March 4, 1901.					
11						
12						
13						
14						
15						
16						
17						

RESIDENCE:	Chickasaw Natn						CARD NO. 5224
POST OFFICE:	Ardmore I.T.	Choctaw **Nation** Choctaw **Roll**					FIELD NO. C 269

Dawes' Roll No.	NAME	Relationship to Person First Named	AGE	SEX	BLOOD	TRIBAL ENROLLMENT		
						Year	County	No.
1	Shelton, Daisy		20	F	1/32			
2	" Frank	Son	5	M				
3	" Emma	Dau	3	F				
4								
5								
6								
7								
8								
9								
10								
11								
12								
13								
14								
15								
16								
17								

CANCELLED

Is a duplication of Choctaw card #216

TRIBAL ENROLLMENT OF PARENTS

	Name of Father	Year	County	Name of Mother	Year	County
1	G.W. Buckholts		Choctaw Citz	Julia Omo		Non Citz
2	John F Shelton		Non Citz	No.1		
3	" " "		" "	No.1		
4						
5						
6						
7						
8	Admitted by U.S. Court Ardmore Dec. 21st 1897 Court Case No. 139					
9						
10	The above named people are supposed to have been enrolled at Ardmore					
11						
12						
13						
14						
15						
16						
17						

Choctaw By Blood Enrollment Cards 1898-1914

RESIDENCE:	Chickasaw Natn				Choctaw **Nation** Choctaw **Roll**				CARD NO. **5225**
POST OFFICE:	Davis Ind.T.								FIELD NO. C 270

Dawes' Roll No.	NAME	Relationship to Person First Named	AGE	SEX	BLOOD	TRIBAL ENROLLMENT		
						Year	County	No.
DP	1 Omo, Julia	First Named	39	F	I.W.			
	2 Buckholts, Nellie	Dau	14	F				
	3							
	4							
	5 #1 DISMISSED							
	6 DEC							
	7							
	8							
	9							
	10							
	11							
	12							
	13							
	14							
	15							
	16							
	17							

Transferred to Choctaw card #982

GRANTED

TRIBAL ENROLLMENT OF PARENTS

	Name of Father	Year	County	Name of Mother	Year	County
1	Robt Biggar		Non Citz	Jane Biggar	Dead	Non Citz
2	G.W. Buckholts		Choctaw Citz	No.1		
3						
4						
5	Nos. 1&2 denied in 1896, case #1407.					
6						
7	Admitted by U.S. Court Ardmore Dec 21, 1898 No 139					
8	No.2 supposed to be enrolled at Ardmore					
9	Nº2 is a duplicate of Nº on Choctaw card #221					
10	Judgement of U.S. Ct admitting No.1 vacated and set aside by [illegible]					
11	No appeal to C.C.C.C.					
12						
13						
14						
15						
16						
17			Date of Application for Enrollment	9-26-98		

125

RESIDENCE: Chickasaw Natn

POST OFFICE: Davis Ind. Terr.

Choctaw **Nation**   Choctaw **Roll**

CARD NO. **5226**

FIELD NO. C 271

Dawes' Roll No.	NAME	Relationship to Person First Named	AGE	SEX	BLOOD	TRIBAL ENROLLMENT Year	County	No.
1	Agee, W. E.	Named	35	M	I.W.			
2	" Annie	Wife	24	F				
3	" Florence	Dau	10	F				
4	" Abera	Dau	8	F				
5	" Zora	Dau	6	F				
6	" Hester L	Dau	4	F				
7	" Pearl	Dau	2					
8	" William H	Son	2 mo	M				
9								
10								
11								
12								
13								
14								
15								
16								
17								

CANCELLED

April 11th 1950

Is a duplicate of Choctaw Card (illegible)

TRIBAL ENROLLMENT OF PARENTS

	Name of Father	Year	County	Name of Mother	Year	County
1	Wm Agee		Non Citz	Mary Agee	Dead	Non Citz
2	G.W. Buckholts		Choctaw Citz	Julia Buckholts		" "
3	No.1			No.2		
4	No.1			No.2		
5	No.1			No.2		
6	No.1			No.2		
7	No.1			No.2		
8	No.1			No.2		
9						
10	No.8 was born Aug 1st 1898					
11	No6 was admitted as "Lee"					
12	The above family is supposed to have been enrolled at Ardmore					
13	Admitted by the U.S. Court at Ardmore Dec. 21st 1897 Court Case 139					
14						
15						
16						
17						

Choctaw By Blood Enrollment Cards 1898-1914

					CARD NO. **5227**
RESIDENCE:	Blue County		Choctaw **Nation**	Choctaw **Roll**	
POST OFFICE:	Fulsom	I.T.			FIELD NO. C 272

Dawes' Roll No.	NAME	Relationship to Person First Named	AGE	SEX	BLOOD	TRIBAL ENROLLMENT		
						Year	County	No.
1	Petty, Elizabeth	Named	54	F	1/8			
2	" Chas. W.	Son	22	M				
3	" George R	"	18	"				
4	" Margaret E	Dau	15	F				
5	" Jacob	Son	12	M				
DP 6	" Pansy	Gran dau	7mo	F				
DP 7	" E. J.	Son of No2	2mo	m				
DP 8	"							
9	No.1 denied by C.C.C.C.							
10	as Elizabeth A. Petty							
11	No.2 denied by C.C.C.C. as Charles W. Petty							
12								
#6-7 13	DISMISSED							
14	NOV 10 1904							
15								
16								
17								

TRIBAL ENROLLMENT OF PARENTS

	Name of Father	Year	County	Name of Mother	Year	County
1	Cary Parr	Dead	Non Citz	Sally Parr	Dead	Non Citz
2	E. J. Petty	"	"	No. 1		
3	" "	"	"	No. 1		
4	" "	"	"	No. 1		
5	" "	"	"	No. 1		
6	No.2			Mattie E. Petty		Non Citizen
7	No. 3			Minnie Ann Petty		
	No.2			Mattie E. Petty		
9	Nos 1 to 5 denied in 1896, case #562					
10	Admitted by the U.S. Court, South McAlester, I.T. Aug 25, 1897, Court Case [illegible]					
11	[Entry illegible]					
12	No. 6 Enrolled July 10, 1900					
13	No.2 is the husband of Mattie E. Petty on Choctaw card #D.596.					
14	No. 3 now is Husband of Minnie Ann Petty, non citizen. Evidence of marriage filed June 23 1902					
15	No.7 Born March 27th 1902; Enrolled June 23rd 1902					
16	No.8 Born May 6th, 1902; Enrolled July 14rh 1902					
17						

DENIED CITIZENSHIP BY THE CHOCTAW AND CHICKASAW CITIZENSHIP COURT

Choctaw By Blood Enrollment Cards 1898-1914

RESIDENCE: Blue County
POST OFFICE: Fulsom   I.T.

Choctaw **Nation**   Choctaw **Roll**

CARD NO. **5228**
FIELD NO. C 273

Dawes' Roll No.		NAME	Relationship to Person First Named	AGE	SEX	BLOOD	TRIBAL ENROLLMENT		
							Year	County	No.
	1	Petty, John L	First Named	38	M	1/8			
	2	" Mary A	Wife	29	F	IW			
	3	" Ella	Dau	8	."				
	4	" Blanche	"	5	"				
	5	" Ruben	Son	3	M				
DP	6	" Willie	Dau	1	F				
DP	7	" Clayton	Son	1mo	M				
DP	8	" Ordrel Amanda	Dau	10das	F				
	9								
	10								
	11								
	12								
	13								
	14								
	15								
	16								
	17								

DISMISSED NOV 12 1904

DISMISSED DEC 2 1904

DENIED CITIZENSHIP BY THE CHOCTAW AND CHICKASAW CITIZENSHIP COURT

TRIBAL ENROLLMENT OF PARENTS

	Name of Father	Year	County	Name of Mother	Year	County
1	E.J. Petty		Non Citz	Elizabeth Petty		Non Citz
2	J. M. Walker		" "	Manda Walker	Dead	" "
3	No1			No2		
4	No1			No2		
5	No1			No2		
6	No1			No2		
7	No1			No2		
8	No1			No2		
9	Nos 1,2,3,4&5 denied in 1896, case #562					
10	Admitted by the U.S. Court, South McAlester, I.T. Aug. 25, 1897, Court Case No22					
11	Judgement of U.S. Court admitting [illegible]					
12	No8 Born Sept. 12, 1902, enrolled Sept. 22, 1902.					
13	[Entry illegible]					
14	No.3 denied by C.C.C.C. as Ella Petty or Ellen Petty.					
15	No.5 " " " " Reuben Petty.					
16						
17						

Choctaw By Blood Enrollment Cards 1898-1914

RESIDENCE:	Blue County				CARD No.	**5229**
POST OFFICE:	Emmett, I.T.	Choctaw **Nation**	Choctaw **Roll**		FIELD No.	C 274

Dawes' Roll No.	NAME	Relationship to Person First Named	AGE	SEX	BLOOD	TRIBAL ENROLLMENT		
						Year	County	No.
1	Matlock, Louisa	Named	32	F	1/16			
2	" John	Son	9	M				
3	" Nellie	Dau	5	F				
4	" Mintie	"	2	"				
5	" Jos G. Ralls	Son	4mo	M				
6								
7	#4-5 DISMISSED							
8								
9								
10								
11								
12								
13	DENIED CITIZENSHIP BY THE CHOCTAW AND							
14	CHICKASAW CITIZENSHIP COURT							
15								
16								
17								

TRIBAL ENROLLMENT OF PARENTS

	Name of Father	Year	County	Name of Mother	Year	County
1	E. J. Petty		Non Citz	Elizabeth Petty		Non Citz
2	G.W. Matlock		" "	No 1		
3	" "		" "	No 1		
4	" "		" "	No 1		
5	" "		" "	No 1		
6						
7	Denied in 1896, case #562					
8	Admitted by the U.S. Court, South McAlester, I.T. Aug. 25, 1897. Court Case No. 22					
9	[Entry illegible]					
10	No.5 Enrolled June 10, 1900.					
11	[Entry illegible]					
12						
13	No 1 denied by C.C.C.C. as Louisa A. Matlock.					
14						
15						
16						
17					Date of Application for Enrollment	9-28-98

Choctaw By Blood Enrollment Cards 1898-1914

RESIDENCE: Blue County
POST OFFICE: Fulsom, I.T.

Choctaw **Nation**   Choctaw **Roll**

CARD No. **5230**
FIELD No. C 275

Dawes' Roll No.	NAME	Relationship to Person First Named	AGE	SEX	BLOOD	TRIBAL ENROLLMENT Year	County	No.
1	Petty, Robert C	Named	28	M	1/16			
DP 2	" Carrie	Wife	28	F	IW			
3	" Luther	Son	5	M	1/32			
DP 4	" Ethel	Dau	2	F	1/32			
DP 5	" Clatie K	"	10mo	"	1/32			
DP 6	" Toel J	Son	2½ mo	M	1/32			
7								
1-5 /8								
9								
#2 10								
11								
12								
13								
14								
15								
16								
17								

DENIED CITIZENSHIP BY THE CHOCTAW AND CHICKASAW CITIZENSHIP COURT

TRIBAL ENROLLMENT OF PARENTS

	Name of Father	Year	County	Name of Mother	Year	County
1	E.J. Petty		Non Citz	Elizabeth Petty		Non Citz
2	J.D. Wharton		" "	Rachel Wharton		" "
3	No 1			No 2		
4	No 1			No 2		
5	No 1			No 2		
6	No.1			No.2		
7	Nos. 1,2&3 denied in 1896, case #562					
8	Admitted by the U.S. Court, South McAlester, I.T. Aug 25, 1897 Court Case No22					
9						
10	No.4 was born Oct. 15, 1896.					
11						
12				No. 6 Born Jany 26, 1902. Enrolled April 8, 1902.		
13						
14						
15				No5 enrolled Oct. 30/99		
16						
17						

130

| RESIDENCE: | Blue County | | Choctaw **Nation** | Choctaw **Roll** | CARD NO. | **5231** |
| POST OFFICE: | Fulsom | I.T. | | | FIELD NO. | 276 |

Dawes' Roll No.	NAME	Relationship to Person First Named	AGE	SEX	BLOOD	TRIBAL ENROLLMENT		
						Year	County	No.
1	Stracner, Amanda P	Named	30	F	1/16			
2	Stracner, Garland Jackson	Son	1	M	1/32			
3	" Otto Carry	Son	1mo	M	1/32			
4	#2-3 DISMISSED							
5								
6	NOV 19 1904							
7								
8								
9								
10								
11								
12	DENIED CITIZENSHIP BY THE CHOCTAW AND							
13	CHICKASAW CITIZENSHIP COURT							
14								
15								
16								
17								

TRIBAL ENROLLMENT OF PARENTS

	Name of Father	Year	County	Name of Mother	Year	County
1	E. J. Petty		Non Citz	Elizabeth Petty		Non Citz
2	L. C. Stracner		" "	No. 1		
3	" "		" "	Nº 1		
4						
5	No.1 denied in 1896, case #562					
6	Admitted by the U.S. Court, South McAlester, I.T. Aug. 25, 1897, Court Case No. 22.					
7	Admitted as "Amanda P. Petty"					
8						
9	Proper post-office address is Marsden, I.T. June 3d, 1901.					
10	Proper spelling of surname is "Stracner"					
11	No.2 born Dec. 10, 1900: Enrolled Jan. 8, 1902					
12	Nº3 Born Aug. 20, 1902; enrolled Sept 19, 1902.					
13						
14	No.1 denied by C.C.C.C. as Amanda P. Petty.					
15						
16						
17				Date of Application for Enrollment		9-28-98

Choctaw By Blood Enrollment Cards 1898-1914

RESIDENCE: Chickasaw Natn
POST OFFICE: Tishomingo, I.T.

Choctaw **Nation**   Choctaw **Roll**

CARD NO. **5232**
FIELD NO.

Dawes' Roll No.	NAME	Relationship to Person First Named	AGE	SEX	BLOOD	TRIBAL ENROLLMENT Year	County	No.
1	Mickle, Nicholas J	First Named	40	M				
2	" Nora	Wife	37					
3	" Lawrence	Son	18					
4	" John	"	11					
5								
6								
7								
8								
9								
11								
12								
13								
14								
15								
16								
17								

DENIED CITIZENSHIP BY THE CHOCTAW AND CHICKASAW CITIZENSHIP COURT

TRIBAL ENROLLMENT OF PARENTS

	Name of Father	Year	County	Name of Mother	Year	County
1	Harmon Mickle	Dead	Choc. Citz	Joanna Mickle		Non Citz
2	John Roberts		Non Citz	[Name illegible]		" "
3	No 1			Anna Mickle	Dead	" "
4	No 1			" "	"	" "
5						
6	Nos 1 to 4 denied in 1896, case #400.					
7	Admitted by the U.S. Court, South McAlester, I.T. Aug. 25, 1897. Court Case No. 240					
8						
9	The father of No1 married a Choctaw Citizen about 1850, who died.					
10	He then married a white woman to whom No1 was born.					
11	Mother of No1 is Joanna Mickle on Choctaw card #4521.					
12	No2 is a white woman.					
13						
14						
15						
16						
17						

132

Choctaw By Blood Enrollment Cards 1898-1914

| RESIDENCE: | Chickasaw Natn | | | | | | | | CARD NO. **5233** |
| POST OFFICE: | Tishomingo, I.T. | | Choctaw **Nation** | | | Choctaw **Roll** | | | FIELD NO. 0278 |

Dawes' Roll No.	NAME	Relationship to Person First Named	AGE	SEX	BLOOD	TRIBAL ENROLLMENT		
						Year	County	No.
1	Mickle, William	Named	28	M	IW			
2								
3								
4								
5								
6								
7								
8								
9								
10								
11								
12								
13								
14								
15								
16								
17								

DENIED CITIZENSHIP BY THE CHOCTAW AND CHICKASAW CITIZENSHIP COURT

TRIBAL ENROLLMENT OF PARENTS

	Name of Father	Year	County	Name of Mother	Year	County
1	Karmon Mickle	Dead	Choc Citz	Joanna Mickle		Non Citz
2						
3						
4						
5						
6	No.1 denied in 1896, case #400					
7	Admitted by the U.S. Court, South McAlester, I.T. Aug. 25, 1897					
8	Court Case No 2					
9				Mother of No.1 is Joanna Mickle on Choctaw card #4521.		
10						
11						
12						
13						
14						
15						
16						
17						

Choctaw By Blood Enrollment Cards 1898-1914

RESIDENCE:	Chickasaw Natn					CARD NO. 5234
POST OFFICE:	Norton, I.T.	Choctaw **Nation**	Choctaw **Roll**			FIELD NO.

Dawes' Roll No.	NAME	Relationship to Person First Named	AGE	SEX	BLOOD	TRIBAL ENROLLMENT		
						Year	County	No.
() ✓ 1	Leard, Julius M		29	M	1/4			
() ✓ 2	" Frank	Son	9	"	1/8			
() ✓ 3	" Sudie	Dau	7	F	1/8			
() ✓ 4	" Nannie	"	5	"	1/8			
✓ 5	" Barney Edward	Son	2mo	M	1/8			
✓ 6	" David	Son	6wks	M	1/8			
7								
#5-6 8								
9								
10								
11								
12								
13								
14								
15								
16								
17								

DENIED CITIZENSHIP BY THE CHOCTAW AND
CHICKASAW CITIZENSHIP COURT

TRIBAL ENROLLMENT OF PARENTS

	Name of Father	Year	County	Name of Mother	Year	County
1	D.J. Leard		Non Citz	Susanna Leard	Dead	Non Citz
2	No.1			Mary C. Leard	Dead	Non Citz
3	No.1			" " "	" " "
4	No.1			" " "	" " "
5	No.1			" " "	" " "
6	No.1			" " "	" " "
7						
8	Nos. 1 to 4 denied in 1896, case #850.					
9	Admitted by the U.S. Curt, South McAlester, I.T. Jan 19, 1898					
10	Court Case No.[illegible]					
11	No.5 Enrolled Aug. 6th, 1900					
12	No.6 Born September 22, 1901; Enrolled November [illegible]					
13						
14						
15						
16						
17						

Choctaw By Blood Enrollment Cards 1898-1914

RESIDENCE: Chickasaw Natn
POST OFFICE: Tishomingo, I.T.

Choctaw **Nation**   Choctaw **Roll**

CARD NO. **5235**
FIELD NO. C 280

Dawes' Roll No. DEAD.	NAME	Relationship to Person First Named	AGE	SEX	BLOOD	TRIBAL ENROLLMENT Year	County	No.
1	Cobb, W. F. DEAD.		50	M				
2	" Ida M	Wife	37	F	I.W.			
3	" Grace M	Dau	18	"				
4	" Hugh T	Son	11	M				
5	" Lillian B	Dau	9	F				
6	" Sailie B	"	7	"				
7	" George A	"[sic]	4	"				
8	" Townsend	Son	4m	M				
9	Pautsky, William Allen	Son of No3	1mo	M				
10								
11	#840							
12								
13								
14								
15								
16								
17								

DISMISSED MAY 27 1904

DENIED CITIZENSHIP BY THE CHOCTAW AND CHICKASAW CITIZENSHIP COURT

TRIBAL ENROLLMENT OF PARENTS

	Name of Father	Year	County	Name of Mother	Year	County
1	S.B. Cobb	Dead	Non Citz	Missiana Cobb	Dead	Non Citz
2	D. [illegible]		[illegible]	Sailie Bell[illegible]		[Illegible]
3	No1			No2		
4	No1			No2		
5	No1			No2		
6	No1			No2		
7	No1			No2		
8	No1			No2		
9	J.A. Pautsky		noncitizen	No3		
10	Nos. 1 to 7 denied in 1896, case #734					
11	Admitted by the U.S. Court, Ardmore, I.T. Jan. 18, 1898, Court Case No. 140					
12	[Entry illegible]					
13	No.8 was born June 25th 1898					
14	No1 died Feby 1, 1894. Proof of death filed Aug. 19, 1901.					
15	No3 is now the wife of J.A. Pautsky a noncitizen. Evidence of marriage filed Aug. 21, 1901					
16	No9 enrolled Aug. 21, 1901					
17	For child of No3 see NB #10 16 See Act Apr 26-06					

Date of Application for Enrollment 9-29-98

135

RESIDENCE:	Chickasaw Natn								

Choctaw Nation   Choctaw **Roll**

CARD NO. **5236**

FIELD NO.

Dawes' Roll No.	NAME	Relationship to Person First Named	AGE	SEX	BLOOD	TRIBAL ENROLLMENT		
						Year	County	No.
1	Mickle, Peter		31	M	I.W.			
2								
3								
4								
5								
6								
7								
8								
9								
10								
11								
12								
13								
14								
15								
16								
17								

POST OFFICE: Tishomingo, I.T.

TRIBAL ENROLLMENT OF PARENTS

	Name of Father	Year	County	Name of Mother	Year	County
1	Harman Mickle	Dead	Choc Citz	Joanna Mickle		Non Citz
2						
3						
4						
5						
6						
7	No.1 denied in 1896, case #400					
8	Admitted by the U.S. Court, South McAlester, I.T.					
9	Aug. 25, 1897, Court Case No. 240.					
10						
11						
12						
13						
14						
15						
16						
17						

Choctaw By Blood Enrollment Cards 1898-1914

Dawes' Roll No.	NAME	Relationship to Person First Named	AGE	SEX	BLOOD	TRIBAL ENROLLMENT		
						Year	County	No.
1	Davis, John A		36	M	1/8			
2	" Samuel	Son	12	"	1/16			
3	" William	"	10	"	1/16			
4	" Frank	"	8	"	1/16			
5	" Pearl	Dau	3	F	1/16			
6	" Lillie May	"	1	"	1/16			
7	" Lou Ella	"	2mo	"	1/16			
8								
9								
10								
11								
12								
13								
14								
15								
16								
17								

FEB 5 1902

CANCELLED

TRIBAL ENROLLMENT OF PARENTS

	Name of Father	Year	County	Name of Mother	Year	County
1	Henry Davis	Dead	Non Citz	Ellen P. Davis		Non Citz
2	No 1			Mollie Davis		" "
3	No 1			" "		" "
4	No 1			" "		" "
5	No 1			" "		" "
6	No 1			" "		" "
7	No 1			" "		" "
8						
9	Admitted by the U.S. Court, South McAlester, I.T. Aug 30, 1897					
10	Court Case No 66.					
11	No6 was born September 14, 1897,					
12	No.7 enrolled Dec 14/99 subject to receipt of evidence of marriage of					
13	parents which has been requested. See Card No 3400					
14						
15						
16						28
17						9-29-98

137

Choctaw By Blood Enrollment Cards 1898-1914

RESIDENCE: Chickasaw Natn						CARD NO. 5238
POST OFFICE: Lebanon, I.T.		Choctaw **Nation**		Choctaw **Roll**		FIELD NO.

Dawes' Roll No.	NAME Osborn	Relationship to Person First Named	AGE	SEX	BLOOD	TRIBAL ENROLLMENT		
						Year	County	No.
1	Schockley[sic], Mattie		42	F	I.W.	18[??]	Choc Dist	307A
2	" John E	Son	12	M	1/16			
3								
4	DECISION RENDERED							
5								
6	GRANTED							
7								
8	COPY OF DECISION FORWARDED APPLICANT							
9								
10	COPY OF DECISION FORWARDED ATTORNEYS FOR CHOCTAW AND CHICKASAW NATIONS.							
11								
12								
13								
14								
15	RECORD FORWARDED DEPARTMENT.							
16	NOTICE OF DEPARTMENTAL ACTION FORWARDED ATTORNEY FOR APPLICANT							

TRIBAL ENROLLMENT OF PARENTS

	Name of Father	Year	County	Name of Mother	Year	County
1	Moses Lunsford	Dead	Non Citz	Eliza Lunsford	Dead	Non Citz
2	John Shockley	"	" "	No1		
3						
4						
5						
6	Nos. 1&2 admitted in 1896, case #955.					
7	Admitted by the U.S. Court S. McAlester, I.T. Aug. 30, 1899 Court Case No 221					
8	No2 was admitted Eddie Shockley					
9	No1 on 1896 roll as Mattie Shockley					
10	[Entry illegible]					
11						
12						
13						
14						
15						
16						
17						

DENIED CITIZENSHIP BY THE CHOCTAW AND CHICKASAW CITIZENSHIP COURT

and transferred to Choctaw Card #6034 May 20-06

138

Choctaw By Blood Enrollment Cards 1898-1914

RESIDENCE: Chickasaw Natn
POST OFFICE: Oakland, I.T.

Choctaw **Nation** Choctaw **Roll**

CARD NO. **5239**
FIELD NO. 284

Dawes' Roll No.	NAME	Relationship to Person First Named	AGE	SEX	BLOOD	TRIBAL ENROLLMENT		
						Year	County	No.
1	Dutton, Henry		72	M	IW			
2								
3								
4								
5								
6								
7								
8								
9								
10								
11								
12								
13								
14								
15								
16								
17								

TRIBAL ENROLLMENT OF PARENTS

	Name of Father	Year	County	Name of Mother	Year	County
1	Peter Dutton	Dead	Non Citz	Barbara Dutton	Dead	Non Citz
2						
3						
4						
5						
6	Rejected by the Dawes Com.		Appealed to the U.S. Court, Ardmore, I.T. and			
7	admitted June 23, 1897, Court Case No. 132					
8	Appealed to the U.S. Court					
9						
10						
11						
12						
13						
14						
15						
16						
17						

139

Choctaw By Blood Enrollment Cards 1898-1914

RESIDENCE: Chickasaw Natn		Choctaw **Nation**		Choctaw **Roll**		CARD NO. 5240	
POST OFFICE: Willis, I.T.						FIELD NO.	

Dawes' Roll No.	NAME	Relationship to Person First Named	AGE	SEX	BLOOD	TRIBAL ENROLLMENT		
						Year	County	No.
1	Buck, J. G.		68	M	I.W.			
2	" Martha Jane	Wife	60	F				
3	" Fitzgerald	Son	21	M				
4	" Wm R.	"	18	"				
5	" Clarence	"	15	"				
6	" Homer Jiri	G.Son	2mo	M				
7								
8								
9								
10								
11								
12								
13								
14								
15								
16								
17								

DENIED CITIZENSHIP BY THE CHOCTAW AND CHICKASAW CITIZENSHIP COURT June 29/04

	TRIBAL ENROLLMENT OF PARENTS					
	Name of Father	Year	County	Name of Mother	Year	County
1	Abram Buck	Dead	Non Citz	Katie Buck	Dead	Non Citz
2	Thos Taylor	"		Catherine Taylor	"	" "
3	No1			No2		
4	No1			No2		
5	No1			No2		
6	No3			Sallie Buck		noncitizen
7						
8	Rejected by the Dawes Com. case #631. Appealed to the U.S. Court, Ardmore, I.T.					
9	and admitted June 23, 1897. Court Case No. 132					
10	Appealed to the U.S. Supreme Court.					
11	[Entries illegible.]					
12	No.2 was admitted as Martha Buck					
13	No.3 is now the husband of Sallie Buck, a non citizen. Evidence of marriage filed Sept.20,1901					
14	No.6 Enrolled Sept 20, 1901. For child of No4 see NB 958 (Act Apr 26-06)					
15	For children of No5 see " 959 " " "					
16						
17	No.6 Dismissed 97					

140

Choctaw By Blood Enrollment Cards 1898-1914

RESIDENCE:	Chickasaw Natn
POST OFFICE:	Willis, I.T.

Choctaw **Nation**   Choctaw **Roll**

CARD NO. **5241**

FIELD NO. C 286

Dawes' Roll No.	NAME	Relationship to Person First Named	AGE	SEX	BLOOD	TRIBAL ENROLLMENT		
						Year	County	No.
1	Buck, George Piper		36	M	1/32			
2	" Rosa	Dau	11	F				
3								
4								
5								
6								
7								
8								
9								
10								
11								
12								
13								
14								
15								
16								
17								

DENIED CITIZENSHIP BY THE CHOCTAW AND CHICKASAW CITIZENSHIP COURT June 29/04

TRIBAL ENROLLMENT OF PARENTS

	Name of Father	Year	County	Name of Mother	Year	County
1	J. G. Buck		Non Citz	Martha J. Buck		Non Citz
2	No.1			Cynda Buck		" "
3						
4						
5	Rejected by the Dawes Com. case #631. Appealed to the U.S. Court, Ardmore, I.T.					
6	and admitted June 23, 1897, Court Case No 132					
7	Appealed to the U.S. Supreme Court					
8						
9	No.1 is now the husband of Ada C. Buck on Choctaw card #D.773; Aug. 21, 1902.					
10						
11	P.O. address: Oakland, I.T.					
12						
13	For child of No1 see NB #1038 (Act Apr 26 06)					
14						
15						
16						
17						Date of Application for Enrollment 10-4-98

Choctaw By Blood Enrollment Cards 1898-1914

RESIDENCE: Chickasaw Natn

POST OFFICE: Willis, I.T.

Choctaw **Nation** Choctaw **Roll**

CARD No. **5242**

FIELD No.

Dawes' Roll No.	NAME	Relationship to Person First Named	AGE	SEX	BLOOD	TRIBAL ENROLLMENT		
						Year	County	No.
1	Dutton, James H	First Named	43	M	1/8			
2	" Virgie	Son	8	"	1/16			
3	" Mary	Dau	6	F	1/16			
4	" Jessie	"	4	"	1/16			
5	" Zella	"	2	"	1/16			
6	" Dorsey	Son	3wks	M	1/16			
7	" Dora Cordelia	Dau	3wks	F	1/16			
8								
9								
10								
11								
12								
13								
14								
15								
16								
17								

DENIED CITIZENSHIP BY THE CHOCTAW AND CHICKASAW CITIZENSHIP COURT

	TRIBAL ENROLLMENT OF PARENTS					
	Name of Father	Year	County	Name of Mother	Year	County
1	Henry Dutton		Non Citz	Harriet Dutton	Dead	Non Citz
2	No 1			Rutha J Dutton		" "
3	No 1			" "		" "
4	No 1			" "		" "
5	No 1			" "		" "
6	No 1			" "		" "
7	No 1			" "		" "
8						
9	Rejected by the Dawes Com case #319. Appealed to the U.S. Court, Ardmore, I.T. and					
10	admitted June 23, 1897. Court Case No 132. Appealed to the U.S. Supreme Court					
11						
12	No.5 was born November 25, 1896					
13	No5 Affidavit of attending Physician to be supplied. Filed Oct. 30/99.					
14	No.6 was enrolled Oct. 30/99					
15	No.7 Enrolled Aug. 24, 1901.					
16	Evidence of marriage of parents of No. 6 to be supplied. Filed Dec. 14/99.					
17						

Choctaw By Blood Enrollment Cards 1898-1914

RESIDENCE: Chickasaw Natn						CARD NO. **5243**		
POST OFFICE: Willis, I.T.		Choctaw **Nation**	Choctaw **Roll**			FIELD NO. C 288		

Dawes' Roll No.	NAME	Relationship to Person First Named	AGE	SEX	BLOOD	TRIBAL ENROLLMENT		
						Year	County	No.
1	Dutton, Robert	Named	42	M	1/8			
2	" Dora V	Dau	13	F				
3	" Maggie	"	7	"				
4	" Monta	"	3	"				
5	" Charley B	Son	3wk	M				
6								
7								
8								
9								
10								
11								
12								
13								
14								
15								
16								
17								

No DISMISSED OCT

DENIED CITIZENSHIP BY THE CHOCTAW AND CHICKASAW CITIZENSHIP COURT

TRIBAL ENROLLMENT OF PARENTS

	Name of Father	Year	County	Name of Mother	Year	County
1	Henry Dutton		Non Citz	Harriet Dutton	Dead	Non Citz
2	No 1			Alice Dutton		" "
3	No 1			" "		" "
4	No 1			" "		" "
5	No 1			" "		" "
6						
7	Rejected by the Dawes Com case #319. Appealed to the U.S. Court, Ardmore, I.T. and					
8	admitted June 23, 1897. Court Case No 132. Appealed to the U.S. Supreme Court.					
9						
10	No.5 was born Sept. 13, 1898					
11						
12	No5 - Affidavit of attending Physician to be supplied.					
13						
14						
15						
16						
17						

Choctaw By Blood Enrollment Cards 1898-1914

RESIDENCE: Chickasaw Natn	Choctaw **Nation** Choctaw **Roll**	CARD NO. **5244**
POST OFFICE: Oakland, I.T.		FIELD NO.

Dawes' Roll No.	NAME	Relationship to Person First Named	AGE	SEX	BLOOD	TRIBAL ENROLLMENT Year	County	No.
1	Dutton, Stephen A		37	M	1/8			
2	" Delia	Dau	11	F				
3	" Beulah	"	9	"				
4	" Berta	"	7	"				
5	" Sherman E	Son	3	M				
6	" Willis	"	1	"				
7	" Hughlin	"	2mo	M				
8								
9								
10								
11								
12								
13								
14								
15								
16								
17								

DENIED CITIZENSHIP BY THE CHOCTAW AND
CHICKASAW CITIZENSHIP COURT

TRIBAL ENROLLMENT OF PARENTS

	Name of Father	Year	County	Name of Mother	Year	County
1	Henry Dutton		Non Citz	Harriet Dutton	Dead	Non Citz
2	No 1			Elie Dutton		" "
3	No 1			" "		" "
4	No 1			" "		" "
5	No 1			" "		" "
6	No 1			" "		" "
7	No. 1			" "		" "
8	Rejected by the Dawes Com case #319. Appealed to the U.S. Court, Ardmore, I.T. and					
9	admitted June 23, 1897 Court Case No 132. Appealed to the U S Supreme Court					
10						
11	No6 was born Aug 14, 1897					
12	No6 - Affidavit of attending Physician to be supplied. Filed Jany 17, 1900					
13						
14	No7 Enrolled June 23d 1901					
15						
16						
17						

144

Choctaw By Blood Enrollment Cards 1898-1914

RESIDENCE:	Blue County							CARD NO.	**5245**
POST OFFICE:	Boggy Depot, I.T.		Choctaw **Nation**			Choctaw **Roll**		FIELD NO.	

Dawes' Roll No.	NAME	Relationship to Person First Named	AGE	SEX	BLOOD	TRIBAL ENROLLMENT		
						Year	County	No.
1	Dutton, David C	Named	27	M	1/8			
2	" Lela Edna	Dau	1m	F				
3								
4	No2 ~~DISMIS~~							
5								
6								
7								
8								
9								
10								
11								
12								
13								
14								
15								
16								
17								

DENIED CITIZENSHIP BY THE CHOCTAW AND CHICKASAW CITIZENSHIP COURT

#1

TRIBAL ENROLLMENT OF PARENTS

	Name of Father	Year	County	Name of Mother	Year	County
1	Henry Dutton		Non Citz	Harriet Dutton	Dead	Non Citz
2	No1			Emma Dutton		" "
3						
4						
5	Rejected by the Dawes Com case #319. Appealed to the U.S. Court, Ardmore, I.T. and					
6	admitted June 23, 1897. Court Case No 132. Appealed to the U.S. Supreme Court.					
7						
8	No.2 was born Aug. 18, 1898					
9						
10	No2 - Affidavit of attending Physician to be supplied. Received Oct. 13, 1898					
11						
12						
13						
14						
15						
16						
17						

Choctaw By Blood Enrollment Cards 1898-1914

RESIDENCE: Chickasaw Natn

POST OFFICE: Willis, I.T.

Choctaw **Nation**   Choctaw **Roll**

CARD No. **5246**

FIELD No.

Dawes' Roll No.	NAME	Relationship to Person First Named	AGE	SEX	BLOOD	TRIBAL ENROLLMENT		
						Year	County	No.
1	Thorn, Lelia	Named	23	F	1/8			
2	" Hattie B	Dau	6	"	1/16			
3	" William Earnest	Son	4mo	M	1/16			
4	" James Burris	Son	1mo	M	1/16			
5								
6								
7								
8								
9								
10								
11								
12								
13								
14								
15								
16								
17								

DENIED CITIZENSHIP BY THE CHOCTAW AND CHICKASAW CITIZENSHIP COURT

	TRIBAL ENROLLMENT OF PARENTS					
	Name of Father	Year	County	Name of Mother	Year	County
1	Henry Dutton		Non Citz	Harriet Dutton	Dead	Non Citz
2	Willie Thorn		" "	No 1		
3	" "		" "	No 1		
4	W.A. Thorn		" "	No 1		
5						
6	Rejected by the Dawes Com case #319 Appealed to the U.S. Court, Ardmore, I.T. and					
7	admitted June 23, 1897 Court Case No 132. Appealed to the U.S. Supreme Court.					
8						
9	Post office address of No1 is Kingston, I.T.					
10						
11	No.4 Enrolled June 28, 1901.					
12						
13						
14						
15					No3 Enrolled Dec. 14/99	
16						
17						

Choctaw By Blood Enrollment Cards 1898-1914

RESIDENCE: Atoka County
POST OFFICE: Coalgate, I.T.

Choctaw **Nation**   Choctaw **Roll**

CARD NO. **5247**
FIELD NO. (29?

Dawes' Roll No.	NAME	Relationship to Person First Named	AGE	SEX	BLOOD	TRIBAL ENROLLMENT		
						Year	County	No.
1	Dutton, Roy		5	M	1/16			
2								
3								
4								
5								
6								
7								
8								
9								
10								
11								
12								
13								
14								
15								
16								
17								

TRIBAL ENROLLMENT OF PARENTS

	Name of Father	Year	County	Name of Mother	Year	County
1	John Dutton	Dead	Non Citz	Mary Dutton		Non Citz
2						
3						
4						
5						
6						
7	Rejected by the Dawes Com case #319. Appealed to the U.S. Court, Ardmore, I.T. and					
8	admitted June 23, 1897. Court Case No 132. Appealed to the U.S. Supreme Court.					
9						
10						
11						
12						
13						
14						
15						
16						763
17					Date of application for enrollment	10-4-98

RESIDENCE: Chickasaw Natn
POST OFFICE: Willis, I.T.

Choctaw **Nation**   Choctaw **Roll**

CARD NO. **5248**
FIELD NO.

Dawes' Roll No.	NAME	Relationship to Person First Named	AGE	SEX	BLOOD	TRIBAL ENROLLMENT		
						Year	County	No.
1	Taylor, Mary C		43	F				
2	" Andrew	Son	16	M				
3	" Jesse	"	14	"				
4	" Ida	Dau	9	F				
5	" Oscar	Son	12	M				
6	" Ora	"	6	"				
7	" Marion	"	3	"				
8								
9								
10								
11								
12								
13								
14								
15								
16								
17								

TRIBAL ENROLLMENT OF PARENTS

	Name of Father	Year	County	Name of Mother	Year	County
1	Geo. Buck		Non Citz	Martha Buck		Non Citz
2	Sam Taylor	Dead	" "	No 1		
3	" "	"	" "	No 1		
4	" "	"	" "	No 1		
5	" "	"	" "	No 1		
6	" "	"	" "	No 1		
7	" "	"	" "	No 1		
8						
9	Rejected by the Dawes Com, case #631. Appealed to U.S. Court Ardmore, I.T. and					
10	admitted June 23, 1898, Court Case No 132. Appealed to U.S. Supreme Court.					
11						
12						
13						
14						
15						
16						
17						

DENIED CITIZENSHIP BY THE CHOCTAW AND CHICKASAW CITIZENSHIP COURT

Choctaw By Blood Enrollment Cards 1898-1914

RESIDENCE: Chickasaw Natn							CARD NO. **5249**
POST OFFICE: I.T.	Choctaw **Nation** Choctaw **Roll**						FIELD NO. 294

Dawes' Roll No.	NAME	Relationship to Person First Named	AGE	SEX	BLOOD	TRIBAL ENROLLMENT		
						Year	County	No.
1	Taylor, Robert	Named	24	M				
2	" Rutha Lou	Dau	2mo	F				
3	" Dovey Lee	Dau	7wks	F				
4								
5	Nos DIS							
6	2&3							
7								
8								
9								
10								
11		DENIED CITIZENSHIP BY THE CHOCTAW AND						
#2-3 12		CHICKASAW CITIZENSHIP COURT						
13								
14								
15								
16								
17								

TRIBAL ENROLLMENT OF PARENTS

	Name of Father	Year	County	Name of Mother	Year	County
1	Sam Taylor	Dead	Non Citz	Mary [?] Taylor	Dead	Non Citz
2	No 1			Martha C. Taylor	" "	
3	Nº 1			" "	" "	
4						
5						
6	Rejected by the Dawes Com, case #631. Appealed to U.S. Court Ardmore, I.T. and					
7	admitted June 23, 1898, Court Case No 132. Appealed to U.S. Supreme Court.					
8						
9	No.2 enrolled Oct 30/99 subject to receipt of evidence of marriage of parents					
10	Letter requesting same this day Rec'd and filed Nov. 23/99					
11	Nº 3 Born Aug. 19, 1902, enrolled Oct. 10, 1902.					
12						
13						
14						
15						
16						
17					Date of Application for Enrollment. 10-4-98	

149

Choctaw By Blood Enrollment Cards 1898-1914

RESIDENCE: Chickasaw Natn
POST OFFICE: Oakland, I.T.

Choctaw **Nation**   Choctaw **Roll**

CARD NO. **5250**
FIELD NO.

Dawes' Roll No.	NAME	Relationship to Person First Named	AGE	SEX	BLOOD	TRIBAL ENROLLMENT Year	County	No.
1	Bardin, Virgie		20	F				
2	" Callie	Dau	1mo	"				
3								
4								
5								
6								
7								
8								
9								
10								
11								
12								
13								
14								
15								
16								
17								

DENIED CITIZENSHIP BY THE CHOCTAW AND CHICKASAW CITIZENSHIP COURT

TRIBAL ENROLLMENT OF PARENTS

	Name of Father	Year	County	Name of Mother	Year	County
1	Sam Taylor	Dead	Non Citz	Mary C. Taylor		Non Citz
2	William Bardin	"	"	No. 1		
3						
4						
5						
6						
7	Rejected by the Dawes Com. case #631. Appealed to U.S. Court Ardmore, I.T. and					
8	admitted June 23, 1898, Court Case No 132. Appealed to U.S. Supreme Court.					
9						
10						
11						
12						
13						
14						
15						
16						
17						

150

Choctaw By Blood Enrollment Cards 1898-1914

| RESIDENCE: | Chickasaw Natn | | | | | CARD NO. | **5251** |
| POST OFFICE: | Willis, I.T. | Choctaw **Nation** | Choctaw **Roll** | | | FIELD NO. | |

Dawes' Roll No.	NAME	Relationship to Person First Named	AGE	SEX	BLOOD	TRIBAL ENROLLMENT		
						Year	County	No.
1	Buck, Joseph F		34	M				
2	" Erastus	Son	4	"				
3	" Ceicil[sic] Martin	Son	1mo	M				
4								
5								
6								
7								
8								
9								
10								
11								
12								
13								
14								
15								
16								
17								

DISMIS

DENIED CITIZENSHIP BY THE CHOCTAW AND CHICKASAW CITIZENSHIP COURT

TRIBAL ENROLLMENT OF PARENTS

	Name of Father	Year	County	Name of Mother	Year	County
1	Geo. Buck		Non Citz	Martha Buck		Non Citz
2	No 1			Julia A. Buck		" "
3	No.1			" "		" "
4						
5						
6	Rejected by the Dawes Com. case #631. Appealed to U.S. Court Ardmore, I.T. and					
7	admitted June 23, 1898, Court Case No 132. Appealed to U.S. Supreme Court.					
8	No.3 Born March 27, 1902; Enrolled April 14, 1902					
9						
10						
11						
12						
13						
14						
15						
16						
17						

Choctaw By Blood Enrollment Cards 1898-1914

RESIDENCE: Chickasaw Natn   Choctaw **Nation**   Choctaw **Roll**   CARD NO. **5252**

POST OFFICE: Holder, I.T.   FIELD NO.

Dawes' Roll No.	NAME	Relationship to Person First Named	AGE	SEX	BLOOD	TRIBAL ENROLLMENT		
						Year	County	No.
1	Bingham, Elizabeth	Named	23	F				
2	" William P	Son	1/2	M				
3	" Charles B	Son	6wks	M				
4								
5								
No.6								
263 7								
8								
9								
10								
11								
12								
13								
14								
15								
16								
17								

DENIED CITIZENSHIP BY THE CHOCTAW AND CHICKASAW CITIZENSHIP COURT

TRIBAL ENROLLMENT OF PARENTS

	Name of Father	Year	County	Name of Mother	Year	County
1	Sam Taylor	Dead	Non Citz	Mary C. Taylor		Non Citz
2	B.Z. Bingham		" "	No. 1		
3	" "		" "	No. 1		
4						
5						
6						
7	Rejected by the Dawes Com. case #631. Appealed to U.S. Court Ardmore, I.T. and					
8	admitted June 23, 1897[sic], Court Case No 132. Appealed to U.S. Supreme Court					
9						
10	No2 was born March 2, 1898					
11						
12	No2 - Affidavit of attending Physician to be supplied					
13	Received and filed Feby 21st, 1900.					
14	No.3 Enrolled Dec. 26th, 1900					
15	Correct spelling of surname is Bigham; See letter of Jan. 10, 1901					
16						
17						

152

Choctaw By Blood Enrollment Cards 1898-1914

RESIDENCE: Chickasaw Natn

POST OFFICE: Willis, Ind. Ter.

Choctaw **Nation**   Choctaw **Roll**

CARD NO. **5253**

FIELD NO. C 298

Dawes' Roll No.	NAME	Relationship to Person First Named	AGE	SEX	BLOOD	TRIBAL ENROLLMENT		
						Year	County	No.
1	Jacks, Ora A		23	F	1/16			
2	" George W	Son	3	M				
3	" John Alfred	Son	1	"				
4	" Janie Magnolia	Dau	6mo	F				
5								
6								
7								
8								
9								
10								
11								
12								
13								
14								
15								
16								
17								

Nos. DISM #1&4

DENIED CITIZENSHIP BY THE CHOCTAW AND CHICKASAW CITIZENSHIP COURT #1&2

TRIBAL ENROLLMENT OF PARENTS

	Name of Father	Year	County	Name of Mother	Year	County
1	George Buck		Non Citizen	Martha Buck		Non Citizen
2	W. P. Jacks		" "	No1		
3	" " "		" "	No1		
4	" " "		" "	No.1		
5						
6	Rejected by the Dawes Commission case #631. Appealed to United States Court at Ardmore,					
7	and admitted June 23d, 1898, Court Case No 132. Appealed to U.S. Supreme Court.					
8	No.4 Enrolled June 27, 1901					
9						
10						
11						
12						
13						
14						
15						
16						
17						

Choctaw By Blood Enrollment Cards 1898-1914

RESIDENCE: Chickasaw Natn
POST OFFICE: Willis, Ind. Ter.

Choctaw **Nation**   Choctaw **Roll**

CARD NO. **5254**
FIELD NO.

Dawes' Roll No.	NAME	Relationship to Person First Named	AGE	SEX	BLOOD	TRIBAL ENROLLMENT Year	County	No.
1	Parker, Lela G		26	F	1/16			
2	" Linden	son	4	M				
3	" Clarence Hubbard	son	5mo	M	1/32			
4								
5								
6								
7								
8								
9								
10								
11								
12								
13								
14								
15								
16								
17								

#1&2 DENIED CITIZENSHIP BY THE CHOCTAW AND CHICKASAW CITIZENSHIP COURT

TRIBAL ENROLLMENT OF PARENTS

	Name of Father	Year	County	Name of Mother	Year	County
1	George Buck		Non Citizen	Martha Buck		Non Citizen
2	J. W. Parker		" "	No. 1		
3	J. W. Parker			No 1		
4						
5						
6	Rejected by the Dawes Commission case #631. Appealed to United States Court at Ardmore,					
7	and admitted June 23d 1898, Court Case No 132. Appealed to U.S. Supreme Court.					
8						
9	No.3 Born Oct 7, 1898. Erroneously enrolled on Chickasaw card #997 Nov. 6, 1899					
10	No3 transferred to this card February 9, 1904.					
11						
12						
13						
14						
15						
16						
17						

Choctaw By Blood Enrollment Cards 1898-1914

RESIDENCE: Chickasaw Natn
POST OFFICE: Willis, Ind. Ter.

Choctaw **Nation**   Choctaw **Roll**

CARD NO. **5255**
FIELD NO. C 300

Dawes' Roll No.	NAME	Relationship to Person First Named	AGE	SEX	BLOOD	TRIBAL ENROLLMENT Year	County	No.
1	Buck, Thomas J	Named	30	M				
2	" Ora M	dau	8	F				
3	" Clinton	son	5	M				
4	" Alma	dau	3	F				
5	" Ray	son	3mo	M				
6	" Stonewall	son	2½mo	M				
7								
8	Nos 5&6							
9								
10								
11								
12								
13								
14								
15	#1 2,3,4							
16								
17								

DENIED CITIZENSHIP BY THE CHOCTAW AND CHICKASAW CITIZENSHIP COURT

TRIBAL ENROLLMENT OF PARENTS

	Name of Father	Year	County	Name of Mother	Year	County
1	George Buck		non citizen	Martha Buck		non citizen
2	No 1			Becky "		" "
3	No 1			" "		" "
4	No 1			" "		" "
5	No 1			" "		" "
6	Nº 1			" "		" "
7						
8	Rejected by the Dawes Commission case #631 Appealed to United States Court at Ardmore,					
9	and admitted June 23ᵈ 1898, Court Case No 132 Appealed to U.S. Supreme Court.					
10	Nº6 Born June 19, 1901; enrolled Sept. 4, 1902.					
11						
12						
13						
14						
15					No5 enrolled July 1/99	
16						
17						10/4/98

155

RESIDENCE:	Chickasaw Natn							

RESIDENCE: Chickasaw Natn
POST OFFICE: Silo, I.T.

Choctaw **Nation**   Choctaw **Roll**

CARD NO. **5256**
FIELD NO.

Dawes' Roll No.	NAME	Relationship to Person First Named	AGE	SEX	BLOOD	TRIBAL ENROLLMENT		
						Year	County	No.
X o ✓	1 Kizer, Sarah E	Named	57	F	1/8			
X ✓	2 " Cordelia	Dau	20	"	1/16			
X ✓	3 " Julia A	"	18	"	1/16			
X o ✓	4 " Arthur A	Son	15	M	1/16			
X	5 " Hannah B	Dau	13	F	1/16			
DP	6 Roller, Joseph Wayne	G.Son	2mo	M	1/32			
"	7 McFarland, Nevaloy	G.Dau	1mo	F	1/32			
"	8 Roller, Robert Loyce	Son[sic]	1mo	M	1/32			
	9							
	10							
	11							
	12							
	13							
	14							
	15							
	16 Nos. 1 to 5 denied in 1896, case #231.							
	17							

DENIED CITIZENSHIP BY THE CHOCTAW AND
CHICKASAW CITIZENSHIP COURT

TRIBAL ENROLLMENT OF PARENTS

	Name of Father	Year	County	Name of Mother	Year	County
1	W.H. Harrison	Dead	Non Citz	Mahulda Harrison	Dead	Non Citz
2	Valentine Kizer	" "		No1		
3	" "	" "		No1		
4	" "	" "		No1		
5	" "	" "		No1		
6	J.S. Roller	" "		No2		
7	W.B. McFarland	" "		No3		
8	J.S. Roller	" "		No2		
9	Admitted by the U.S. Court, South McAlester, I.T. Jany 18, 1898 Court Case No [illegible]					
10	No2 states in affidavit attached, relative to birth of No6, that she is wife of J.S. Roller					
11	No3 is now the wife of W.B. McFarland, non-citizen. Evidence of marriage filed Jan. 3, 1902.					
12	No7 Born Dec. 3, 1901; enrolled Jany. 3, 1902.					
13	No.8 Born Feby 24, 1902; enrolled March 25, 1902					
14	Evidence of marriage between No.2 and J.S. Roller a noncitizen filed April 2, 1902.					
15				No6 enrolled Oct. 30/99		
16						
17						

Choctaw By Blood Enrollment Cards 1898-1914

RESIDENCE:	Chickasaw Natn								
POST OFFICE:	Silo, I.T.								

Choctaw **Nation** Choctaw **Roll**

CARD No. **5257**
FIELD No. C 302

Dawes' Roll No.	NAME	Relationship to Person First Named	AGE	SEX	BLOOD	TRIBAL ENROLLMENT		
						Year	County	No.
X O 1	Trimmer, Lucinda F	First Named	31	F	1/16			
X O 2	" David B	Son	13	M				
X O 3	" Luther W	"	11	"				
X O 4	" Carlos S	"	7	"				
X 5	" Browdie E. F.	"	5	"				
X O 6	" Zellia	Dau	3	F				
DP O 7	" James V	Son	9mo	M				
X O 8	" Marvin A	"		"				
DP O 9	" Ethel Ardith	Dau	5mo	F				
O 10	" Argie Eunice	Dau	1mo	F				
Nos. 9 & 10 11	DISMISSED OCT 25 1904							
13								
#7 14	DISMISSED							
15	FEB 1[?] 1905	Nos. 1 to 6 denied in 1896, case #231.						
16								
17	For children of No2 see NB #1030. (Act Apr. 26 '06)							

TRIBAL ENROLLMENT OF PARENTS

	Name of Father	Year	County	Name of Mother	Year	County
1	Val Kizer		Non Citz	Sarah E. Kizer		Non Citz
2	J.S. Trimmer		" "	No 1		
3	" "		" "	No 1		
4	" "		" "	No 1		
5				No 1		
6	" "		" "	No 1		
7	" "		" "	No 1		
8	" "		" "	No 1		
9	" "		" "	No 1		
10	" "		" "	No 1		

DENIED CITIZENSHIP BY THE CHOCTAW AND CHICKASAW CITIZENSHIP COURT

11	Admitted by the U.S. Court, South McAlester, I.T. Jany 18, 1898 Court Case No 77
12	No.7 was born Feby 8, 1898. Not in decree.
13	No3 was admitted as Luther Trimmer
14	No.10 born Oct. 24, 1901; Enrolled Nov. 30, 1901
15	
16	See 7-5256 for Record
17	P.O. Folsum I.T. No.9 Enrolled May 24, 1900.

RESIDENCE:	Chickasaw Natn					Choctaw **Nation**		Choctaw **Roll**	CARD NO. 5258	
POST OFFICE:	Silo, I.T.								FIELD NO.	

Dawes' Roll No.	NAME	Relationship to Person First Named	AGE	SEX	BLOOD	TRIBAL ENROLLMENT		
						Year	County	No.
1	Kizer, Joseph V		30	M	1/16			
2								
3								
4								
5								
6								
7								
8								
9								
10								
11								
12								
13								
14								
15								
16								
17								

DENIED CITIZENSHIP BY THE CHOCTAW AND CHICKASAW CITIZENSHIP COURT

TRIBAL ENROLLMENT OF PARENTS

	Name of Father	Year	County	Name of Mother	Year	County
1	Val. Kizer		Non Citz	Sarah E. Kizer		non Citz
2						
3						
4						
5						
6	No.1 denied in 1896, case #231.					
7	Admitted by the U.S. Court, South McAlester, I.T. Jany 18, 1898					
8	Court Case No. 77					
9						
10						
11						
12						
13						
14						
15						
16						
17						

Choctaw By Blood Enrollment Cards 1898-1914

RESIDENCE: Chickasaw Natn
POST OFFICE: Silo, I.T.

Choctaw **Nation**   Choctaw **Roll**

CARD NO. **5259**
FIELD NO. C 304

Dawes' Roll No.	NAME	Relationship to Person First Named	AGE	SEX	BLOOD	TRIBAL ENROLLMENT		
						Year	County	No.
1	Kizer, Francis M		27	M	1/16			
DP 2	" Edgar O.	Son		"	1/32			
DP 3	" Foy Elbert	Son	1mo	"	1/32			
4								
Nos 5								
2&3 6								
7								
8								
9								
10								
11								
13								
14								
15								
16								
17								

DENIED CITIZENSHIP BY THE CHOCTAW AND CHICKASAW CITIZENSHIP COURT

TRIBAL ENROLLMENT OF PARENTS

	Name of Father	Year	County	Name of Mother	Year	County
1	Val. Kizer		Non Citz	Sarah E. Kizer		Non Citz
2	No.1			Julia A. Kizer		" "
3	No.1			" " "		" "
4						
5						
6	No.1 denied in 1896, case #231.					
7	Admitted by the U.S. Court, South McAlester, I.T. Jany 18, 1898.					
8	Court Case No. 77					
9						
10	No2 was born Oct. 5, [illegible]					
11	Evidence of marriage of No.1 and Julia A. Kizer to be supplied.					
12	Received and filed Oct. 25th, 1900.					
13	No.3 Enrolled Oct. 16th, 1900 subject to evidence of marriage of					
14	parents.					
15						
16	P.O. address is given as Mead, I.T.					Date of Application for Enrollment.
17	Oct. 15, 1900					

159

Choctaw By Blood Enrollment Cards 1898-1914

RESIDENCE: Chickasaw Natn

POST OFFICE: Silo, I.T.

Choctaw **Nation**   Choctaw **Roll**

CARD No. **5260**

FIELD No.

Dawes' Roll No.	NAME	Relationship to Person First Named	AGE	SEX	BLOOD	TRIBAL ENROLLMENT		
						Year	County	No.
✓	1 Kizer, James S		26	M	1/16			
DP	2 " Jesse E	Son	10mo	"				
"	3 " Lonnie Evert	Son	2mo	"				
	4							
No?	5							
	6							
	7							
	8							
	9							
	10							
	11							
	12							
	13							
	14							
	15							
	16							
	17							

TRIBAL ENROLLMENT OF PARENTS

	Name of Father	Year	County	Name of Mother	Year	County
1	Val Kizer		Non Citz	Sarah E Kizer		Non Citz
2	No 1			Amy Kizer		" "
3	No 1			Emma L Kiser[sic]		" "
4						
5						
6	No1 denied in 1896, case #231					
7	Admitted by the U.S. Court, South McAlester, I.T. Jany 18, 1898.					
8	Court Case No 77					
9						
10	No2 was born December 11, 1897.					
11						
12						
13						
14						
15						
16				No3 Enrolled May 24, 1900		
17						

Choctaw By Blood Enrollment Cards 1898-1914

| RESIDENCE: | Blue County | | | | | | | | |

RESIDENCE: Blue County
POST OFFICE: Durant, I.T.

Choctaw **Nation** Choctaw **Roll**

CARD NO. **5261**
FIELD NO.

Dawes' Roll No.	NAME	Relationship to Person First Named	AGE	SEX	BLOOD	TRIBAL ENROLLMENT		
						Year	County	No.
1	Jennings, Mary L		22	F	1/16			
DP 2	" Elizabeth F	Dau	6mo	"	1/32			
DP 3	" Francis Jas	Son	2mo	M	1/32			
4								
5								
6								
7								
8								
9								
10								
11								
12								
13								
14								
15								
16								
17								

DISMISSED OCT 15 1904

No.1

DENIED CITIZENSHIP BY THE CHOCTAW AND CHICKASAW CITIZENSHIP COURT

TRIBAL ENROLLMENT OF PARENTS

	Name of Father	Year	County	Name of Mother	Year	County
1	Val Kizer		Non Citz	Sarah E. Kizer		Non Citz
2	Fred P. Jennings		" "	No.1		
3	" " "		" "	No.1		
4						
5	No.1 denied in 1896, case #231					
6	Admitted by the U.S. Court, South McAlester, I.T. Jany 18, 1898.					
7	Court Case No. 77					
8						
9	Married to Fred Jennings August 14, 1898, under license issued by the Clerk of the					
10	U.S. Court, South McAlester, I.T.					
11						
12	Admitted as Mary L Kizer					
13	No.3 Enrolled Sept. 4, 1901.					
14						
15				No3 enrolled Oct 30/99		
16	See Decision of C.C.C. in Case 126T [... illegible]					
17				Date of Application for Enrollment		10-12-98

RESIDENCE: Gaines County

POST OFFICE: Viereton[sic], I.T.

Choctaw **Nation**   Choctaw **Roll**

CARD NO. **526**

FIELD NO.

Dawes' Roll No.	NAME	Relationship to Person First Named	AGE	SEX	BLOOD	TRIBAL ENROLLMENT		
						Year	County	No.
✓	1 Miller, Thomas		26	M	1/16			
	2							
	3							
	4							
	5							
	6							
	7							
	8							
	9							
	10							
	11							
	12							
	13							
	15							
	16							
	17							

TRIBAL ENROLLMENT OF PARENTS

Name of Father	Year	County	Name of Mother	Year	County
1 H. E. Miller		Non Citz	Sally Miller		Non Citz
2					
3					
4					
5					
6 No.1 denied in 1896, case #1282					
7 Admitted by the U.S. Court, South McAlester, I.T. August 25, [illegible]					
8 Court Case No. [?]					
9					
10					
11					
12					
13					
14					
15					
16					
17					

Choctaw By Blood Enrollment Cards 1898-1914

| RESIDENCE: | Gaines County | | | | | Choctaw **Nation** | | Choctaw **Roll** | | CARD No. **5263** |
| POST OFFICE: | Vireton, I.T. | | | | | | | | | FIELD No. C 308 |

Dawes' Roll No.	NAME	Relationship to Person	AGE	SEX	BLOOD	TRIBAL ENROLLMENT		
						Year	County	No.
✓ *	1 Miller, William	First Named	23	M	1/16			
✓	2 " Vicey J	Wife	21	f	IW			
✓	3 " Fenus M	Dau	8mo	f	1/32			
	4							
No2	5 DISMISSED							
	6 MAY 13 1904							
	7							
	8							
No3	9 DISMISSED							
	10							
	11 MAY 27 1904							
	12							
	13 DENIED CITIZENSHIP BY THE CHOCTAW AND							
	14 CHICKASAW CITIZENSHIP COURT							
	15							
	16							
	17							

TRIBAL ENROLLMENT OF PARENTS

Name of Father	Year	County	Name of Mother	Year	County
1 H. E. Miller		Non Citz	Sally Miller		Non Citz
2 L.B. Shockley	US Citz		Rebecca Shockley		" "
3 No1			No2		
4					Sept 8/99[sic]
5					
6 No.1 denied in 1896, case #1282					
7 Admitted by the U.S. Court, South McAlester, I.T. August 26, 1897					
8 Court Case No [illegible]					
9					
10 See No2 testimony					
11					
12					
13					
14					
15					
16					
17					

RESIDENCE:	Chickasaw Natn						CARD NO. **5264**	
POST OFFICE:	Woodville, I.T.	Choctaw **Nation**		Choctaw **Roll**		FIELD NO.		

Dawes' Roll No.	NAME	Relationship to Person	AGE	SEX	BLOOD	TRIBAL ENROLLMENT		
						Year	County	No.
✓	1 Crowson, A. J.	First Named	53	M				
✓	2 " Andrew J.	Son		M				
	3							
	No2 DISMISSED							
	5 MAY 27 1904							
	6							
	7							
	8							
	9							
	10							
	11							
	12							
	13							
	14							
	15							
	16							
	17							

DENIED CITIZENSHIP BY THE CHOCTAW AND CHICKASAW CITIZENSHIP COURT

TRIBAL ENROLLMENT OF PARENTS

	Name of Father	Year	County	Name of Mother	Year	County
1	John Crowson	Dead	Non Citz	Sally Crowson	Dead	Non Citz
2	No 1			Lizzie Crowson		" "
3						
4						
5						
6	No 1 denied by Com in 1896 case # in 1896, case #719					
7	Admitted by the U.S. Court, South McAlester, I.T. August 27, 1897.					
8	Court Case No. 74					
9						
10	No.2 was born Feby 23, 1898					
11	No1 Denied by C.C.C.C. [remainder illegible]					
12	No.2 Dismissed [remainder illegible]					
13						
14	Children of A. J. Crowson on Choctaw card R.590					
15						
16						
17						

Choctaw By Blood Enrollment Cards 1898-1914

RESIDENCE:	Chickasaw Natn								CARD NO. **5265**
POST OFFICE:	Colbert, I.T.	Choctaw **Nation**		Choctaw **Roll**					FIELD NO.

Dawes' Roll No.	NAME	Relationship to Person First Named	AGE	SEX	BLOOD	TRIBAL ENROLLMENT		
						Year	County	No.
DP	1 Hill, Louis	Named	38	M	1/4			
O O	2 " William B	Son	24	"				
O O	3 Blagg, Joseph L	G.Son		"				
	4							
#1	5 DISMISSED JAN 26 1905							
	6							
	7							
	8							
	9							
	10							
	11 No3 "Joseph Lewis Blog or Joseph Lewis Blagg"							
	12 No2 "V.B. Hill or W.B. Hill"							
	13							
	14 DENIED CITIZENSHIP BY THE CHOCTAW AND							
	15 CHICKASAW CITIZENSHIP COURT							
	16							
	17							

TRIBAL ENROLLMENT OF PARENTS

	Name of Father	Year	County	Name of Mother	Year	County
1	Ben Hill		Non Citz	Piety Hill	Dead	Non Citz
2	No 1			Sarah J Hill		" "
3	G.J. Blagg		Non Citz	Sarah J Blagg		
4						
5						
6	Nos 1,2 & 3 denied by Com in 1896 case # in 1896, case #61					
7	Admitted by the U.S. Court, South McAlester, I.T. Jany 18, 1898					
8	Court Case No. 58					
9						
10						
11						
12						
13						
14						
15						
16	See Petition #C-109					
17					Date of Application for Enrollment	10-13-98

165

Choctaw By Blood Enrollment Cards 1898-1914

						CARD No.	**5266**

RESIDENCE: Blue County
POST OFFICE: Durant, I.T.

Choctaw **Nation**   Choctaw **Roll**

FIELD No.

Dawes' Roll No.	NAME	Relationship to Person First Named	AGE	SEX	BLOOD	TRIBAL ENROLLMENT		
						Year	County	No.
O O ₁	Palmer, Elizabeth	Named	34	F	1/8			
O O ₂	" George A	Son	16	M				
O O ₃	" Lee H	"	7	"				
O O ₄	" Earl A	"	4	"				
DP x ₅	" Josie A	"	2	"				
DP x ₆	" Netty May	Dau	7mo	F				
₇								
₈								
₉	DISMISSED							
₁₀	JAN 2							
₁₁	No2 "Georgia Allen Palmer"							
₁₂	" 4 "Earl Palmer"							
₁₃								
₁₄								
₁₅	DENIED CITIZENSHIP BY THE CHOCTAW AND							
₁₆	CHICKASAW CITIZENSHIP COURT							
₁₇								

TRIBAL ENROLLMENT OF PARENTS

	Name of Father	Year	County	Name of Mother	Year	County
₁	Louis Hill		Non Citz	Sarah J Hill	Dead	Non Citz
₂	Gus Palmer		" "	No i		
₃	" "		" "	No i		
₄	" "		" "	No i		
₅	" "		" "	No i		
₆	" "		" "	No i		

7 Nos 1 to 4 denied in 1896, case #61.
8 Admitted by the U.S. Court, South McAlester, I.T. Jan. 18, 1898, Court Case No. 54
9
10 No 2 was admitted as Georgia A Palmer
11 No 4 " " " Earl Palmer
12 No5 was born November 23, 1896
13 Correct name of No.1 is Pairlee Elizabeth Palmer. See letter Of A.A. Palmer filed Feby 23,1901
14 Record in Choctaw #5365
15 For child of No2-see NB "10 5 (Act Apr 26 '06)
16
17 5&6 Dismissed by C.C.C.C. Nov 28 '04 132 T [illegible]

Choctaw By Blood Enrollment Cards 1898-1914

RESIDENCE: **Blue County**
POST OFFICE: **Durant, I.T.**

Choctaw **Nation**   Choctaw **Roll**

CARD NO. **5267**
FIELD NO. C 312

Dawes' Roll No.	NAME	Relationship to Person First Named	AGE	SEX	BLOOD	TRIBAL ENROLLMENT		
						Year	County	No.
x 1	Hill, J. Wesley	Named	31	M	1/8			
x 2	" Birtie B	Dau	7	F	1/16			
DP x 3	" William L	Son	19mo	M	1/16			
DP x 4	" Pairlee Jane	Dau	6mo	F	1/16			
DP x 5	" Roy Velt	Son	1mo	M	1/16			
6								
#3&4-5 DISMISSED 7								
8	JAN							
9	No2 "Bertie Bell Hill"							
10	" 1 "J.W. Hill or J Wesley Hill"							
11								
12	DENIED CITIZENSHIP BY THE CHOCTAW AND							
13	CHICKASAW CITIZENSHIP COURT							
14								
15								
16	Record in Choctaw #5265							
17	See C-109							

TRIBAL ENROLLMENT OF PARENTS

	Name of Father	Year	County	Name of Mother	Year	County
1	Louis Hill		Non Citz	Sarah J Hill	Dead	Non Citz
2	No 1			Dollie Hill		" "
3	No 1			" "		" "
4	No 1			" "		" "
5	No 1			" "		" "
6						
7	No1&2 denied in 1896, case #61					
8	Admitted by the U.S. Court, South McAlester, I.T. Jan 18, 1898					
9	Court Case No 54					
10	No3 was born Jany 26, 1896					
11	No4 was born April 8/99; Enrolled Oct. 30/99 subject to receipt of evidence of marriage of					
12	parents. Letter requesting same this day Rec'd & filed April 23/[sic]					
13						
14	No.5 born Oct 9th, 1901 Enrolled Nov. 25, 1901					
15						
16						
17						

Choctaw By Blood Enrollment Cards 1898-1914

RESIDENCE:	Atoka County							
POST OFFICE:	Coalgate, I.T.							

Choctaw **Nation** Choctaw **Roll**

CARD No. **5268** FIELD No.

Dawes' Roll No.	NAME	Relationship to Person First Named	AGE	SEX	BLOOD	TRIBAL ENROLLMENT Year	County	No.
O O X 1	Humphrey, G. J.		31	M	1/8			
O O X 2	" William	Son	9	"	1/16			
O O X 3	" Cullis M	"	7	"	1/16			
O O X 4	" Emmett L	"	5	"	1/16			
DP 5	" Willie Ollie	Wife	23	F	IW			
DP 6	" Johnson	son	1mo	M	1/16			
7	Nos 1 to 4 denied in 1896 case #1364							
8	Admitted by the U.S. Court, South McAlester, I.T	Jany 18, 1898						

DENIED CITIZENSHIP BY THE CHOCTAW AND CHICKASAW CITIZENSHIP COURT

TRIBAL ENROLLMENT OF PARENTS

	Name of Father	Year	County	Name of Mother	Year	County
1	M.B. Humphrey		Non Citz	Mary Humphrey	Dead	Non Citz
2	No 1			Minnie Humphrey	"	" "
3	No 1			" "	"	" "
4	No 1			" "	"	" "
5	Jim Beck		Non citizen	Alginie Beck		Non citizen
6	No 1			No 5		
8	No3 was admitted as Cullus Humphrey					
9	No4 " " " Ellett Leroy Humphrey					
10	No.5 Enrolled as an intermarried citizen December 7th 1900.					
11	No.6 born Oct 7, 1901; Enrolled Nov. 21, 1901.					
16	For children of No1&5 see NB 998 (Act Apr 26-06)					

168

Choctaw By Blood Enrollment Cards 1898-1914

RESIDENCE:	Chickasaw Natn		Choctaw **Nation** Choctaw **Roll**		CARD NO.	**5269**
POST OFFICE:	Duncan I.T.				FIELD NO.	

Dawes' Roll No.	NAME	Relationship to Person First Named	AGE	SEX	BLOOD	TRIBAL ENROLLMENT		
						Year	County	No.
1	Lockett, H B	Named	30	M	IW			
2	" Eula	Wife	24	F	1/16			
3	" Luther Lee	Son	1	M				
4								
5								
6								
7								
8								
9								
10								
11								
12								
13								
14								
15								
16								
17								

#3 DISMISSED JAN 24

TRIBAL ENROLLMENT OF PARENTS

	Name of Father	Year	County	Name of Mother	Year	County
1	G. Lockett		Non Citz	Martha Lockett	Dead	Non Citz
2	John Boon		" "	Abbey Boon		" "
3		No 1			No 2	
4						
5	Nos 1&2 denied in 1896 case #18					
6	Admitted by the U.S. Court, Ardmore, I.T. December 21, 1897. Case No 88					
7						
8	No3 was born August 21, 1897.					
9	No2 was admitted as Beulah Lockett					
10						
11						
12	DENIED CITIZENSHIP BY THE CHOCTAW AND					
13	CHICKASAW CITIZENSHIP COURT					
14						
15						
16	For child of No1 see NB (Apr 26 '06) #1125					
17						

Date of Application For Enrollment 10-13-98

Choctaw By Blood Enrollment Cards 1898-1914

RESIDENCE: Chickasaw Natn   Choctaw **Nation**   Choctaw **Roll**   CARD NO. **5270**

POST OFFICE: Ryan   I.T.   FIELD NO.

Dawes' Roll No.	NAME	Relationship to Person First Named	AGE	SEX	BLOOD	TRIBAL ENROLLMENT		
						Year	County	No.
1	Sanders, L.A.		28	M	I.W.			
2	" Dennie	Wife	26	F	1/16			
3	" Harold	Son	10mo	M				
4	No1 Dismissed by C.C.C.C. [illegible]							
5								
6	#3							
7								
8								
9								
10								
11								
12								
13								
14								
15								
16								
17								

DENIED CITIZENSHIP BY THE CHOCTAW AND CHICKASAW CITIZENSHIP COURT

TRIBAL ENROLLMENT OF PARENTS

	Name of Father	Year	County	Name of Mother	Year	County
1	Clark Sanders	Dead	Non Citz	Amanda Sanders		Non Citz
2	Jonathan Barefoot	"	" "	Adeline Barefoot		" "
3	No 1			No 2		
4						
5						
6	Nos 1&2 denied in 1896, case #18					
7	Admitted by the U.S. Court, Ardmore, I.T. December 21, 1897. Court Case No 88					
8						
9	No3 was born December 31, 1897.					
10						
11						
12						
13						
14						
15						
16						
17						

Choctaw By Blood Enrollment Cards 1898-1914

RESIDENCE:	Chickasaw Natn								CARD No. **5271**
POST OFFICE:	Ryan, I.T.		Choctaw **Nation**			Choctaw **Roll**			FIELD No. C316

Dawes' Roll No.	NAME	Relationship to Person First Named	AGE	SEX	BLOOD	TRIBAL ENROLLMENT		
						Year	County	No.
1	Branson, J. W.	Named	48	M				
2	" Rebecca Adeline	Wife	32	F				
3								
4								
5								
6								
7	Nos 1&2 denied in 1896 case #18							
8	Admitted by the U.S. Court, Ardmore, I.T. Dec. 21, 1897 Court Case No 88							
9								
10								
11	No2 was admitted as Adeline [Illegible]							
12								
13								
14								
15								
16								
17								

TRIBAL ENROLLMENT OF PARENTS

	Name of Father	Year	County	Name of Mother	Year	County
1	[?] A. Branson	Dead	Non Citz	Darcus Branson	Dead	Non Citz
2	Thos Boone	"	" "	Louisa Boone	"	" "
3						
4				ACTION APPROVED BY		
5				SECRETARY OF INTERIOR.		
6						
7						
8						
9						
10						
11						
12						
13						
14						
15						
16						
17						

Date of Application for Enrollment 10-14-98

171

Choctaw By Blood Enrollment Cards 1898-1914

RESIDENCE: Chickasaw Natn
POST OFFICE: Comanche, I.T.

Choctaw **Nation**　　Choctaw **Roll**

CARD NO. **5272**
FIELD NO.

Dawes' Roll No.	NAME	Relationship to Person First Named	AGE	SEX	BLOOD	TRIBAL ENROLLMENT		
						Year	County	No.
1	Johnson, G. W.	First Named	48	M	I.W.			
2	"　Nancy A	Wife		F	"			
3	"　Jessie B.	Dau	1/2	"				
4						ACTION APPROVED BY		
5						SECRETARY OF INTERIOR. FEB 27 1907		
6	No2					NOTICE OF DEPARTMENTAL ACTION		
7	REFUSED					FORWARDED ATTORNEYS FOR CHOCTAW		
8	APR 19 1906					AND CHICKASAW NATIONS. MAR 27 1907		
9	No2 Apr 19, 1906 Record					NOTICE OF DEPARTMENTAL ACTION		
10	forwarded Dept.					FORWARDED ATTORNEY FOR APPLICANT.		
11	No3							
12	REFUSED							
13	JAN 26 1907					NOTICE OF DEPARTMENTAL ACTION MAILED APPLICANT.		
14								
15	RECORD FORWARDED DEPARTMENT.							
16	JAN 26 1907							
17								

	TRIBAL ENROLLMENT OF PARENTS					
	Name of Father	Year	County	Name of Mother	Year	County
1	Pleas. Johnson	Dead	Non Citz	Nancy Johnson	Dead	Non Citz
2	D. [?] McGrew			[illegible] McGrew		
3	No1			No2		
4						
5	No1 admitted in 1896 case #1046					
6	Admitted by the U.S. Court, South McAlester, I.T. October [?], 1897 Court Case No 22					
7	No1 a United States citizen married a Choctaw Indian, who obtained a divorce from him. He					
8	then married No2 - Nancy A. McGrew, a United States Citizen who is the mother of his child					
9	Jessie B. Johnson					
10	No1 now in C.C.C.C. Case #[?]					
11	No3 was born April 10, 1898 - Not in [illegible]					
12	Oct 16, 1906 Dept affirmed decision					
13	No1 transferred to Choctaw card #5785 July [illegible]					
14	For child of No.2 see NB (March 3, 1905) #1482.					
15						
16						
17						

Choctaw By Blood Enrollment Cards 1898-1914

Choctaw **Nation** Choctaw **Roll**

CARD NO. **5273**
FIELD NO. C318

Dawes' Roll No.	NAME	Relationship to Person First Named	AGE	SEX	BLOOD	TRIBAL ENROLLMENT		
						Year	County	No.
1	Tucker, Nancy	First Named	42	F	I.W.			
Void 2	" Minnie D	Dau	5mo	"				
3		No 1 is mother of						
No 4	~~DISMISSED~~	Charles Dibrell on						
5	~~OLP 23 1904~~	Choctaw card #137 and of James Dibrell on						
6		Choctaw card #408						

No 1 admitted in 1896, case #298.
Admitted by the U.S. Court, South McAlester, I.T. Jany 18, 1898, Court Case No. [?]
No 2 was born May 24, 1898

No 1 a United States Citz intermarried with Joe Dibrell a Choctaw Citz
After his death she intermarried with James A Tucker, a United States Citz by whom she has four children admitted by the Dawes Commission and child Minnie D. Tucker. Has resided in Chickasaw Nation 26 [remainder illegible]

TRIBAL ENROLLMENT OF PARENTS

	Name of Father	Year	County	Name of Mother	Year	County
1	Bannister Stone		Non Citz	Katie Stone		Non Citz
2	James Tucker			No 1		
3						
4	Dec 4/99 No2 is born of James A and Nancy Tucker					
5						
6						
7	No2 is duplicate of No6 on Choctaw rejected card #R311. Entry of No2 cancelled Feb 10" 1901					
8	Husband and children of No1 all enrolled on Choctaw #R311					
9						
10	No1 was admitted as an Intermarried Choctaw by C.C.C.C. Case #128T, Oct 2, '04					
11						
12						
13						
14						
15						
16						
17						

Date of Application for Enrollment 10-17-98

Choctaw By Blood Enrollment Cards 1898-1914

RESIDENCE: Chickasaw Natn
POST OFFICE: Belmont, I.T.

Choctaw **Nation**   Choctaw **Roll**

CARD NO. **5274**
FIELD NO.

Dawes' Roll No.	NAME	Relationship to Person First Named	AGE	SEX	BLOOD	Year	County	No.
1	Davenport, Jane		24	F				
2	" Hattie	Dau		"	1/16			
3	" Eva May	Dau	2mo	F	1/16			
4								
5								
6								
7								
8								
9								
10								
11								
12								
13								
14								
15								
16								
17								

DENIED CITIZENSHIP BY THE CHOCTAW AND CHICKASAW CITIZENSHIP COURT

TRIBAL ENROLLMENT OF PARENTS

Name of Father	Year	County	Name of Mother	Year	County
1 Geo McFatridge		Non Citz	Harriet McFatridge		Non Citz
2 Stiiweii Davenport		" "	Noi		
3 " "		" "	Noi		
4					
5 Admitted by the U.S. Court, Ardmore, I.T. Jan 20, 1898					
6					
7					
8 Made application to the Dawes Commission and was rejected case #1005. Appealed					
9 to U.S. Court at Ardmore, I.T. Has resided in the Territory seventeen years.					
10					
11 No2 was born April 24, 1897.					
12					
13 P.O. address of No.1 now seems to be Velma, I.T.					
14 No.3 Enrolled Oct. 1st, 1900.					
15					
16					
17					

174

Choctaw By Blood Enrollment Cards 1898-1914

RESIDENCE: Chickasaw Natn
POST OFFICE: Duncan, I.T.

Choctaw **Nation**   Choctaw **Roll**

CARD No. **5275**
FIELD No. C 320

Dawes' Roll No.	NAME	Relationship to Person First Named	AGE	SEX	BLOOD	TRIBAL ENROLLMENT		
						Year	County	No.
1	Tapp, Rosa							
2	" Onley							
3								
4								
5								
6								
7								
8								
9								
10								
11								
12								
13								
14								
15								
16								
17								

TRIBAL ENROLLMENT OF PARENTS

	Name of Father	Year	County	Name of Mother	Year	County
1	Geo McFatridge		Non Citz	Harriet McFatridge		Non Citz
2	P.L. Tapp			Noi		
3						
4						
5	No1 denied in 1896, case #1398					
6	Admitted by the U.S. Court, Ardmore, I.T. Jan 20, 1898					
7						
8	No1 has resided in the Territory [remainder illegible]					
9						
10	No.2 denied by C.C.C.C. as Onley Tapp or Anley Tapp					
11						
12						
13						
14						
15						
16						
17						

Date of Application for Enrollment   10-17-98

Choctaw By Blood Enrollment Cards 1898-1914

RESIDENCE: Chickasaw Natn
POST OFFICE: Duncan, I.T.

Choctaw **Nation** Choctaw **Roll**

CARD NO. **5276**
FIELD NO.

Dawes' Roll No.	NAME	Relationship to Person First Named	AGE	SEX	BLOOD	TRIBAL ENROLLMENT Year	TRIBAL ENROLLMENT County	TRIBAL ENROLLMENT No.
1	Lowrance, Florence	Named			1/8			
2	" Jessie	Dau						
3								
4								
5								
6								
7								
8								
9								
10								
11								
12								
13								
14								
15								
16								
17								

TRIBAL ENROLLMENT OF PARENTS

	Name of Father	Year	County	Name of Mother	Year	County
1	Geo McFatridge		Non Citz	Harriet McFatridge		Non Citz
2	Willie Lowrance			No 1		
3						
4						
5						
6	No1 denied in 1896, case #1005					
7	Admitted by U.S. Court Ardmore, I.T. Jany 20, 1898 Court Case No [?]					
8						
9	No2 was born Oct 20, 1897					
10						
11	No1 has lived in the Territory [illegible]					
12	No.1 denied by C.C.C.C. as Florence Lowrance or Florence Lawrance					
13						
14						
15						
16						
17						

Choctaw By Blood Enrollment Cards 1898-1914

RESIDENCE: Chickasaw Natn
POST OFFICE: Arthur, I.T.

Choctaw **Nation**   Choctaw **Roll**

CARD NO. **5277**
FIELD NO. C 322

Dawes' Roll No.	NAME	Relationship to Person First Named	AGE	SEX	BLOOD	TRIBAL ENROLLMENT		
						Year	County	No.
1	Marier, Ida		29	F	1/16			
2	" Bessie	Dau	7	"				
3	" Carl	Son	5	M				
4	" Nannie	Dau						
5								
6								
7								
8								
9								
10								
11								
12	No4							
13								
14								
15								
16								
17								

DENIED CITIZENSHIP BY THE CHOCTAW AND CHICKASAW CITIZENSHIP COURT

DISMISSED

TRIBAL ENROLLMENT OF PARENTS

	Name of Father	Year	County	Name of Mother	Year	County
1	Harrington Gray		Non Citz	Emeline Gray		
2	John Marier		" "	No 1		
3	" "		" "	No 1		
4	" "		" "	No 1		
5						
6						
7	Admitted by the U.S. Court, Ardmore, I.T. March 18, 1898, Court Case #153					
8						
9	No4 was born Mar 18, 1898					
10						
11	No1 has lived in the Territory all her life.					
12	For child of No1 see N.B. #1056 (Act Apr 26 '06)					
13						
14						
15						
16						124
17					Date of Application for Enrollment	10-17-98

177

Choctaw By Blood Enrollment Cards 1898-1914

RESIDENCE: Chickasaw Natn

POST OFFICE: Center I.T.

Choctaw **Nation** Choctaw **Roll**

CARD NO. 5278

FIELD NO. C 323

Dawes' Roll No.	NAME	Relationship to Person First Named	AGE	SEX	BLOOD	TRIBAL ENROLLMENT		
						Year	County	No.
1	Rhoades, L. F.		53	M	I.W.			
2								
3								
4								
5								
6								
7								
8								
9								
10								
11								
12								
13								
14								
15								
16								
17								

TRIBAL ENROLLMENT OF PARENTS

	Name of Father	Year	County	Name of Mother	Year	County
1	Elisha Rhoades	Dead	Non Citz	Julia Rhoades	Dead	Non Citz
2						
3						
4						
5						
6	No.1 denied on 1896, case #59.					
7	Admitted under Suplemental[sic] Judgement rendered at Ardmore, I.T. September 28, 1898.					
8	Court Case No. 128					
9						
10	Has lived in the Territory about [illegible]					
11						
12						
13						
14						
15						
16						
17						

Choctaw By Blood Enrollment Cards 1898-1914

RESIDENCE: Chickasaw Natn					CARD NO. 5279
POST OFFICE: Addington, I.T.	Choctaw **Nation**	Choctaw **Roll**			FIELD NO. C 324

Dawes' Roll No.	NAME	Relationship to Person First Named	AGE	SEX	BLOOD	TRIBAL ENROLLMENT Year	County	No.
1	Boone, Ewalt	Named	23	M	1/16			
2	" Cora	Wife	20	F	I.W.			
3	" Leo L	Son	4mo	M				
4								
5	#2-3 DISMISSED							
6	JAN							
7								
8								
9								
10								
11								
12								
13	DENIED CITIZENSHIP BY THE CHOCTAW AND							
14	CHICKASAW CITIZENSHIP COURT							
15								
16								
17								

TRIBAL ENROLLMENT OF PARENTS

	Name of Father	Year	County	Name of Mother	Year	County
1	John Boone		Non Citz	Abbie Boone		Non Citz
2	M.C. Short		" "	Hester Short		" "
3	No1			No2		
4						
5	Denied in 1896 case #18					
6	Admitted by the U.S. Court, Ardmore, I.T. December 2, 1897, Court Case No 88					
7						
8	No3 was born June 3, 1898. Not in decree.					
9						
10	No1 has lived in Chickasaw Nation four years. Married to Cora Short, a United States					
11	Citz., September 12, 1897, under license issued by the United States.					
12						
13						
14						
15						
16						7/36
17					Date of Application for Enrollment	10-17-98

179

Choctaw By Blood Enrollment Cards 1898-1914

Dawes' Roll No.	NAME	Relationship to Person First Named	AGE	SEX	BLOOD	TRIBAL ENROLLMENT		
						Year	County	No.
1	Keith, G. Jones		45	M	I.W.			
2	" Pink O.	Wife	38	F	1/16			
3	" James L	Son	18	M	1/32			
4	" Dennie M	Dau	16	F	1/32			
5	" Lennie	"	8	"	1/32			
6	" Hensley O	Son	1 mo	M	1/32			
7								
8	#6 DISMISSED							
9								
10	No2 denied by C.C.C.C. as "Pinkie Keith"							
11	" 4 " " " " "Denny " "							
12	" 5 " " " " "Lemmie " or Lennie Keith"							
12	1 " [illegible]							
13								
14								
15								
16								
17								

TRIBAL ENROLLMENT OF PARENTS

	Name of Father	Year	County	Name of Mother	Year	County
1	Porter Keith	Dead	Non Citz	Elizabeth Keith	Dead	Non Citz
2	Henry Hensley	"	"	Elizabeth Hensley	"	"
3	No1			No2		
4	No1			No2		
5	No1			No2		
6	No1			No2		
7	Nos 1 to 5 denied in 1896, case #18					
8	Admitted by the U.S. Court, Ardmore, I.T. December 21, 1897, Court Case No 88					
9	No1 was admitted as Jones Keith					
10	No2 " " " Pinkie Keith					
11	No3 " " " Lennie Keith					
12	Above family has lived in the Territory for two years					
13						
14	No6 enrolled Dec 18/99. Affidavit irregular					
15	and returned for correction. Recd & filed Jany 17, 1900					
16						
17						

DENIED CITIZENSHIP BY THE CHOCTAW AND CHICKASAW CITIZENSHIP COURT

Choctaw By Blood Enrollment Cards 1898-1914

RESIDENCE: Chickasaw Natn
POST OFFICE: Duncan I.T.

Choctaw **Nation**   Choctaw **Roll**

CARD NO. **5281**
FIELD NO. C 326

Dawes' Roll No.	NAME	Relationship to Person First Named	AGE	SEX	BLOOD	TRIBAL ENROLLMENT		
						Year	County	No.
1	Jones, Brinkley W	Named	[?]8	M			Do's	
2	" Elizabeth M	Dau	[?]	F			Do's	
3	" Sallie F	"	2[?]	"			Do's	
4	" Herman Hampton	Son of Nº3	2	M				
5	" Donal Wilburn	Son of Nº3	7mo	M				
6								
7	DECISION RENDERED							
8	**REFUSED**							
9								
10								
11								
12								
13								
14								
15								
16								
17								

TRIBAL ENROLLMENT OF PARENTS

	Name of Father	Year	County	Name of Mother	Year	County
1	James Jones		Non Citz	Elizabeth Jones	Dead	Non Citz
2	No 1			[Illegible] Jones	"	"
3	No 1			"	"	"
4	Gus B Jones			No 3		
5	" " "			No 3		
6						
7	Admitted by the U.S. Court, Ardmore, I.T., Jany 17, 1898, Court Case No 148					
8						
9	Removed from Georgia to the Chickasaw Nation, October 1, 1898.					
10						
11	Nos. 4 and 5 placed hereon Dec. 9, 1902 evidence of birth having been filed.					
12						
13						
14						
15						
16	See Choctaw 5053					
17						

181

RESIDENCE:	Chickasaw Natn						CARD NO. **5282**	
POST OFFICE:	Tatum, I.T.	Choctaw **Nation**			Choctaw **Roll**		FIELD NO. C 327	

Dawes' Roll No.	NAME	Relationship to Person First Named	AGE	SEX	BLOOD	TRIBAL ENROLLMENT		
						Year	County	No.
1	Jones, Mary M.		5[sic]		1/16		D	
2								
3								
4								
5								
6								
7								
8								
9								
10								
11								
12								
13								
14								
15								
16								
17								

DISMISSED FEB 11 190?

DENIED CITIZENSHIP BY THE CHOCTAW AND CHICKASAW CITIZENSHIP COURT

TRIBAL ENROLLMENT OF PARENTS

	Name of Father	Year	County	Name of Mother	Year	County
1	James Jones	Dead	Non Citz	Eliz. Jones	Dead	Non Citz
2						
3						
4						
5	No.1 denied in 1896, case #18					
6	Admitted by the U.S. Court, Ardmore, I.T. Jany 17, 1898.					
7	Court Cast #[?]					
8	Has lived in Territory five years.					
9						
10	C.C.C.C. case #107T 3/14/03					
11						
12						
13						
14						
15						
16	For records see 7-6068 - see Petition #C-52					
17						

Choctaw By Blood Enrollment Cards 1898-1914

RESIDENCE:	Chickasaw Natn
POST OFFICE:	Duncan, I.T.

Choctaw **Nation**   Choctaw **Roll**

CARD NO. **5283**
FIELD NO. C 328

Dawes' Roll No.	NAME	Relationship to Person First Named	AGE	SEX	BLOOD	TRIBAL ENROLLMENT		
						Year	County	No.
1	Jones, Amanda M	Named	54	F	1/16			
2								
3								
4								
5								
6	DECISION RENDERED							
7	**REFUSED**							
8								
9								
10								
11								
12								
13								
14								
15								
16								
17								

TRIBAL ENROLLMENT OF PARENTS

	Name of Father	Year	County	Name of Mother	Year	County
1	James Jones	Dead	Non Citz	Eliz. Jones	Dead	Non Citz
2						
3				ACTION APPROVED BY		
4				SECRETARY OF INTERIOR.		
5						
6	Admitted by the U.S Court Ardmore, I.T. Jany 17, 1898					
7	Court Case No 148					
8						
9	Has lived in the Chickasaw Natn since December 1897					
10						
11						
12						
13						
14						
15						
16	See Choctaw 5055					144
17						Date of Application for Enrollment 10-17-98

Choctaw By Blood Enrollment Cards 1898-1914

RESIDENCE: Chickasaw Natn

POST OFFICE: I.T.

Choctaw **Nation**   Choctaw **Roll**

CARD NO. **5284**

FIELD NO. 329

Dawes' Roll No.	NAME	Relationship to Person First Named	AGE	SEX	BLOOD	TRIBAL ENROLLMENT		
						Year	County	No.
O O	1 Gamblin, Eliza Ann		48	F	1/16	1896	Blue	4915
	2							
	3							
	4							
	5							
	6							
	7							
	8							
	9							
	10							
	11							
	12							
	13							
	14							
	15							
	16							
	17							

GRANTED

TRIBAL ENROLLMENT OF PARENTS

	Name of Father	Year	County	Name of Mother	Year	County
1	James Jones	Dead	Non Citz	Eliz. Jones	Dead	Non Citz
2						
3						
4						
5	Not an original applicant before Com. in 1896, in case #56					
6	Admitted under Suplemental [sic] Judgement rendered at Ardmore, I.T.					
7	October 15, 1898. Court Case [illegible]					
8	Has lived in the Chickasaw Nation for five or six years					
9						
10	On 1896 roll as Ann Gamblin					
11			No1 Stricken from original judgement by the U.S. Court			
12			Ardmore, I.T. Jan 20, 1900. Court Case 148 as Eliza Ann			
13						
14						
15						
16						
17						

Choctaw By Blood Enrollment Cards 1898-1914

RESIDENCE: Chickasaw Natn
POST OFFICE: Duncan, I.T.

Choctaw **Nation**   Choctaw **Roll**

CARD NO. **5285**
FIELD NO. C 330

Dawes' Roll No.	NAME	Relationship to Person First Named	AGE	SEX	BLOOD	TRIBAL ENROLLMENT		
						Year	County	No.
O O 1	Gamblin, Joseph M	First Named	24	M	1/32	1896	Blue	4916
O 2	" Emma	Wife	38	F		1896	"	4917
O O 3	" Indian[illegible]	Dau	2		1/64	1896	"	4918
4								
5								
6								
7								
8								
9								
10								
11								
12								
13								
14								
15								
16								
17								

GRANTED

DENIED CITIZENSHIP BY THE CHOCTAW AND CHICKASAW CITIZENSHIP COURT

TRIBAL ENROLLMENT OF PARENTS

	Name of Father	Year	County	Name of Mother	Year	County
1	John Gamblin		Non Citz	Jane Gamblin		Non Citz
2	Bob P[illegible]	Dead	" "	Emily P[illegible]	Dead	" "
3	No 1					
4				ACTION APPROVED BY SECRETARY OF INTERIOR.		
5						
6	Not original applicants before Com. in 1896 in case #56					
7	Nos 1-3 were admitted in the original Judgement rendered at Ardmore, I.T.					
8	Jany 17, 1898, Court Case No 148. No2 was admitted in the Suplemental[sic] Judgement					
9	rendered at Armore, I.T. March 24, 1898, Court Case No 14[?]					
10						
11	No1 has resided in Chickasaw Natn for six years. Was married to No2 April 2, 1895					
12	under United States					
13	No1 on 1896 roll as Joseph Gamblin					
14						
15						
16	No2 Dismissed by C.C.C.C. for want of Jurisdiction.					
17					Date of Application for Enrollment	10-17-98

Choctaw By Blood Enrollment Cards 1898-1914

RESIDENCE:	Chickasaw Natn					CARD NO. **5286**
POST OFFICE:	Duncan, I.T.	Choctaw **Nation**	Choctaw **Roll**			FIELD NO. C 331

Dawes' Roll No.	NAME	Relationship to Person First Named	AGE	SEX	BLOOD	TRIBAL ENROLLMENT		
						Year	County	No.
1	Henson, Minnie M	Named	25	F				
2	" Marshal V	Son	2	M				
3	" Clyde E	"						
4						ACTION APPROVED BY		
5						SECRETARY OF INTERIOR.		
6								
7								
8								
9								
10								
11								
12								
13								
14								
15	All of the above parties were stricken from the rolls by corrected judgement of							
16	U.S. Court Case No. 148, by removing name of Minnie Mildred Henson, see copy of letter attached. Feby. 24th, 1900.							
17								

TRIBAL ENROLLMENT OF PARENTS

	Name of Father	Year	County	Name of Mother	Year	County
1	Brinkley Jones		Non Citz	Mildred Jones		Non Citz
2	Burt V Henson		" "	No i		
3	" " "		" "	No i		
4						
5						
6	No1 was admitted on the Original Judgement rendered at Ardmore, I.T					
7	Jany 17, 1898, as Minnie Mildred Jones. Court Case No [?] and in					
8	the Suplemental[sic] Judgement, rendered at Ardmore, I.T. October 12, 1898,					
9	No1 was admitted as Mrs. Minnie Mildred Henson, Court Case No 148					
10						
11	No2 was born September 27, 1896					
12	No3 " " April 7, 1898					
13						
14	No1 lived in Georgia until August 1898					
15						
16						
17						

186

Choctaw By Blood Enrollment Cards 1898-1914

RESIDENCE: Chickasaw Natn			Choctaw **Nation** Choctaw **Roll**				CARD No. **5287**	
POST OFFICE: Duncan, I.T.							FIELD No. C 332	

Dawes' Roll No.	NAME	Relationship to Person First Named	AGE	SEX	BLOOD	TRIBAL ENROLLMENT		
						Year	County	No.
1	Jones, Charles M		2[?]	M	1/32			
2	" Lynn P	Son		"				
3								
4					ACTION APPROVED BY			
5					SECRETARY OF INTERIOR			
6								
7								
8	DECISION RENDERED							
9	REFUSED							
10								
11								
12								
13								
14								
15								
16								
17								

TRIBAL ENROLLMENT OF PARENTS

	Name of Father	Year	County	Name of Mother	Year	County
1	Brinkley Jones		Non Citz	Mildred Jones		Non Citz
2	No 1			Belle Jones		
3						
4						
5						
6						
7	Admitted by the U.S. Court, Ardmore, I.T. Jany 17, 1898, Court Case No 148					
8						
9	No2 was born November 4th 1897					
10						
11	Removed from Georgia to the Territory August 18th 1898					
12						
13						
14						
15						
16				Date of Application for Enrollment		150
17						10-17-98

187

Choctaw By Blood Enrollment Cards 1898-1914

RESIDENCE: Chickasaw Natn
POST OFFICE: Tatum, I.T.

Choctaw **Nation**   Choctaw **Roll**

CARD NO. **5288**
FIELD NO. C 333

Dawes' Roll No.	NAME	Relationship to Person First Named	AGE	SEX	BLOOD	TRIBAL ENROLLMENT Year	County	No.
1	Jones, Garland R		23	M	1/32			
2	" Jennie F	Dau	2	F				
3	" Ruth C	"		"				
4								
5					ACTION APPROVED BY			
6					SECRETARY OF INTERIOR.			
7								
8								
9		DECISION RENDERED						
10		REFUSED						
11								
12								
13								
14								
15								
16								
17								

TRIBAL ENROLLMENT OF PARENTS

	Name of Father	Year	County	Name of Mother	Year	County
1	M T Jones		Non Citz	Jennie Jones		Non Citz
2	No 1			Emma Jones		" "
3	No 1			" "		" "
4						
5						
6	Admitted by the U.S. Court, Ardmore, I.T. Jany 17, 1898 Court Case No 148					
7						
8	No2 was born September 23, 1896 Not in decree					
9	No3 " " " 17, 1898					
10						
11	No1 has lived in the Territory since December 17, 1897					
12						
13						
14						
15						
16	See Choctaw 5053.					
17						

Choctaw By Blood Enrollment Cards 1898-1914

RESIDENCE: Chickasaw Natn	Choctaw **Nation** Choctaw **Roll**	CARD NO. **5289**
POST OFFICE: Addington, I.T.		FIELD NO. C 334

Dawes' Roll No.	NAME	Relationship to Person First Named	AGE	SEX	BLOOD	TRIBAL ENROLLMENT Year	County	No.
1	Boone, John	Named	4[?]	M	1/8			
2	" Abbie	Wife	4[?]	F				
3	" Belle	Dau						
4	" Ethel							
5								
6								
7								
8								
9								
10								
11								
12								
13								
14								
15								
16								
17								

TRIBAL ENROLLMENT OF PARENTS

	Name of Father	Year	County	Name of Mother	Year	County
1	[illegible] Boone		Non Citz	Louis Boone	Dead	Non Citz
2	[Name illegible]			Dora Lu[illegible]		
3	No1			No2		
4	No1			No2		
5						
6						
7	Nos 1 to 4 denied in 1896, case #18.					
8	Admitted by the U.S. Court, Ardmore, I.T. December 21, 1897, Court Case No 88					
9						
10	John Boone was married to No2 in Texas in 1872, under the laws of Texas					
11	Have lived in the chickasaw Nation for thirteen years					
12						
13						
14						
15						
16						
17					Date of Application for Enrollment	10-17-98

Choctaw By Blood Enrollment Cards 1898-1914

| RESIDENCE: | Chickasaw Natn | | | | | | | CARD NO. | **5290** |
| POST OFFICE: | Addington, | I.T. | Choctaw **Nation** | Choctaw **Roll** | | | | FIELD NO. | C 335 |

Dawes' Roll No.	NAME	Relationship to Person First Named	AGE	SEX	BLOOD	TRIBAL ENROLLMENT		
						Year	County	No.
1	Hensley, Henry		36	M				
2	" Dorcas	Wife		F				
3	" Willie R	Dau		"				
4								
5								
6								
7								
8								
9								
10								
11								
12								
13								
14								
15								
16								
17								

TRIBAL ENROLLMENT OF PARENTS

	Name of Father	Year	County	Name of Mother	Year	County
1	Henry Hensley		Non Citz	Eliz. Hensley		Non Citz
2	William [illegible]			Francis [illegible]		
3						
4						
5						
6	Nos 1,2&3 denied in 1896, case #18					
7	Admitted by the U.S. Court, Ardmore, I.T. Dec. 21, 1897 Court Case No 88					
8						
9	No2 was admitted as Dora Hensley					
10						
11	No1 was married to No2 in Texas in 1893 under the Laws of that State					
12	They have [sic] in the Chickasaw Nation 11 years					
13						
14						
15						
16						
17						

190

Choctaw By Blood Enrollment Cards 1898-1914

RESIDENCE: Chickasaw Natn
POST OFFICE: Addington, I.T.

Choctaw **Nation**   Choctaw **Roll**

CARD NO. **5291**
FIELD NO. C 336

Dawes' Roll No.	NAME	Relationship to Person First Named	AGE	SEX	BLOOD	TRIBAL ENROLLMENT		
						Year	County	No.
Denied 1	Price, John S	Named	49	M	I.W.			
4-17-05 2	" Eva R	Wife	39	F	1/16			
3	" Henry O.	Son	20	M				
4								
5								
6								
7								
8								
9								
10								
11								
12								
13								
14								
15								
16								
17								

TRIBAL ENROLLMENT OF PARENTS

	Name of Father	Year	County	Name of Mother	Year	County
1	Angie Price	Dead	Non Citz	Caroline Price	Dead	Non Citz
2	Henry Hensley	"	" "	Eliz. Hensley	"	" "
3	No1			No2		
4						
5	Nos. 1,2&3 denied in 1896, case #18.					
6	Admitted by the U.S. Court, Ardmore, I.T. December 21, 1897, Court Case No 88.					
7						
8	No1 was admitted as John Price					
9	No2 " " " Eva Price					
10	No3 " " " Henry Price					
11						
12	No1 married No2 in Texas June 10, 1876 under the Laws of that state.					
13	They have been living in the Chickasaw Nation since May 1895.					
14						
15						
16					Date of Application for Enrollment	10-17-98
17						

191

Choctaw By Blood Enrollment Cards 1898-1914

RESIDENCE: Chickasaw Natn
POST OFFICE: Ryan, I.T.

Choctaw **Nation**   Choctaw **Roll**

CARD NO. **5292**
FIELD NO. C 337

Dawes' Roll No.	NAME	Relationship to Person First Named	AGE	SEX	BLOOD	TRIBAL ENROLLMENT Year	County	No.
Refused 1	Edmondson, Thos E	First Named	35	M	I.W.		Dis	
2	" Lizzie	Wife	30	F	1/16		D	
3	" Ethel E	Dau	10	"			D	
4	" Thos. L	Son	8	M			D	
5	" Oliver L	"	7	"			D	
6	" Henry W	"	5	M			D	
7	" Emma B	Dau	3	F				
8	" Ivy	"	18mo	"				
9	" Oia	"	2mo	"				
10	" Forest	Son	2mo	M				

Nos 1 to 7 denied in 1896, case #18

DISMISSED JAN 1905

No1 was married to No3 in Texas, October 20, 1887, under laws of that State
No10 Born Aug. 26, 1901: Enrolled Nov. 7, 1901.
For child of No 1&2 see NB #1054 (Act Apr 26, '06)

TRIBAL ENROLLMENT OF PARENTS

Name of Father	Year	County	Name of Mother	Year	County
1 Peter Edmondson	Dead	Non Citz	Minerva Edmondson		Non Citz
2 John Brummitt[sic]		" "	Eliz. Brummett	Dead	" "
3 No1			No2		
4 No1			No2		
5 No1			No2		
6 No1			No2		
7 No1			No2		
8 No1			No2		
9 No1			No2		
10 No1			No2		

DENIED CITIZENSHIP BY THE CHOCTAW AND CHICKASAW CITIZENSHIP COURT

11 Admitted by the U.S. Court, Ardmore, I.T. December 21, 1897, Court Case No 88
12 No1 was admitted as T.E. Edmondson
13 No8 was born March 29, 1897 Not in decree
14 No9 "   " Sept. 8, 1898 "   "   "
15 No.5 died August 24th, 1900 See letter filed herewith
16 Above family has lived in Chickasaw Nation for eleven years
17 C.C.C.C. case #64 T 3/10/03 Nos 1 to 7

192

Choctaw By Blood Enrollment Cards 1898-1914

RESIDENCE: State of Texas
POST OFFICE: Jacksboro, Texas

Choctaw **Nation** Choctaw **Roll**

CARD NO. **5293**
FIELD NO. C 338

Dawes' Roll No.	NAME	Relationship to Person First Named	AGE	SEX	BLOOD	TRIBAL ENROLLMENT		
						Year	County	No.
1	Dodson, J. W.	First Named	62	M	I.W.		Non citizen	
2	" Elizabeth	wife	61	F	1/8		" "	
3						ACTION APPROVED BY		
4						SECRETARY OF INTERIOR.		
5								
6								
7								
8								
9								
10								
11								
12								
13								
14								
15								
16								
17								

DENIED CITIZENSHIP BY THE CHOCTAW AND CHICKASAW CITIZENSHIP COURT

TRIBAL ENROLLMENT OF PARENTS

	Name of Father	Year	County	Name of Mother	Year	County
1	Enoch Dodson		Non citizen	Frances Dodson	dead	Non Citizen
2	Thomas Boone	dead	" "	Elezean Boone	dead	" "
3						
4						
5	Nos 1&2 denied in 1896, case #18					
6						
7	No1 admitted by intermarriage					
8						
9	Nos 1&2 married in Texas under Texas law 17 years ago & have					
10	never removed from Texas to the Territory					
11						
12	Admitted by U.S. Court of Ardmore December 21st 1897, Court Case No. 88					
13						
14	No 17/99 No1 said to have been [illegible] from Judgement by U.S. Court.					
15						
16						
17	C.C.C.C. case #64 T 3/10/03				Date of Application for Enrollment	10-17-98

Choctaw By Blood Enrollment Cards 1898-1914

RESIDENCE: Chickasaw Natn
POST OFFICE: Sugden, Ind. Ter.

Choctaw **Nation**   Choctaw **Roll**

CARD NO. **5294**
FIELD NO. C 339

Dawes' Roll No.	NAME	Relationship to Person First Named	AGE	SEX	BLOOD	TRIBAL ENROLLMENT Year	TRIBAL ENROLLMENT County	TRIBAL ENROLLMENT No.
1	Brummett, William		29	M	1/16		Non Citizen	
2	" Lizzie	wife	22	F				
3	" Thurston	son	3	M				
4	" Stannie	dau	5mo	F				
5								
6								
7								
8								
9								
10			ACTION APPROVED BY		MAR 23 1905			
11			SECRETARY OF INTERIOR.					
12			NOTICE OF DEPARTMENTAL ACTION MAILED APPLICANT.	APR 4 1905				
13			NOTICE OF DEPARTMENTAL ACTION FORWARDED ATTORNEYS FOR CHOCTAW AND CHICKASAW NATIONS.		APR 04 1905			
14								
15								
16			RECORD FORWARDED DEPARTMENT.	FEB 21 1905				
17								

DENIED CITIZENSHIP BY THE CHOCTAW AND CHICKASAW CITIZENSHIP COURT

DISMISSED

JAN 1905

TRIBAL ENROLLMENT OF PARENTS

	Name of Father	Year	County	Name of Mother	Year	County
1	Wesley Brummett		Non Citizen	Elizabeth Dodson		Non Citizen
2	Crisp	dead	" "	Crisp	dead	
3	No 1			No 2		
4	No 1			No 2		
5						
6	Nos 1, 2 & 3 denied in 1896, case #18		**REFUSED**	FEB 21 1905		
7	Have lived in the Chickasaw Nation 12 years					
8			COPY OF DECISION FORWARDED APPLICANT	FEB 21 1905		
9	William Brummett admitted by intermarriage.		COPY OF DECISION FORWARDED			
10			ATTORNEYS FOR CHOCTAW AND CHICKASAW NATIONS.	FEB 21 1905		
11	William & Lizzie married in 1894, under United States law.					
12						
13	Admitted by U.S. Court at Ardmore December 21st 1897 Court Case No. 88					
14						
15						
16			No4 Enrolled May 24, 1900			
17						

194

Choctaw By Blood Enrollment Cards 1898-1914

| RESIDENCE: | Chickasaw Natn |
| POST OFFICE: | Addington, I.T. |

Choctaw **Nation**   Choctaw **Roll**

CARD NO. **5295**
FIELD NO. C 340

Dawes' Roll No.	NAME	Relationship to Person First Named	AGE	SEX	BLOOD	TRIBAL ENROLLMENT		
						Year	County	No.
1	King, Charles	Named	29	S M			Non Citizen	
2	" Belle	wife	25	F	1/16			
3	" Lela	dau	5	F				
4	" Lila	"	4	"				
5	" Lang	son	2	M				
6	" Willie K	"	8mo	"				
7	" Charley Bartley	Son	4mo	"				
8	" James Homer	son	2mo	M				
9								
10	#6-7-8 DISMISSED					No.8 born Sept 1st, 1901 and Enrolled		
11	JAN 24 1905					Nov. 22d, 1901.		
12						No.7 Enrolled June 23d, 1900.		
13	No1 Dismissed by CCCC for want of Jurisdiction							
14								
15	No2 Denied by CCCC as Belle King or Bell King							
16	4 " " " " Lila " or Lilla King							
17						C.C.C.C. Case #64T 3/10/03		

TRIBAL ENROLLMENT OF PARENTS

	Name of Father	Year	County	Name of Mother	Year	County
1	Richard King	dead	Non Citizen	Mary King		Non Citizen
2	John Brummett		" "	Elizabeth Dodson		" "
3	No1			No2		
4	No1			No2		
5	No1			No2		
6	No1			No2		
7	No1			No2		
8	No1			No2		
9	No6 born Jan. 26th 1898 Not in decree.					
10	Nos 1to5 denied in 1896, #18					
11	No1 admitted by intermarriage					
12						
13	Nos 1&2 married in Texas under Texas law, December 20th 1892					
14	Have lived in Territory since July 1897					
15						
16	Admitted by U.S. Court, Ardmore, December 21st 1897					
17						

DENIED CITIZENSHIP BY THE CHOCTAW AND CHICKASAW CITIZENSHIP COURT

195

Choctaw By Blood Enrollment Cards 1898-1914

RESIDENCE:	Chickasaw Natn								
POST OFFICE:	I.T.		Choctaw **Nation**		Choctaw **Roll**		CARD NO. **5296** FIELD NO. 341		

Dawes' Roll No.	NAME	Relationship to Person First Named	AGE	SEX	BLOOD	TRIBAL ENROLLMENT		
						Year	County	No.
✓ 1	Mullins, Mary M		26	F	1/8			
✓ 2	" Vister L	Dau	2	"	1/16			
✓ 3	" Joseph R	Son		M	1/16			
✓ 4	" Charles L	"	8mo	M	1/16			
✓ 5	" James E	Son	15mo	M				
6								
7	2-3-4 & 5							
8	DISMISSED							
9	MAY 27 1904							
10								
11								
12								
13								
14								
15								
16								
17								

DENIED CITIZENSHIP BY THE CHOCTAW AND CHICKASAW CITIZENSHIP COURT

	TRIBAL ENROLLMENT OF PARENTS					
	Name of Father	Year	County	Name of Mother	Year	County
1	J H Womack		Non Citz	[Illegible] Womack		Non Citz
2	Allen Mullens		" "	No 1		
3	" "		" "	No 1		
4	" "		" "	No 1		
5	" "		" "	No 1		

6 Admitted by the U.S. Court, Ardmore, I.T. Jany 18, 1898

7

8 No1 was admitted as Mary M. Womack. Was married to Allen Mullens under the laws of the
9 United States September 20, 1893. Has lived in the Chickasaw Nation for thirteen years.
10 No2 was born October 12, 1896. Not in decree
11 No3 " " March 2, 1898. " " "
12 No5 Born June 26, 1901. Enrolled Sept. 30, 1902
13 No1 denied in 1896, case #498
14 No1 denied by Judgement of the C.C.C.C. Feb. 23 '04 case #17
15 No4 enrolled Oct 30, '99
16
17

Choctaw By Blood Enrollment Cards 1898-1914

RESIDENCE:	Chickasaw Natn						CARD NO.	5297
POST OFFICE:	Hope, I.T.		Choctaw **Nation**	Choctaw **Roll**			FIELD NO.	C 342

Dawes' Roll No.	NAME	Relationship to Person First Named	AGE	SEX	BLOOD	TRIBAL ENROLLMENT		
						Year	County	No.
	1 Parks, I. E.		52	M	1/2			
DEAD	2 " Martha	wife	48	F	IW			
	3 " Sam, Jr	Son	18	M				
	4 " Willard	"	12	"				
	5 " Jesse	"	10	"				
	6 " Nora	Dau	6	F				
	7 " Susan	dau	5mo	F				
	8							
	9							
#7	10 DISMISSED							
	11							
	12							
	13							
	14							
	15							
	16 DENIED CITIZENSHIP BY THE CHOCTAW AND							
	17 CHICKASAW CITIZENSHIP COURT							

TRIBAL ENROLLMENT OF PARENTS

	Name of Father	Year	County	Name of Mother	Year	County
1	M J Parks	Dead	Non Citz	Rebecca Parks	Dead	Non Citz
2	Reuben Barber	"	" "	Betsy Barber	"	" "
3	No 1			No 2		
4	No 1			No 2		
5	No 1			No 2		
6	No 1			No 2		
7	No 1			Nancy Parks		non-citizen

8 Nos 1 to 6 denied in 1896, case #552
9 Admitted by the U.S. Court, Ardmore, I.T. Jany 20, 1898, Court Case No 133
10 No 1 was married to No 2 in Texas in 1867 under the laws of that state, have lived in the
11 Chickasaw Nation for eighteen years
12   No 2 Died April 15, 1900. See affidavit of Mary A Donaho filed April 21, 1902
13   No 1 is now the husband of Nancy Parks, a non-citizen. Evidence of marriage
14   filed April 21, 1902
15   No 7 Born Nov. 10, 1901; enrolled April 21, 1902
16
17

197

Choctaw By Blood Enrollment Cards 1898-1914

RESIDENCE: Chickasaw Natn

POST OFFICE: Marlow, I.T.

Choctaw **Nation**   Choctaw **Roll**

CARD NO. **5298**

FIELD NO. (342)

Dawes' Roll No.	NAME	Relationship to Person First Named	AGE	SEX	BLOOD	TRIBAL ENROLLMENT		
						Year	County	No.
1	Woods, Allie	First Named	21	F	1/32			
2	" Clara	Dau		"	1/64			
3	" Lillian	Dau	3mo	F	1/64			
4								
5								
6	#2-6 DISMISSED							
7								
8								
9								
10								
11								
12								
13								
14	DENIED CITIZENSHIP BY THE CHOCTAW AND							
15	CHICKASAW CITIZENSHIP COURT							
16								
17								

TRIBAL ENROLLMENT OF PARENTS

	Name of Father	Year	County	Name of Mother	Year	County
1	S. E. Parks		Non Citz	Martha Parks		Non Citz
2	Geo Woods		" "	No 1		
3	" "		" "	No 1		
4	No1 denied in 1896, case #552					
5						
6	[Entry illegible] Has lived in the Chickasaw Nation					
7	Admitted by the U.S. Court, Ardmore, I.T. Jany 20, 1898 Court Case No 133					
8						
9	No2 was born September 19, 1898. Not in decree					
10						
11	No.3 Enrolled July 6, 1900					
12						
13						
14						
15						
16	No1 Denied in 100T as "Alvis Woods or Allie Woods"					
17						

Choctaw By Blood Enrollment Cards 1898-1914

RESIDENCE: Chickasaw Natn			Choctaw **Nation** Choctaw **Roll**				CARD NO. **5299**	
POST OFFICE: Hope, I.T.							FIELD NO. C 344	

Dawes' Roll No.	NAME	Relationship to Person First Named	AGE	SEX	BLOOD	TRIBAL ENROLLMENT		
						Year	County	No.
1	Hallis, Bettie	Named	27	F	1/32			
2	Ward, Thomas	Son	10	M				
3	" Cora	Dau	8	F				
4	" Willie	"	6	"				
5	Hallis, Ruby	"	2	"				
6	Cox, Mollie	Dau	4mo	F				
7								
8	DISMISSED							
9	DEC							
10								
11								
12								
13								
14	DENIED CITIZENSHIP BY THE CHOCTAW AND							
15	CHICKASAW CITIZENSHIP COURT							
16								
17								

#56

TRIBAL ENROLLMENT OF PARENTS

	Name of Father	Year	County	Name of Mother	Year	County
1	S.E. Parks		Non Citz	Martha Parks		Non Citz
2	John Ward	Dead	" "	No 1		
3	" "	"	" "	No 1		
4	" "	"	" "	No 1		
5	John Hallis			No 1		
6	Marion L Cox			No 1		
7	Nos 1to4 denied in 1896, case #552					
8	Admitted by the U.S. Court, Ardmore, I.T. Jany 20, 1898, Court Case No 133					
9						
10	The children Thomas, Cora and Willie Ward are by the first husband of No1 -					
11	John Ward, non dead					
12						
13	No1 was married to John Hallis December 18, 1895 under the laws of the United States and has					
14	lived in the Chickasaw Nation for eighteen years. No1 is now the wife of M. L. Cox					
15	[Entry illegible]					
16						
17	No6 Born Dec. 10, 1901, enrolled April 22, 1902					

for Enrollment.

199

Choctaw By Blood Enrollment Cards 1898-1914

RESIDENCE:	Chickasaw Natn							
POST OFFICE:	Hope, I.T.							

Choctaw **Nation** Choctaw **Roll**

CARD NO. **5300**
FIELD NO. C 345

Dawes' Roll No.	NAME	Relationship to Person First Named	AGE	SEX	BLOOD	TRIBAL ENROLLMENT		
						Year	County	No.
1	Parks, W. J.		28	M	1/32			
2	" Joe	Son	2	"				
3	" Selma	Dau	1	F				
4	" Isaac Irvin	Son	2 1/2	M				
5	" Sarrah Estella	Dau	8mo	F				
6								
7	4-5 DISMISSED							
8								
9								
10								
11								
12								
13								
14								
15								
16								
17								

DENIED CITIZENSHIP BY THE CHOCTAW AND CHICKASAW CITIZENSHIP COURT

TRIBAL ENROLLMENT OF PARENTS

	Name of Father	Year	County	Name of Mother	Year	County
1	S E Parks		Non Citz	Martha Parks		Non Citz
2	No 1			Emma Parks		" "
3	No 1			" "		" "
4	No 1			" "		" "
5	No 1			" "		" "
6	No1 denied in 1896 case #552					
7	Admitted by the U.S. Court, Ardmore, I.T. Jany 20, 1898 Court Case No 133					
8	[Entries illegible...]					
9	No3 was born December 1, 189[?]					
10	No4 Enrolled Sept 23, 1901					
11	No5 Enrolled Sept 23, 1901					
12						
13						
14	No2 was denied by C.C.C.C. Case [?]					
15						
16						
17						

Choctaw By Blood Enrollment Cards 1898-1914

RESIDENCE: Chickasaw Natn		COUNTY. **Choctaw Nation**				**Choctaw Roll** *(Not Including Freedmen)*	CARD No. **5301**	
POST OFFICE: Hope, I.T.							FIELD No. C 346	

Dawes' Roll No.	NAME	Relationship to Person First Named	AGE	SEX	BLOOD	TRIBAL ENROLLMENT		
						Year	County	No.
DP 1	Leonard, Bert	Named	42	M	I.W.			
2	" Abbie	Wife	31	F	1/32			
3	" Clara	Dau	11	"				
4	" Preston	Son	7	M				
5	" Perry	"	4	"				
DP 6	" Emmett	"	5mo	"				
DP 7	" Floy Frank	Dau	3mo	F				
8								
9 #1-6-7 DISMISSED								
10 DEC								
11								
12								
13								
14 DENIED CITIZENSHIP BY THE CHOCTAW AND								
15 CHICKASAW CITIZENSHIP COURT								
16								
17								

TRIBAL ENROLLMENT OF PARENTS

	Name of Father	Year	County	Name of Mother	Year	County
1	William Leonard	Dead	Non Citz	Clarida Leonard	Dead	Non Citz
2	S.E. Parks		" "	Martha Parks		" "
3	No1			No2		
4	No1			No2		
5	No1			No2		
6	No1			No2		
7	R.A. Leonard		non-citizen	No2		
8	Nos 2 to 5 denied in 1896, case #552					
9	Admitted by the U.S. Court, Ardmore, I.T. Jany 20, 1898 Court Case No 133					
10	Above family has lived in the Chickasaw Nation fourteen years					
11						
12	No6 was born May 22, 1898. Not in the decree					
13						
14	No7 Born Jany 16, 1902; enrolled April 21, 1902					
15						
16						
17						

Date of Application for Enrollment 10-18-98

201

Choctaw By Blood Enrollment Cards 1898-1914

RESIDENCE: Chickasaw Natn   COUNTY. **Choctaw Nation**   **Choctaw Roll** *(Not Including Freedmen)*   CARD NO. **5302**

POST OFFICE: Ryan, I.T.   FIELD NO. C 347

Dawes' Roll No.	NAME	Relationship to Person First Named	AGE	SEX	BLOOD	TRIBAL ENROLLMENT		
						Year	County	No.
1	Mallory, Agnes O		61	F	1/4			
2								
3								
4								
5								
6								
7								
8								
9								
10								
11								
12								
13								
14								
15								
16								
17								

TRIBAL ENROLLMENT OF PARENTS

	Name of Father	Year	County	Name of Mother	Year	County
1	Sam'l Foster	Dead	Non Citz	Agnes Foster	Dead	Non Citz
2						
3						
4						
5						
6	No.1 denied in 1896, case #352					
7	Admitted by the U.S. Court, Ardmore, I.T. Jany 20, 1898, Court Case No 112					
8						
9	Has been living in the Territory for four years					
10						
11						
12						
13						
14						
15						
16						
17						

Choctaw By Blood Enrollment Cards 1898-1914

RESIDENCE: Chickasaw Natn   COUNTY.   **Choctaw Nation**   Choctaw Roll   CARD NO. **5303**
POST OFFICE: Ryan, I.T.   *(Not Including Freedmen)*   FIELD NO. C 348

Dawes' Roll No.	NAME	Relationship to Person First Named	AGE	SEX	BLOOD	TRIBAL ENROLLMENT Year	County	No.
1	Prichard, Cassie O	Named	39	F	1/8			
2	" Booker M	Son	18	M				
3	" Jessie A	Dau	16	F				
4								
5								
6								
7								
8								
9								
10								
11								
12								
13								
14								
15								
16								
17								

TRIBAL ENROLLMENT OF PARENTS

	Name of Father	Year	County	Name of Mother	Year	County
1	[Illegible] K Saunders	Dead	Non Citz	Agnes O Saunders		Non Citz
2	Booker Prichard	"	" "	No 1		
3	" "	"	" " "	No 1		
4						
5						
6	Nos 1, 2 & 3 denied in 1896 case #352					
7	Admitted by the U.S. Court, Ardmore, I.T. Jany 20, 1898, Court Case No 112					
8	No1 was admitted as Cassie Prichard					
9	No3 " " " Jessie Prichard					
10						
11						
12						
13						
14						
15						
16						
17					Date of Application for Enrollment	10-18-98

DENIED CITIZENSHIP BY THE CHOCTAW AND CHICKASAW CITIZENSHIP COURT

Choctaw By Blood Enrollment Cards 1898-1914

| RESIDENCE: Chickasaw Natn | COUNTY. | Choctaw Nation | Choctaw Roll | CARD NO. 5304 |
| POST OFFICE: Comanche, I.T. | | | (Not Including Freedmen) | FIELD NO. C 349 |

Dawes' Roll No.	NAME	Relationship to Person First Named	AGE	SEX	BLOOD	TRIBAL ENROLLMENT		
						Year	County	No.
1	Saunders, S. F.	First Named	36	M	1/8			
2	" Fannie	Wife	34	F	I.W.			
3	" Bessie O	Dau	9	"	1/16			
4	" Drucilla	"	7	"	1/16			
5	" Eva	"	6	"	1/16			
6	" Claude	Son	4	M	1/16			
7	" Ella	Dau	2	F	1/16			
8	" Ruth	"	4mo	"	1/16			
9	" Lucile	Dau	[?]mo	F	1/16			
10								
11	#8-9-14 DISMISSED							
12	JAN 24							
13								
14	Saunders, Jesse H	Son	1mo	M	1/16			
15								
16								
17								

TRIBAL ENROLLMENT OF PARENTS

	Name of Father	Year	County	Name of Mother	Year	County
1	[Illegible] Saunders	Dead	Non Citz	Agnes Saunders		Non Citz
2	[Name Illegible]		" "	Becky Miller	Dead	" "
3	No1			No2		
4	No1			No2		
5	No1			No2		
6	No1			No2		
7	No1			No2		
8	No1			No2		
9	No1			No2		
10	Admitted by the U.S. Court, Ardmore, I.T. Jany 20, 1898 Court Case No 112					
11	No1 was married to No2 Jany 8, 1889 under the laws of Mississippi					
12	Have been living in the Territory four years.					
13						
14	No1			No2		
15	Nos1 to 7 denied in 1896 case #352			No8 enrolled June 1/99		
16	No9 Born Jany 6, 1901. Enrolled Oct. 15, 1902					
17	No14 Born Sept 4, 1902. Enrolled Oct. 15, 1902					

DENIED CITIZENSHIP BY THE CHOCTAW AND CHICKASAW CITIZENSHIP COURT

Choctaw By Blood Enrollment Cards 1898-1914

RESIDENCE: Chickasaw Natn	COUNTY.	Choctaw Nation	Choctaw Roll	CARD NO.	5305
POST OFFICE: Minco, I.T.			*(Not Including Freedmen)*	FIELD NO.	C 350

Dawes' Roll No.	NAME	Relationship to Person First Named	AGE	SEX	BLOOD	TRIBAL ENROLLMENT		
						Year	County	No.
✓	1 Marlow, Jasper	First Named	41	M	1/4			
✓	2 " Robert C	Son	12	"				
✓	3 " Haley	Dau	10	F				
✓	4 " Ernest J	Son	8	M				
✓	5 " Roy	"	"	"				
	6							
	7							
	8							
	9							
	10							
	11							
	12							
	13							
	14							
	15							
	16							
	17							

DENIED CITIZENSHIP BY THE CHOCTAW AND CHICKASAW CITIZENSHIP COURT

TRIBAL ENROLLMENT OF PARENTS

	Name of Father	Year	County	Name of Mother	Year	County
1	Bailey Marlow	Dead	Non Citz	Margaret Marlow		Non Citz
2	No 1			Emma Marlow		" "
3	No 1			" "		" "
4	No 1			" "		" "
5	No 1			" "		" "
6						
7	Nos 1 to 5 denied in 1896 case #545					
8	Admitted by the U.S. Court, South McAlester, I.T. Jany 13, 1897 Court Case No 6[?]					
9	[Entry illegible] Have lived in the Territory [illegible]					
10	[Remainder illegible]					
11						
12						
13						
14						
15						
16						
17					Date of Application for Enrollment	10-21-98

Choctaw By Blood Enrollment Cards 1898-1914

RESIDENCE: Chickasaw Natn   COUNTY.   **Choctaw Nation**   Choctaw Roll   CARD NO. **5306**
POST OFFICE: Chickasha,   I.T.   *(Not Including Freedmen)*   FIELD NO. C 351

Dawes' Roll No.	NAME	Relationship to Person First Named	AGE	SEX	BLOOD	TRIBAL ENROLLMENT Year	County	No.
1	Barefoot, George W				I.W.			
2	" Sallie M	Wife			1/8			
3	" Burton	Son						
4	" Clifford	"						
5								
6					No2 Denied by C.C.C. as Sallie Barefoot			
7			" 4 "	"	"	" Clifton [Illegible]		
8								
9	ACTION APPROVED BY SECRETARY OF INTERIOR. MAR 23 1905				COPY OF DECISION FORWARDED APPLICANT FEB 21 1905			
11	NOTICE OF DEPARTMENTAL ACTION MAILED APPLICANT. APR 4 1905				COPY OF DECISION FORWARDED ATTORNEYS FOR CHOCTAW AND CHICKASAW NATIONS. FEB 21 1905			
12	NOTICE OF DEPARTMENTAL ACTION FORWARDED ATTORNEYS FOR CHOCTAW AND CHICKASAW NATIONS. APR 4 1905							
15					RECORD FORWARDED DEPARTMENT. FEB 21 1905			
16	REFUSED FEB 21 1905							
17								

	TRIBAL ENROLLMENT OF PARENTS					
	Name of Father	Year	County	Name of Mother	Year	County
1	[Name Illegible]	Dead	Non Citz	Mahala [Illegible]	Dead	Non Citz
2	Thos Boone			Louisa Boone		
3	No 1			No 2		
4	No 1			No 2		
5						
6	Nos 1 to 4 denied in 1896, case #18					
7	Admitted by the U.S. Court, Ardmore, I.T. [remainder illegible]					
8	No4 was admitted as Clifton Barefoot [Entry illegible]					
9	No1 was married to No2 in Texas March 16, 1867 under the laws of that State					
10	They have lived in the Chickasaw Nation since June 12, 1898					
11						
12						
13						
14						
15						
16						
17						

Choctaw By Blood Enrollment Cards 1898-1914

RESIDENCE: Chickasaw Natn	COUNTY.	**Choctaw Nation**			**Choctaw Roll** *(Not Including Freedmen)*		CARD NO. **5307**	
POST OFFICE: Chickasha, I.T.							FIELD NO. C 352	

Dawes' Roll No.	NAME	Relationship to Person First Named	AGE	SEX	BLOOD	TRIBAL ENROLLMENT		
						Year	County	No.
Refused 1	Woodson, Ed. T.	Named	34	M	I.W.		Dis	
2	" Emma	Wife	25	F	1/16		D	
3	" Guy	Son	4	M	1/32		D	
DP 4	" Clara	Dau	2	F	1/32			
DP 5	" Ruth S	"	2mo	"	1/32			
DP 6	" Samuel William	Son	2mo	M	1/32	REFUSED FEB 21 1905		
7								
8 4-5-6 DISMISSED						COPY OF DECISION FORWARDED APPLICANT FEB 21 1905		
9 JAN								
10 NOTICE OF DEPARTMENTAL ACTION FORWARDED ATTORNEYS FOR CHOCTAW AND CHICKASAW NATIONS. APR 4 1905						COPY OF DECISION FORWARDED ATTORNEYS FOR CHOCTAW AND CHICKASAW NATIONS. FEB 21 1905		
11 RECORD FORWARDED DEPARTMENT FEB 21 1905								
12 NOTICE OF DEPARTMENTAL ACTION MAILED APPLICANT. APR 1 1905						ACTION APPROVED BY SECRETARY OF INTERIOR. MAR 23 1905		
14								
15 DENIED CITIZENSHIP BY THE CHOCTAW AND								
16								
17 CHICKASAW CITIZENSHIP COURT								

TRIBAL ENROLLMENT OF PARENTS

	Name of Father	Year	County	Name of Mother	Year	County
1	[Illegible] Woodson	Dead	Non Citz	[Illegible] S Woodson		Non Citz
2	G.W. Barefoot		" "	Sallie M Barefoot		" "
3	No1			No2		
4	No1			No2		
5	No1			No2		
6	No1			No2		
7						
8	Admitted by the U.S. Court, Ardmore, I.T. December 21, 1897 Court Case No 88					
9	No1 was admitted as Ed Woodson					
10	No3 was born March 4 1897					
11	[... illegible] C.C.C.C. Case #64					
12	Nos 1-2 were married in Texas under the laws of that State.					
13	They have lived in the Territory since February 1898 No6 Born April 25" 1902: Enrolled July 1st 1902					
14	Nos 1,2 & 3 denied in 1896, case #18.					
15				No5 enrolled Oct 31/99		
16						1/92
17						10-21-98

207

Choctaw By Blood Enrollment Cards 1898-1914

RESIDENCE: Chickasaw Natn   COUNTY.   **Choctaw Nation**   Choctaw Roll   CARD NO. **5308**

POST OFFICE: Minnekah, I.T.   *(Not Including Freedmen)*   FIELD NO. C 353

Dawes' Roll No.	NAME	Relationship to Person	AGE	SEX	BLOOD	TRIBAL ENROLLMENT Year	County	No.
✓ 1	Nail, Abraham H	First Named	80	M				
✓ 2	" Matilda J	Wife	73	F				
✓ 3	" John	Son	40	M				
✓ 4	" Aaron L		35					
5								
6								
8								
9								
10								
11								
12								
13								
14								
15								
16								
17								

TRIBAL ENROLLMENT OF PARENTS

	Name of Father	Year	County	Name of Mother	Year	County
1	William Nail	Dead	Non Citz	Delilah Nail	Dead	Non Citz
2	Isaac Robinson			Clara Robinson	"	" "
3	No1			No2		
4	No1			No2		

5

6 Nos 1 to 4 denied in 1896, case #51

7 Admitted by the U.S. Court, Ardmore, I.T. August 26, 1897 Court Case No [?]

8

9 No1 was married in Tenn. under the laws of that State. Have lived in the Chickasaw Nation four years.

10

11 See report to Department of June 6, 1905.

12

13

14 GRANTED FEB 21 190

15

16

17

208

RESIDENCE: Chickasaw Natn   COUNTY.
POST OFFICE: Chickasha,   I.T.

Choctaw Nation

Choctaw Roll
(Not Including Freedmen)

CARD NO. **5309**
FIELD NO. C 354

Dawes' Roll No.	NAME	Relationship to Person First Named	AGE	SEX	BLOOD	TRIBAL ENROLLMENT		
						Year	County	No.
✓	1 Nail, James P		34	M	1/16			
✓	2 " Lizzie	Wife	16	F	I.W.			
	4							
	5							
	6							
	7							
	8							
	9							
	10							
	11							
	12							
	13							
	14							

DENIED CITIZENSHIP BY THE CHOCTAW AND CHICKASAW CITIZENSHIP COURT

Transferred to Choctaw Cas No 6079 2/21/07

GRANTED

TRIBAL ENROLLMENT OF PARENTS

	Name of Father	Year	County	Name of Mother	Year	County
1	Abraham H Nail		Non Citz	Matilda J Nail		
2	[Name Illegible]			Martha [Illegible]		
3						
4						
5	Nos 1&2 denied in 1896, case #57					
6	Admitted by the U.S. Court, Ardmore, I.T. August 26, 1897 Court Case No 84					
7	Were married in Texas December 25, 1885 under the laws of that State.					
8						
9	See report to Department of June 6, 1905.					
10						
11						
12						
13						
14						
15						
16						
17					Date of Application for Enrollment	10-21-98

GRANTED FEB 21 1907

| RESIDENCE: Chickasaw Natn | COUNTY. | Choctaw Nation | Choctaw Roll | CARD NO. 5310 |
| POST OFFICE: Chickasha, I.T. | | | (Not Including Freedmen) | FIELD NO. C 355 |

Dawes' Roll No.	NAME	Relationship to Person First Named	AGE	SEX	BLOOD	TRIBAL ENROLLMENT		
						Year	County	No.
1	Paul, Robert		23	M	1/8			
2	" Annie	Sister	18	F	1/8			
3	" Vivian	Brother		M	1/8			
4								
5								
6								
7								
8								
9								
10								
11								
12								
13								
14								
15								
16								
17								

DENIED CITIZENSHIP BY THE CHOCTAW AND CHICKASAW CITIZENSHIP COURT

TRIBAL ENROLLMENT OF PARENTS

	Name of Father	Year	County	Name of Mother	Year	County
1	Geo Paul	Dead	Non Citz	Sarah Paul	Dead	Non Citz
2	" "	"	" "	" "	" "	" "
3	" "	"	" "	" "	" "	" "
4						
5						
6	Nos 1,2 & 3 denied in 1896, case #558					
7	Admitted by the U.S. Court, South McAlester, I.T. June 25, 1897 Court Case No 103					
8						
9	Have lived in the Territory for 6 years					
10						
11						
12						
13						
14						
15						
16						
17						

Choctaw By Blood Enrollment Cards 1898-1914

| RESIDENCE: | Chickasaw Natn | | | | | | | | CARD No. | **5311** |
| POST OFFICE: | I.T. | Choctaw **Nation** | | | Choctaw **Roll** | | | | FIELD No. | C356 |

Dawes' Roll No.	NAME	Relationship to Person First Named	AGE	SEX	BLOOD	TRIBAL ENROLLMENT		
						Year	County	No.
1	Hart, Nora	Named	21	F	1/8			
2	" Dewey L	Son	5mo	M				
3								
4								
5								
6								
7	No2 DISMISSED							
8	JAN 18 1905							
9								
10								
11								
12	DENIED CITIZENSHIP BY THE CHOCTAW AND							
13	CHICKASAW CITIZENSHIP COURT							
14								
15								
16								
17								

TRIBAL ENROLLMENT OF PARENTS

	Name of Father	Year	County	Name of Mother	Year	County
1	Geo Paul	Dead	Non Citz	Sarah Paul	Dead	Non Citz
2	Solomon Hart			No 1		
3						
4						
5						
6	No1 denied in 1896, case #558					
7	Admitted by the U.S. Court, South McAlester, I.T. August 25, 1897, Court Case No 103					
8						
9	No2 was born March 22, 1898					
10	No1 now in C.C.C.C. Case No [?]					
11	Have lived in the Territory six years					
12						
13						
14						
15						
16				Date of Application for Enrollment		10-21-98
17						

211

Choctaw By Blood Enrollment Cards 1898-1914

RESIDENCE:	Chickasaw Natn								
POST OFFICE:	Chickasha, I.T.			Choctaw **Nation**	Choctaw **Roll**		CARD NO. **5312** FIELD NO. 357		

Choctaw **Nation** Choctaw **Roll**

CARD NO. **5312**
FIELD NO. 357

Dawes' Roll No.	NAME	Relationship to Person First Named	AGE	SEX	BLOOD	TRIBAL ENROLLMENT		
						Year	County	No.
1	Collei, Laura		21	F	1/16			
2	" Georgia H.	Dau	2½	"	1/32			
3								
4								
5								
6								
7								
8								
9								
10								
11								
12	No. 1 HEREON DISMISSED UNDER ORDER OF THE COMMISSIONER TO THE FIVE CIVILIZED TRIBES OF JULY 18, 1905.							
15								
16								
17								

TRIBAL ENROLLMENT OF PARENTS

	Name of Father	Year	County	Name of Mother	Year	County
1	Wᵐ Kirkland	Dead	Non Citz	[Illegible] Kirkland		Non Citz
2	A. B. Collett[sic] Jr		" "	No 1		
3						
4						
5	No1 denied in 1896, case #8.					
6	Admitted by the U.S. Court, Ardmore, I.T. December 22, 1897, Court Case No 115					
7	Was admitted as Laura Kirkland					
8						
9	Has lived in the Territory all her life.					
10						
11	No1 Died Nov. 7, 1898 See affidavit of A.B. Collet, Jr, relative to her death and the					
12	birth of No2					
13	No2 born May 21.97,					
14						
15					No2 enrolled Dec 19/99	
16						
17						

212

Choctaw By Blood Enrollment Cards 1898-1914

RESIDENCE:	Chickasaw Natn					
POST OFFICE:	Chickasha, I.T.					

Choctaw **Nation**   Choctaw **Roll**

CARD NO. **5313**
FIELD NO. *C358*

Dawes' Roll No.	NAME	Relationship to Person First Named	AGE	SEX	BLOOD	TRIBAL ENROLLMENT		
						Year	County	No.
1	Ofolter, Amanda J	First Named	25	F	1/16			
2	" Charley J	Son	11	M	1/32			
3	" John F.	"	5	"	1/32			
4	" Amanda M	Dau	3	F	1/32			
5	" Ermer Lee	"	10mo	"	1/32			
6	" Oleo Ophelia	Dau	2mo	F	1/32			
7								
8								
9								
10	#5-6 DISMISSED							
11	DEC							
12								
13	DENIED CITIZENSHIP BY THE CHOCTAW AND							
14								
15	CHICKASAW CITIZENSHIP COURT							
16								
17	Aug 25-1900 Naples I.T.							

TRIBAL ENROLLMENT OF PARENTS

	Name of Father	Year	County	Name of Mother	Year	County
1	Geo Campbell	Dad	Non Citz	Narcissa Campbell	Dead	Non Citz
2	Albert Ofoiter		" "	No1		
3	" "		" "	No1		
4	" "		" "	No1		
5	" "		" "	No1		
6	" "		" "	No1		
7						
8	Nos 1 to 4 denied in 1896, case #1418					
9	Admitted by the U.S. Court, Ardmore, I.T. December 20, 1897 Court Case No 96					
10						
11	No5 was born January 30, 1898					
12						
13	Have lived in the Chickasaw Nation four years.					
14						
15	No.6 Enrolled Aug 30th, 1900					
16				Date of Application for Enrollment	10-21-98	
17						

213

RESIDENCE:	Chickasaw Natn							
POST OFFICE:	Velma, I.T.							

Choctaw **Nation**   Choctaw **Roll**

CARD NO. **5314**
FIELD NO. (359)

Dawes' Roll No.	NAME	Relationship to Person First Named	AGE	SEX	BLOOD	TRIBAL ENROLLMENT		
						Year	County	No.
1	Sledge, William	Named	35	M	1/4			
2	" Mattie	Wife	25	F	I.W.			
3	" Conza	Son	3	M				
4	" Maggie	Dau	3mo	F				
5	" Anna Pearie	Dau	3mo	F				
6								
7								
8								
9	#4-5 DISMISSED							
10	NOV							
11								
12								
13								
14	DENIED CITIZENSHIP BY THE CHOCTAW AND							
15	CHICKASAW CITIZENSHIP COURT							
16								
17	P.O. Arthur I.T. 11/21/06							

TRIBAL ENROLLMENT OF PARENTS

	Name of Father	Year	County	Name of Mother	Year	County
1	Zebbon Sledge	Dead	Non Citz	Jane Sledge	Dead	Non Citz
2	John Pridmore	"	" "	Jennie Pridmore	"	" "
3	No 1			No 2		
4	No 1			No 2		
5	No 1			No 2		
6						
7	Nos 1,2 & 3 admitted by Com in 1896, Case #817					
8	Admitted by the U.S. Court, South McAlester, I.T. October 8, 1897, Court Case No 229 & 203					
9						
10	Nos 1-2 were married at Ft. Smith, Arkansas under the laws of that State					
11	Have lived in the Territory for several years					
12	No.5 Born Dec. 28, 1901: enrolled April 4, 1902					
13	No4 was born April 22, 1898. Not in the decree					
14	No3 denied by C.C.C.C. as Conzer Sledge or Conza Sledge					
15	No4 affidavit of attending Physician to be supplied. Received Nov 17/98.					
16						
17	For child of No1&2 see NB #1036 (Act Apr 26 '06)					

Choctaw By Blood Enrollment Cards 1898-1914

RESIDENCE: Chickasaw Natn		CARD NO. **5315**
POST OFFICE: Purdy, Ind. Ter.	Choctaw **Nation** Choctaw **Roll**	FIELD NO. C360

Dawes' Roll No.	NAME	Relationship to Person First Named	AGE	SEX	BLOOD	TRIBAL ENROLLMENT		
						Year	County	No.
1	Worley, Nancy H	Named	38	F	1/8			
2	Rose, Lillie Lee	dau	18	"				
3	" Mary Ann	"	15	"				
4	Houston, Jim Albert	son	8	M				
5								
6								
7								
8								
9								
10								
11								
12								
13								
14								
15								
16								
17								

DENIED CITIZENSHIP BY THE CHOCTAW AND CHICKASAW CITIZENSHIP COURT

TRIBAL ENROLLMENT OF PARENTS

	Name of Father	Year	County	Name of Mother	Year	County
1	Mauser Tidwell	dead	Non Citizen	Harriet Tidwell	dead	Non Citizen
2	Frank Rose	"	" "	No 1		
3	" "	"	" "	No 1		
4	" "	"	" "	No 1		
5						
6	Nos 1 to 4 denied in 1896, case #1301					
7	Admitted by the U.S. Court, Ardmore, Court Case 120					
8						
9	Have lived in the Territory seventeen years.					
10						
11	No1 admitted as "Nancy H Houston"					
12	Sept 11-99 - Lived in Oklahoma when enrolled as above, moved to Territory about					
13	Christmas 1898 - see testimony of husband of #1, William A. Worley, and his					
14	enrollment 7D479					
15						
16						721
17				Date of Application for Enrollment		10-22-98

Choctaw By Blood Enrollment Cards 1898-1914

RESIDENCE:	Chickasaw Natn					CARD NO. **5316**
POST OFFICE:	Comanche, Ind. Ter.	Choctaw **Nation**	Choctaw **Roll**			FIELD NO. 361

Dawes' Roll No.	NAME	Relationship to Person First Named	AGE	SEX	BLOOD	TRIBAL ENROLLMENT Year	County	No.
1	Boen, George W		48	M	1/8			
2	" Mary	wife	40	F	I.W.			
3	" Leona M	Dau	7	"	1/16			
4	" Rosa E	"	5	"	1/16			
5	" Jesse A	son	2	M	1/16			

DENIED CITIZENSHIP BY THE CHOCTAW AND CHICKASAW CITIZENSHIP COURT

TRIBAL ENROLLMENT OF PARENTS

Name of Father	Year	County	Name of Mother	Year	County
1 Jesse A. Boen	Dead	non citizen	Polly Boen	Dead	1/4 Choctaw
2 Mark R Callahan	"	" "	Jane Callahan		non citizen
3 No1			No2		
4 No1			No2		
5 No1			No2		

Nos 1 to 5 denied in 1896, case #1418

Admitted by U. S. Court, Southern District in case of Nancy J. Cooper, et. al vs Choctaw Nation No 96

No1 married to Mary in Arkansas in 1890, Removed to Chickasaw Nation in July 1896.

216

Choctaw By Blood Enrollment Cards 1898-1914

RESIDENCE: Chickasaw Natn
POST OFFICE: Comanche, Ind. Ter.

Choctaw **Nation**   Choctaw **Roll**

CARD NO. **5317**
FIELD NO. C362

Dawes' Roll No.	NAME	Relationship to Person First Named	AGE	SEX	BLOOD	TRIBAL ENROLLMENT		
						Year	County	No.
1	Sanders, Elijah M	Named	38	M	1/8			
2								
3								
4								
5								
6								
7								
8								
9								
10								
11								
12								
13								
14								
15								
16								
17								

TRIBAL ENROLLMENT OF PARENTS

	Name of Father	Year	County	Name of Mother	Year	County
1	Newton Sanders		non citizen	Artenuncie Sanders		1/4 Choctaw
2						
3						
4						
5						
6	No 1 denied by Com in 1896 case # in 1896, case #1418					
7	Admitted by U.S. Court, Southern District Case No 96 Nancy J Cooper					
8	et al vs. Choctaw Nation					
9						
10	Came from Arkansas four years ago.					
11						
12						
13						
14						
15						
16						
17						

Nov 21/98

217

Choctaw By Blood Enrollment Cards 1898-1914

RESIDENCE: Chickasaw Natn
POST OFFICE: Hart I.T.

Choctaw **Nation** Choctaw **Roll**

CARD NO. 5318
FIELD NO. C363

Dawes' Roll No.	NAME	Relationship to Person First Named	AGE	SEX	BLOOD	TRIBAL ENROLLMENT Year	County	No.
1	Taylor, Nancy H		30	F	1/8			
2	" Willie B	Son		M	1/16			
3	" Sarah E	Dau	6	F	1/16			
4	Hale, Stephen A	nephew	13	M	1/8			
5								
6								
7								
8								
9								
10								
11								
12								
13								
14								
15								
16								
17								

GRANTED

Transferred to Choctaw Card No 6082 Feb 27'07
See decision of same date

TRIBAL ENROLLMENT OF PARENTS

	Name of Father	Year	County	Name of Mother	Year	County
1	J. [?] Husbands		Non Citz	Frances E. Husbands		Non Citz
2	J H Taylor		" "	No i		
3	" "		" "	No i		
4	John C Hale		" "	Melissa Hale		dead non citz
5						
6						
7	Nos 1-2-3 admitted by the Dawes Commission Case No [illegible]					
8						
9	See evidence attached May 24/99					
10	No4 transferred from Choctaw card No D992 Dec 10.1903					
11						
12						
13						
14						
15					# 1to3 inc	
16						
17						

Choctaw By Blood Enrollment Cards 1898-1914

RESIDENCE: Pontotoc County Chick Natn
POST OFFICE: Hart I.T.
CARD NO. 5319
FIELD NO. C364

Choctaw **Nation**   Choctaw **Roll**

Dawes' Roll No.	NAME	Relationship to Person First Named	AGE	SEX	BLOOD	TRIBAL ENROLLMENT Year	TRIBAL ENROLLMENT County	TRIBAL ENROLLMENT No.
1	Husbands, Thos J	Named	35	M	1/8			
2	" Johny M	Dau	1mo	F	1/16			
3	" James A	Son	2mo	M	1/16			
4	" Sarah Malissa	Dau	2mo	F	1/16			
5	Mathews, Alexander P	Bro	50	M	1/8			
6								
7								
8	Nos 1-2-3&4 GRANTED							
9	FEB 27 1907							
10								
11								
12								
13								
14								
15								
16								
17								

TRIBAL ENROLLMENT OF PARENTS

	Name of Father	Year	County	Name of Mother	Year	County
1	J. A. Husbands		Non Citz	Frances E. Husbands		Non Citz
2	No1			[?]atherine J Husbands		" "
3	No1			" " "		" "
4	No1			" " "		" "
5	Alexander Matthews	dead	non-citizen	Fannie E Husbands		admitted in 1896
6						
7	No1 was admitted by the Dawes Commission Case No [?]					
8	No2 was born July 25, 1898					
9	See evidence attached May 24/99					
10						
11	No3 Enrolled June 23d, 1900					
12	Wife of No1 on Choctaw Rejected Card #72					
13	No4 Born Jany 5, 1902; enrolled March 7, 1902					
14	No5 transferred from Choctaw card #D770 Dec. 10, 1903					
15	Nos 1 to 4 inclusive transferred to Choctaw Card No 6083 Feby 27, 1907					
16	No2 Born July 25, 1898 proof of birth filed Nov 28 1904					
17						

Date of Application for Enrollment   9-7-98

219

RESIDENCE:	Chickasaw Natn		Choctaw **Nation**	Choctaw **Roll**	CARD NO. **5320**	
POST OFFICE:	Elmore, I.T.				FIELD NO. C365	

Dawes' Roll No.	NAME	Relationship to Person First Named	AGE	SEX	BLOOD	TRIBAL ENROLLMENT		
						Year	County	No.
Granted	1 Meek, Jacob		56	M				
"	2 " James H	Son	22	"				
"	3 " Calvin W	"	11	"				
	4							
	5 DECISION RENDERED OCT 15 1904							
	6							
	7							
	GRANTED							
	9							
	10							
	11 NOTICE OF DECISION FORWARDED							
	12 ATTORNEY FOR APPLICANTS.							
	13 OCT 15 1904							
	14							
	15 COPY OF DECISION FORWARDED							
	16 ATTORNEYS FOR CHOCTAW AND							
	17 CHICKASAW NATIONS OCT 15 1904							

GRANTED and transferred to Choctaw Card #5850, Oct. 3d, 1904

TRIBAL ENROLLMENT OF PARENTS

	Name of Father	Year	County	Name of Mother	Year	County
1	Simon Meek	Dead	Non Citz	Laura Meek	Dead	Non Citz
2	No i			Sarah E Meek	"	" "
3	No i			Eliza A Meek	"	" "
4						
5						
6	Nos 1-2-3 were admitted by the Dawes Commission, Dec. 2, 189[?] Case #373					
7	Appealed U.S. Court, Central District, Ind. Ter. Appeal dismissed					
8	Sept. 3rd, 1897: Court case #189					
9	See evidence attached May 24/99					
10						
11	No.2 is the husband of Ada Meek. Choctaw card #D691 Dec. 4, 1901					
12						
13						
14						
15						
16						
17						

Choctaw By Blood Enrollment Cards 1898-1914

| RESIDENCE: | Choctaw Nation | | | | | CARD NO. | **5321** |
| POST OFFICE: | Lehigh, I.T. | Choctaw **Nation** | Choctaw **Roll** | | | FIELD NO. | C367 |

Dawes' Roll No.	NAME	Relationship to Person First Named	AGE	SEX	BLOOD	TRIBAL ENROLLMENT		
						Year	County	No.
Dead	1 Miner, Sarah	First Named	33	F	1/4			
	2 " Thomas J Jr	Son	8	M	1/8			
	3 " Sarah F	Dau	3mo	F	1/8			
	4							
	5							
	6							
	7							

No 1 HEREON DISMISSED UNDER ORDER OF THE COMMISSIONER TO THE FIVE CIVILIZED TRIBES OF MARCH 31, 1905.

Transferred from Chick Card C-208 Dec 20/99.

~~CANCELLED~~

| | 17 | | | | | | | |

TRIBAL ENROLLMENT OF PARENTS

	Name of Father	Year	County	Name of Mother	Year	County
1	Bob Sealey	Dead	Chick Ind	Lucy Sealey	Dead	Non Citz
2	T. J. Miner		Non Citz	No 1		
3	" "		" "	No 1		
4						
5						
6	Admitted by the U.S. Court, Ardmore, I.T. Feby 1, 1898, Court Case No 156					
7						
8	Have lived in the Territory all their lives					
9	No 1 was admitted as Sarah Sealey					
10	No 1 wife of Thomas J. Miner, a United States citz					
11						
12	Oct. 4th, 1899, Contested: see report made on Choctaw Cases by P.B. Hopkins					
13	in March, 1899. Style of case Sarah Sealy[sic] et al vs Choctaw Nation PGR (G)					
14						
15	Nov. 17-99: Judgment shows these people to be Choctaws. No 3 enrolled Nov. 21/99					
16	Enrolled as Chickasaws by error.					
17						

Date of Application for Enrollment 10/21/98

Choctaw By Blood Enrollment Cards 1898-1914

RESIDENCE: Kiamitia COUNTY
POST OFFICE: Goodland, I.T.

Choctaw **Nation** Choctaw **Roll**

CARD NO.
FIELD NO. 5322

Dawes' Roll No.	NAME	Relationship to Person	AGE	SEX	BLOOD	TRIBAL ENROLLMENT		
						Year	County	No.
13508	1 Lawechubbe, William	First Named	41	M	Full	1896	Kiamitia	8100
	2							
	3							
	4							
	5							
	6							
	7							
	8							
	9							
	10	ENROLLMENT						
	11	OF NOS. -----1------ HEREON						
		APPROVED BY THE SECRETARY						
	12	OF INTERIOR Mar 19-1903						
	13							
	14							
	15							
	16							
	17							

TRIBAL ENROLLMENT OF PARENTS

Name of Father	Year	County	Name of Mother	Year	County
1 Charley Lawechubbe	Dead	Kiamitia	Vicey Lawechubbe	Dead	Kiamitia
2					
3					
4					
5 No1 is duplicate of No1 on Choctaw Card #468. Enrollment Cancelled under					
6 Departmental Authority of August 30, 1906 (I.T.D. 14748-1906) D.C. 38130-1906					
7					
8					
9 Wife and child are Chickasaws on					
10 Chickasaw Card 1571.					
11 Testimony filed with Chickasaw Card 1571.					
12					
13					
14					
15				Date of Application for Enrollment.	
16					
17			No1 Enrolled March 6, 1900.		

222

Choctaw By Blood Enrollment Cards 1898-1914

RESIDENCE: Kiamitia   COUNTY. **Choctaw Nation**   **Choctaw Roll** (Not Including Freedmen)   CARD NO.
POST OFFICE: Goodland, I.T.   FIELD NO. **5323**

Dawes' Roll No.	NAME	Relationship to Person	AGE	SEX	BLOOD	TRIBAL ENROLLMENT		
						Year	County	No.
13509	1 Spring, James	First Named	19	M	1/2	1896	Kiamitia	11511
	2							
	3							
	4							
	5							
	6							
	7							
	8							
	9							
	10							
	11							
	12							
	13							
	14							
	15							
	16							
	17							

ENROLLMENT
OF NOS. ---- 1 ----- HEREON
APPROVED BY THE SECRETARY
OF INTERIOR MAR 19 1903

TRIBAL ENROLLMENT OF PARENTS

Name of Father	Year	County	Name of Mother	Year	County
1 James Spring	Dead	Kiamitia	Mary Spring	1896	Kiamitia
2					
3					
4					
5					
6 No. 1 is duplicate of James F. Spring #2 on Choctaw card #1432 Enrollment					
7 cancelled under Departmental authority of Nov. 3, 1906					
8 (I.T.D. 21162-1906) D.C. 48472-1906.					
9					
10					
11					
12					
13					
14					
15				Date of Application for Enrollment.		
16				March 6th 1900		
17						

Choctaw By Blood Enrollment Cards 1898-1914

RESIDENCE: Blue   COUNTY.   **Choctaw Nation**   **Choctaw Roll**   CARD NO.
POST OFFICE: Bennington, I.T.   (Not Including Freedmen)   FIELD NO. **5324**

Dawes' Roll No.		NAME	Relationship to Person	AGE	SEX	BLOOD	TRIBAL ENROLLMENT		
							Year	County	No.
13510	1	Dyer, Sam	First Named	20	M	3/4	1896	Blue	3570
	2								
	3								
	4								
	5								
	6								
	7								
	8								
	9								
	10								
	11	ENROLLMENT							
	12	OF NOS. 1 HEREON APPROVED BY THE SECRETARY							
	13	OF INTERIOR MAR 19 1903							
	14								
	15								
	16								
	17								

TRIBAL ENROLLMENT OF PARENTS

	Name of Father	Year	County	Name of Mother	Year	County
1	Willie Dyer	Dead	Blue	Phoebe Dyer	Dead	Blue
2						
3						
4						
5						
6	No1 is duplicate of Sampson Dyer, Choctaw Card #3482 Approved roll of					
7	Choctaw by blood #9922					
8	Enrollment of No1 cancelled by Secretary of Interior Aug 27-1904 see Departmental letter of that date (I.T.D. 6816-1904, DC 31853-1904)					
9						
10						
11						
12						
13						
14						
15				Date of Application for Enrollment.		
16				March 6th, 1900		
17						

Choctaw By Blood Enrollment Cards 1898-1914

RESIDENCE: Blue
POST OFFICE: Caddo, Ind. Ter.

COUNTY. **Choctaw Nation**

Choctaw Roll
(Not Including Freedmen)

CARD NO.
FIELD NO. **5325**

Dawes' Roll No.	NAME	Relationship to Person	AGE	SEX	BLOOD	TRIBAL ENROLLMENT		
						Year	County	No.
13511	1 Hayes, Edward	First Named	11	M	Full	1896	Blue	5905
	2							
	3							
	4							
	5							
	6							
	7							
	8							
	9							
	10							
	11	ENROLLMENT						
	12	OF NOS. --- 1 ---- HEREON APPROVED BY THE SECRETARY						
	13	OF INTERIOR MAR 19 1903						
	14							
	15							
	16							
	17							

TRIBAL ENROLLMENT OF PARENTS

	Name of Father	Year	County	Name of Mother	Year	County
1	Sidney Hayes	Dead	Blue	Basie Hayes	1896	Blue
2						
3						
4						
5						
6						
7						
8						
9						
10						
11						
12						
13						
14						
15				Date of Application for Enrollment. March 6th, 1900		
16						
17						

Choctaw By Blood Enrollment Cards 1898-1914

RESIDENCE: Towson COUNTY.
POST OFFICE: Doaksville, I.T.

Choctaw Nation

Choctaw Roll
(Not Including Freedmen)

CARD NO.
FIELD NO. **5326**

Dawes' Roll No.		NAME	Relationship to Person First Named	AGE	SEX	BLOOD	TRIBAL ENROLLMENT		
							Year	County	No.
13512	1	Hall, Nicholas		22	M	Full	1896	Towson	5473
13513	2	" Siney	Wife	23	F	Full	1896	"	1297
13514	3	" Dora	Dau	3	F	"			
13515	4	" David	Son	9mo	M	"			
	5								
	6								
	7								
	8								
	9	ENROLLMENT							
	10	OF NOS. 1,2,3 & 4 HEREON APPROVED BY THE SECRETARY							
	11	OF INTERIOR MAR 19 1903							
	12								
	13								
	14								
	15	No2 now wife of Abel Suckky							
	16	#9677 - Card #7-							
	17								

TRIBAL ENROLLMENT OF PARENTS

	Name of Father	Year	County	Name of Mother	Year	County
1	Hall, Greenwood			Emily Greenwood	dead	
2	Mistle Billey	dead		Marsey Billey	dead	
3	No1			No2		
4	No1			No2		
5						
6						
7	No1 also on 1893 Leased district pay roll Towson Co page 1 #7 as Nicholas Austin					
8	See testimony of No1 and others Nov. 25, 1902.					
9	For child of Nos 1&2 see NB (March 3, 1905) #1004					
10	Name of father and mother of No.2 to be supplied by L. V. Bibbs.					
11	No2 also on 1893 Leased district payroll Boktuklo[sic] Co page 5 #42 as Sian Billy					
12	No1 is also known as Nicholas Greenwood. See testimony of No2 Nov 25, 1902. No3 Born Oct. 1, 1899, enrolled Dec. 24, 1902.					
13	No4 Born March 12, 1902, enrolled Dec. 24, 1902					
14						
15						
16						
17						

RESIDENCE: Chickasaw Nation COUNTY.				**Choctaw Nation**		**Choctaw Roll** (Not Including Freedmen)	CARD NO.	
POST OFFICE: Kingston, Ind. Ter.							FIELD NO. **5327**	

Dawes' Roll No.	NAME	Relationship to Person First Named	AGE	SEX	BLOOD	TRIBAL ENROLLMENT		
						Year	County	No.
1035	Bounds, James H		44	M	I.W.	1896	Chick. Dist	14364
15630	" " Young Walker	Son	21	"	1/16	1896	" "	2038
15631	" " James, Jr.	"	20	"	1/16	1895	" "	2016

Nos 1,2 and 3 were admitted by Dawes Commission Case No 863; on appeal from decision of Commission by the Choctaw Nation the U.S. Court, Southern Dist. Ind. Ter. Dec 21, 1897, Court Case No 155 admitted James H, Fannie, Young W, James Jr, Overton M and Frank Bounds. ~~By order of said court Jany 25th, 1900, the judgment was set aside, because of Court having no jurisdiction to render same, on account of appeal not having been perfected in time required by law~~

ENROLLMENT
OF NOS. ---- 2 and 3 ---- HEREON
APPROVED BY THE SECRETARY
OF INTERIOR OCT 21 1904

TRIBAL ENROLLMENT OF PARENTS

	Name of Father	Year	County	Name of Mother	Year	County
1	O. Bounds		Non Citz	Parthenia Bounds		Non Citz
2	No 1			Joanna Bounds	Dead	Choc. Ind.
3	No 1			" "	" "	" " "
4						
5						
6			ENROLLMENT			
7			OF NOS. ---- 1 ---- HEREON			
8			APPROVED BY THE SECRETARY			
9			OF INTERIOR OCT 21 1904			
10	No.1 on 1896 Choctaw roll as J. H. Bond			No.1 transferred from Choctaw card 5134		
11	No.2 " " " " " Y.W. Bonds			and Nos 2 and 3 transferred from Choctaw		
12	~~No.3 " " " " " James Bone.~~			~~Card 271. May 11th, 1900.~~		
13	No.2 1893 Kiamitia Page 125, No. 19					
14	" " " " " " 20					
15						
16					Date of Application for Enrollment.	
17					Sept. 23, 1898	

Choctaw By Blood Enrollment Cards 1898-1914

RESIDENCE: Chickasaw Nation COUNTY. **Choctaw Nation** **Choctaw Roll** CARD NO.
POST OFFICE: Minco, Ind. Ter. *(Not Including Freedmen)* FIELD NO. **5328**

Dawes' Roll No.	NAME	Relationship to Person	AGE	SEX	BLOOD	TRIBAL ENROLLMENT		
						Year	County	No.
15501	1 Schrock, Frances	First Named	19	F	Full		Choctaw residing in Chickasaw Dist	CCR #0 77R102
DEAD 2	" Lila	Dau	9mo	F	1/2			
15502 3	" Arthur Lee	Son	2mo	M	1/2			
4								
5 ENROLLMENT								
OF NOS. 1 and 3 HEREON								
6 APPROVED BY THE SECRETARY			No.1			1893	Gaines	Page 60 No 560
7 OF INTERIOR MAY 9 1904								
8								
9 As to amount of Choctaw blood see copy of								
10 letter of L.L. Schrock of Dec. 21, 1902 filed herein.								
11								
12								
13								
14								
15								
16								
17								

TRIBAL ENROLLMENT OF PARENTS

	Name of Father	Year	County	Name of Mother	Year	County
1	James Williams	Dead	Gaines		Dead	Gaines
2	L. L. Schrock		Non Citz	No1		
3	" " "		" "	No1		
4						
5	#1 On Choctaw roll as Frances Williams					
6	#2 died Sept. 10-1900: Proof of Death filed Oct. 18-02					
7	No.1 was enrolled Oct. 21, '98 on Choctaw card #444 as					
8	Frances Williams, and transferred to this card, May 24, 1900.					
9						
10	No.2 Enrolled May 25, 1900					
11	No.3 Enrolled Jany 11, 1901.					
12	For child of No1 see NB (Apr 26 '06) Card No 221.					
13	" " " " " (Mar 3 '05) " " 388					
14						
15						
16					Date of Application for Enrollment.	
17					Oct 21/98	

Choctaw By Blood Enrollment Cards 1898-1914

RESIDENCE: Sans Bois   COUNTY: **Choctaw Nation**   **Choctaw Roll**   CARD NO.
POST OFFICE: Whitefield, I.T.   *(Not Including Freedmen)*   FIELD NO. **5329**

Dawes' Roll No.	NAME	Relationship to Person First Named	AGE	SEX	BLOOD	TRIBAL ENROLLMENT Year	County	No.
13516	1 McKinney, Sampson	First Named	18	M	Full	1896	Sans Bois	9001
I.W.591	2 " " Leona	Wife	17	F	I.W.			
13517	3 " " Elmer	Son	6wks	M	1/2			
	4							
	5							
	6	ENROLLMENT						
	7	OF NOS. --- 2 ------- HEREON APPROVED BY THE SECRETARY						
	8	OF INTERIOR FEB -8 1904						
	9							
	10							
	11	ENROLLMENT						
	12	OF NOS. 1 & 3 HEREON APPROVED BY THE SECRETARY						
	13	OF INTERIOR MAR 19 1903						
	14							
	15							
	16	P.O. Fort Smith Ark 10/19/05						
	17	P.O. Stigler I.T. 12/28/02						

TRIBAL ENROLLMENT OF PARENTS

	Name of Father	Year	County	Name of Mother	Year	County
1	Philip McKinney	Dead	Sans Bois	Pollie McKinney	Dead	Sans Bois
2	Kelough		Non Citz	Kelough		Non Citz
3	No1			No2		
4						
5	No.3 Enrolled April 20, 1901					
6	No.1 in U.S. Penetentiary[sic] at Atlanta, Ga, until March, 1903.					
7						
8				No.1 was enrolled May 15, 1899 and		
9				transferred from Choctaw card 2731 to		
10				this card May 29, 1900.		
11	No.2 married to #1 May 2d, 1900;					
12	Evidence of marriage exhibited, but defective.					
13	Marriage certificate to be supplied. Certificate of marriage on file					
14						
15				Date of Application for Enrollment.		
16				May 29, 1900		
17						

Choctaw By Blood Enrollment Cards 1898-1914

RESIDENCE:	Blue	COUNTY.								
POST OFFICE:	Ego, I.T.		**Choctaw Nation**			**Choctaw Roll** *(Not Including Freedmen)*		CARD NO. FIELD NO. **5330**		

Dawes' Roll No.	NAME	Relationship to Person	AGE	SEX	BLOOD	TRIBAL ENROLLMENT		
						Year	County	No.
13518	1 Camp, Levander	First Named	16	F	1/64	1896	Blue	7183
13519	2 " Ethel Alta	Dau	3mo	F	1/128			
DEAD	3 " John Herbet[sic]	Son	1mo	M	1/128			
	4							
	5							
	6	ENROLLMENT						
	7	OF NOS. 1 & 2 HEREON						
	8	APPROVED BY THE SECRETARY OF INTERIOR MAR 19 1903						
	9	No. 3 HEREON DISMISSED UNDER						
	10	ORDER OF THE COMMISSION TO THE FIVE CIVILIZED TRIBES OF MARCH 31, 1905.						
	11							
	12							
	13							
	14							
	15							
	16	P.O. Wapanucka I.T.						
	17	P.O. Copeland, I.T. 3/27/05						

TRIBAL ENROLLMENT OF PARENTS

Name of Father	Year	County	Name of Mother	Year	County
1 W.T. Jones		Blue	Mary J Jones		Intermarried
2 John B. Camp		Non Citizen	No1		
3 " " "		" " "	No1		
4					
5					
6 Husband of No.1 is John B. Camp, a non citizen					
7					
8 No.1 on 1896 roll as Levander Jones Her mother was regularly admitted.					
9					
10 Transferred from Choctaw card D.356					
11 No.2 Enrolled June 4, 1900					
12 No3 Born March 25, 1902; enrolled April 29, 1902					
13 No3 died September 3, 1902. Proof of death filed March 6, 1905.					
14 For child of No1 see NB (Mar 3 '05) #473					
15					#1
16			Date of Application for Enrollment.		6/4/1900
17					

230

Choctaw By Blood Enrollment Cards 1898-1914

RESIDENCE: Atoka
POST OFFICE: Atoka, I.T.
COUNTY. **Choctaw Nation**
Choctaw Roll (*Not Including Freedmen*)
CARD NO. FIELD NO. **5331**

Dawes' Roll No.	NAME	Relationship to Person First Named	AGE	SEX	BLOOD	TRIBAL ENROLLMENT		
						Year	County	No.
IW4036	1 Brown, George		49	M	I.W.	1896	Atoka	14341
	2							
	3							
	4							
	5							
	6							
	7	ENROLLMENT						
	8	OF NOS. ----- 1 ------- HEREON APPROVED BY THE SECRETARY						
	9	OF INTERIOR OCT 21 1904						
	10							
	11							
	12							
	13							
	14							
	15							
	16							
	17							

TRIBAL ENROLLMENT OF PARENTS

	Name of Father	Year	County	Name of Mother	Year	County
1	Robert Brown	Dead	Non Citz	Barbara Brown	Dead	Non citz
2						
3						
4						
5						
6	Admitted by Com in 1896; no appeal. Case #891					
7	Husband of Melvina Brown, Choctaw card					
8	#4138 Roll #11605 See his testimony as to intermarriage.					
9						
10						
11						
12						
13						
14						
15						
16	P.O. Wapanucka, I.T.				Date of Application for Enrollment.	
17	P.O. Phillip I.T. 10/28/03				6/4/1900	

Choctaw By Blood Enrollment Cards 1898-1914

RESIDENCE:	Tobucksy		COUNTY.				Choctaw Roll		CARD NO.	
POST OFFICE:	McAlester, I.T.		**Choctaw Nation**				(Not Including Freedmen)		FIELD NO. **5332**	

Dawes' Roll No.	NAME	Relationship to Person Named	AGE	SEX	BLOOD	TRIBAL ENROLLMENT		
						Year	County	No.
IW4037	1 Bond, George M	First Named	53	M	I.W.	1896	Tobucksy	14300
	2							
	3							
	4							
	5							
	6	ENROLLMENT						
	7	OF NOS. ------ 1 ------ HEREON APPROVED BY THE SECRETARY						
	8	OF INTERIOR OCT 21 1904						
	9							
	10							
	11							
	12							
	13	Petition W.92						
	14							
	15							
	16							
	17							

TRIBAL ENROLLMENT OF PARENTS

	Name of Father	Year	County	Name of Mother	Year	County
1	George Bond	Dead	Non-citizen	Rebecca Bond	Dead	Non-citizen
2						
3						
4	On 1896 roll, intermarried list as Geo. M. Bond					
5						
6	Married in Sept. 1875 to Narcissa McClure, a 1/4 blood Choctaw Indian; she died in April, 1891.					
7	Married Lulu Routon, a non citizen white woman,					
8	May 6, 1893					
9						
10	Father of children on Choctaw card #4598					
11	P.O. ADDRESS: TERRAL, I.T. SEPT. 13, 1902 For children of No 1 see NB (Apr 26 ;06) #1102					
12						
13						
14						
15					Date of Application for Enrollment.	
16						
17	P.O. Terral I.T. 3-1-5				June 6, 1900	

Choctaw By Blood Enrollment Cards 1898-1914

RESIDENCE: Tobucksy   COUNTY. **Choctaw Nation**   **Choctaw Roll** CARD NO.
POST OFFICE: Stuart, Ind. Ter.   (Not Including Freedmen)   FIELD NO. 5333

Dawes' Roll No.	NAME	Relationship to Person	AGE	SEX	BLOOD	TRIBAL ENROLLMENT		
						Year	County	No.
13520	1 Jackson, Elum	First Named	48	M	Full	1896	Tobucksy	6663
DEAD	2 " Nancy	Wife	26	F	I.W.			
	3							
	4							
	5 No. 2 HEREON DISMISSED UNDER ORDER OF THE COMMISSION TO THE FIVE CIVILIZED TRIBES OF MARCH 31, 1905.							
	7							
	8							
	9							
	10							
	11	ENROLLMENT OF NOS. ----- 1 ------ HEREON APPROVED BY THE SECRETARY OF INTERIOR MAR 19 1903							
	12							
	13							
	14							
	15							
	16							
	17							

TRIBAL ENROLLMENT OF PARENTS

	Name of Father	Year	County	Name of Mother	Year	County
1	Watkins	Dead	Choctaw	Lucy	Dead	Choctaw
2	Harris	Dead	Non-citizen	Harris		Non-citizen
3						
4						
5						
6	No.1 on 1896 roll as Eli Jackson					
7	No.2 enrolled subject to evidence of					
8	marriage to No.1					
9	No.1 transferred from Choctaw rejected card R. 144.					
10	No.2 Died April, 1902: Proof of death filed Dec. 24, 1902					
11						
12						
13						
14						
15					Date of Application for Enrollment.	
16						
17					June 6,1900	

Choctaw By Blood Enrollment Cards 1898-1914

RESIDENCE: Skullyville   COUNTY.   **Choctaw Nation**   **Choctaw Roll** *(Not Including Freedmen)*   CARD NO.

POST OFFICE: Guertie, Ind. Ter.   FIELD NO. 5334

Dawes' Roll No.		NAME	Relationship to Person First Named	AGE	SEX	BLOOD	TRIBAL ENROLLMENT		
							Year	County	No.
✓	1	Johnson, Alvin		17	M	1/16			
✓ DP	2	" Alice	Wife	18	F	I.W.			
✓ DP	3	" Virgle Benton	Son	1	M	1/32			
	4								
	5								
	6	2 & 3 DISMISSED							
	7								
	8	MAY 27 1904							
	9								
	10								
	11								
	12								
	13								
	14								
	15	DENIED CITIZENSHIP BY THE CHOCTAW AND							
	16	CHICKASAW CITIZENSHIP COURT							
	17								

TRIBAL ENROLLMENT OF PARENTS

	Name of Father	Year	County	Name of Mother	Year	County
1	James C. Johnson		Court citizen	Delilah Johnson		Court citizen
2	Eliza McCoy		Non-citizen	Mary Jane McCoy		Non-citizen
3	No1			No2		
4						
5						
6	No.1 denied in 96 Case #1026					
7	No.1 admitted by U.S. Court, Central District					
8	Sept 11, '97, Court case #672. and transferred from Choctaw care 2207 - June 7, 1900					
9	No.2 Enrolled June 7, 1900					
10	Marriage license and certificate exhibited and filed					
11	No.3 born Jan. 4, 1901- Enrolled Jan. 9, 1902					
12	Judgement of U.S. Ct admitting No1 vacated and set aside by decree of C.C.C.C. Decr 17 02					
13	No1 now in C.C.C.C. Case #65					
14						
15						
16	Duplicate record in Choctaw #4575				Date of Application for Enrollment.	
17	See C#132				June 7, 1900	

234

Choctaw By Blood Enrollment Cards 1898-1914

RESIDENCE:	Kiamitia	COUNTY.	**Choctaw Nation**				**Choctaw Roll**	CARD NO.	
POST OFFICE:	Nelson, Ind. Ter.						*(Not Including Freedmen)*	FIELD NO. **5335**	

Dawes' Roll No.	NAME	Relationship to Person First Named	AGE	SEX	BLOOD	TRIBAL ENROLLMENT		
						Year	County	No.
IW795	1 Skaggs, John	Named	52	M	I.W.			
	2							
	3							
	4							
	5							
	6	ENROLLMENT						
	7	OF NOS. 1 HEREON APPROVED BY THE SECRETARY						
	8	OF INTERIOR MAY 9 1904						
	9							
	10							
	11							
	12							
	13							
	14							
	15							
	16							
	17							

TRIBAL ENROLLMENT OF PARENTS

Name of Father	Year	County	Name of Mother	Year	County
1 Michael Skaggs	Dead	Non-citizen	Ruth Skaggs	Dead	Non-citizen
2					
3					

4
5 No1 admitted in 96 Case #1390
6 Admitted by Dawes Commission Sept. 1896 in case #1390, judgment rendered Dec. 8, 1896
7 Appealed by Choctaw Nation.
8 Admitted by U.S. Court, Central District
9 Ind. Ter., Aug. 24th, 1897, Court Case No. 13, at So. McAlester
10 Judgement of U.S. Ct. admitting No1 vacated and set aside by Decree of C.C.C.C. Dec 17.02
11 No1 now in C.C.C.C. Case #90
12 No1 Admitted by C.C.C.C. March 28'04
13
14
15
16 Date of Application for Enrollment. June 8, 1900
17

Choctaw By Blood Enrollment Cards 1898-1914

RESIDENCE: Atoka COUNTY. **Choctaw Nation** Choctaw Roll CARD NO.
POST OFFICE: Atoka, Ind. Ter. *(Not Including Freedmen)* FIELD NO. 5336

Dawes' Roll No.	NAME	Relationship to Person First Named	AGE	SEX	BLOOD	TRIBAL ENROLLMENT		
						Year	County	No.
13521	1 Frazier, Adline		31	F	3/4	1896	Blue	#4415
13522	2 Colbert, Sam	Son	11/2	M	7/8			
	3							
	4							
	5							
	6							
	7							
	8							
	9							
	10							
	11	ENROLLMENT						
	12	OF NOS. 1 & 2 HEREON APPROVED BY THE SECRETARY						
	13	OF INTERIOR MAR 19 1903						
	14							
	15							
	16							
	17							

TRIBAL ENROLLMENT OF PARENTS

	Name of Father	Year	County	Name of Mother	Year	County
1	Joe Collins	Dead	Kiamitia	Mary Collins	Dead	Kiamitia
2	Allison Colbert		Atoka	No1		
3						
4						
5						
6						
7	No.2 transferred from Choctaw card #4321, June 8, 1900.					
8	Evidence of birth of No.2 filed June 8, 1900					
9	No.1 on 1896 Roll as "Edline" Frazier					
10						
11						
12						
13						
14						
15					Date of Application for Enrollment.	
16						
17					June 8, 1900	

Choctaw By Blood Enrollment Cards 1898-1914

RESIDENCE: Atoka COUNTY. **Choctaw Nation** **Choctaw Roll** CARD No.
POST OFFICE: Atoka, Ind. Ter. *(Not Including Freedmen)* FIELD NO. **5337**

Dawes' Roll No.	NAME	Relationship to Person First Named	AGE	SEX	BLOOD	TRIBAL ENROLLMENT		
						Year	County	No.
13523	1 Homma, Georgian		16	F	7/8	1896	Blue	4414
	2							
	3							
	4							
	5							
	6							
	7							
	8							
	9							
	10							
	11							
	12							
	13							
	14							
	15							
	16							
	17							

ENROLLMENT
OF NOS. 1 HEREON
APPROVED BY THE SECRETARY
OF INTERIOR MAR 19 1903

TRIBAL ENROLLMENT OF

Name of Father	Year	County		Year	County
1 Josiah Homma		Atoka	Adline		Blue
2					
3					
4					
5					
6					
7	No.1 transferred from Choctaw #3446, June 8, 1900.				
8	No.1 lives with Johnson Frazier at Caddo, Ind. Ter.				
9	No.1 is wife of Linis Leflore on Choc. Card #4174				
10					
11					
12					
13					
14					
15					
16					
17			Date of Application for Enrollment		June 8, 1900

237

Choctaw By Blood Enrollment Cards 1898-1914

RESIDENCE: Skullyville   COUNTY. **Choctaw Nation**   **Choctaw Roll**   CARD NO.
POST OFFICE: Walls, I.T.   *(Not Including Freedmen)*   FIELD NO. 5338

Dawes' Roll No.		NAME	Relationship to Person	AGE	SEX	BLOOD	TRIBAL ENROLLMENT		
							Year	County	No.
IW592	1	Martin, Howard	First Named	29	M	I.W.			
13524	2	" Canzada	Wife	17	F	1/4	1896	Skullyville	3155
13525	3	" Howard Lee	son	1mo	M	1/8			
	4								
	5								
	6	ENROLLMENT							
	7	OF NOS. 1 HEREON							
	8	APPROVED BY THE SECRETARY OF INTERIOR FEB -8 1904							
	9								
	10								
	11	ENROLLMENT							
	12	OF NOS. 2 & 3 HEREON APPROVED BY THE SECRETARY							
	13	OF INTERIOR MAR 19 1903							
	14								
	15								
	16								
	17								

TRIBAL ENROLLMENT OF PARENTS

	Name of Father	Year	County	Name of Mother	Year	County
1	W.E. Martin	Dead	Non-citizen	Comelia[sic] Martin		Non-citizen
2	John Drake	"	" "	Palmer Drake	Dead	Sans Bois
3	No1			No2		
4						
5						
6						
7						
8						
9	No.2 was enrolled on Choctaw card 2842 as Cazada Drake					
10	and transferred to this card with her husband					
11	No.3 born Nov. 27th, 1901: Enrolled Dec. 10, 1901 June 30th, 1900. For child of Nos 1&2 see N.B.(Apr. 26, 1906) Card No. 97.					
12						
13						
14						
15						
16				Date of Application for Enrollment.	June 30, 1900	
17	Davis, I.T. 11/13-02					

238

Choctaw By Blood Enrollment Cards 1898-1914

RESIDENCE: COUNTY. **Choctaw N**   Ch

POST OFFICE: Rush Springs, I.T.   5339   FIELD

Dawes' Roll No.		NAME	Relationship to Person First Named	AGE	SEX	TRIBAL ENROLLMENT		
						r	County	No.
IW4038	1	Brooks, William		52	M			
	2							
	3							
	4							
	5							
	6							
	7	ENROLLMENT						
	8	OF NOS. 1 HEREON APPROVED BY THE SECRETARY						
	9	OF INTERIOR OCT 21 1904						
	10							
	11							
	12							
	13							
	14							
	15							
	16							
	17							

TRIBAL ENROLLMENT OF PARENTS

	Name of Father	Year	County	Name of Mother		
				oks		
3						
4						
5						
6						
7						
8	See testimony of No.1 taken Oct. 17, 1902.					
9						
10	No.1 admitted by Dawes Commission in 1896, Case No. 641.					
11						
12						
13						
14						
15						
16				Date of Application for Enrollment	June 21" 1900	
17						

Choctaw By Blood Enrollment Cards 1898-1914

RESIDENCE: Skullyville   COUNTY.   **Choctaw Nation**   **Choctaw Roll**   CARD NO.
POST OFFICE: Milton, I.T.   *(Not Including Freedmen)*   FIELD NO. **5340**

Dawes' Roll No.	NAME	Relationship to Person	AGE	SEX	BLOOD	TRIBAL ENROLLMENT		
						Year	County	No.
13526	1 Dobson, William T	First Named	18	M	1/16	1896	Skullyville	3205
IW593	2 " Josie E	wife	18	F	I.W.			
13527	3 " Jewel Sumpter	Son	6wks	M	1/32			
	4							

ENROLLMENT
OF NOS. 1 & 3 HEREON
APPROVED BY THE SECRETARY
OF INTERIOR MAR 19 1903

ENROLLMENT
OF NOS. 2 HEREON
APPROVED BY THE SECRETARY
OF INTERIOR FEB 8 1904

DEPARTMENT OF THE INTERIOR.
COMMISSION TO THE FIVE CIVILIZED TRIBES.
The application for enrollment of
Jesse E. Dobson

GRANTED

TRIBAL ENROLLMENT OF PARENTS

	Name of Father	Year	County	Name of Mother	Year	County
1	A.E. Dobson	Dead	Non citizen	Laura Dobson	1896	Skullyville
2	--------- Rooks	"	" "	---------- Rooks		Non citizen
3	No 1			No.2		
4						
5						
6	No.3 Enrolled May 2, 1901					
7	For child of Nos. 1&2 see NB (March 3, 1905) #1012					

DEPARTMENT OF THE INTERIOR
COMMISSION TO THE FIVE CIVILIZED TRIBES,
JUDGMENT RENDERED AND COPY
MAILED APPLICANT.
JUL 25 1900
Tams Bixby
ACTING CHAIRMAN

Date of Application for Enrollment.

No 1 enrolled on Choctaw Card 2546 on 6/13/99
No.2 enrolled 7/23-1900.

240

Choctaw By Blood Enrollment Cards 1898-1914

| RESIDENCE: | Choctaw Nation | COUNTY. | | | | | | | | |

RESIDENCE: Choctaw Nation COUNTY. **Choctaw Nation** Choctaw Roll CARD No.
POST OFFICE: Wheelock, Ind. Ter. *(Not Including Freedmen)* FIELD No. **5341**

Dawes' Roll No.	NAME	Relationship to Person First Named	AGE	SEX	BLOOD	TRIBAL ENROLLMENT		
						Year	County	No.
13528	₁ Pebworth, Joseph	First Named	30	M	1/4	1896	Red River	10425
IW1355	₂ " Octavia	Wife	20	F	I.W.			
13529	₃ " John L	Son	3	M	1/8			
13530	₄ " Frank	Son	1mo	M	1/8			
13531	₅ " Maguerite	Dau	4 "	F	1/8			
	6							
	7 ENROLLMENT							
	8 OF NOS. 1-3-4 & 5 HEREON APPROVED BY THE SECRETARY							
	9 OF INTERIOR Mar. 19, 1903							
	10							
	11 ENROLLMENT							
	12 OF NOS. 2 HEREON APPROVED BY THE SECRETARY							
	13 OF INTERIOR Mar. 14, 1905							
	14							
	15							
	16							
	17							

TRIBAL ENROLLMENT OF PARENTS

Name of Father	Year	County	Name of Mother	Year	County
₁ John Pebworth	Dead	Towson	Mary Pebworth	Dead	
₂ Marion Russell	"	Non Citz	Ostrander		Non Citz
₃ No1			No2		
₄ No1			No2		
₅ No1			No2		
₆					
₇					
₈ Marriage license and certificate to be supplied. Filed Oct 1, 1900.					
₉ Evidence of birth of No3 to be supplied					
₁₀ Evidence of birth of No3 received and filed Sept 24ᵗʰ 1900					
No4 Enrolled Sept 24th, 1900					
₁₁ P.O. address seems to be Hartshorne, I.T.					
₁₂ No5 Born Aug 3, 1902: Enrolled Dec. 24, 1902.					
₁₃					
₁₄					
₁₅					
₁₆					#1 to 3 inc
₁₇ P.O. Wilburton I.T. 3/6/05			Date of Application for Enrollment.		July 26, 1900

Choctaw By Blood Enrollment Cards 1898-1914

RESIDENCE:	Jackson							
POST OFFICE:	Mayhew, I.T.	COUNTY. **Choctaw Nation**				**Choctaw Roll** *(Not Including Freedmen)*	CARD NO.	
							FIELD NO. **5342**	

Dawes' Roll No.	NAME	Relationship to Person Named	AGE	SEX	BLOOD	TRIBAL ENROLLMENT		
						Year	County	No.
13532	1 LeFlore, Allen	First Named	21	M	1/4	1896	Jackson	8124
IW1039	2 " Ella	Wife	16	F	I.W.			
13533	3 " Ethel	Dau	2mo	F	1/8			
13534	4 " Viola	Dau	1mo	F	1/8			
	5							
	6							
	7							
	8							
	9							
	10							
	11							
	12							
	13							
	14							
	15							
	16							
	17							

ENROLLMENT
OF NOS. 2 HEREON
APPROVED BY THE SECRETARY
OF INTERIOR OCT 21 1904

ENROLLMENT
OF NOS. 1-3 & 4 HEREON
APPROVED BY THE SECRETARY
OF INTERIOR MAR 19 1903

TRIBAL ENROLLMENT OF PARENTS

	Name of Father	Year	County	Name of Mother	Year	County
1	Phelin LeFlore	1896	Jackson	Sophia LeFlore	1896	Jackson
2	Robert Adair		Non-citizen	Loretta Adair		Non-citizen
3	No1			No2		
4	No1			No2		
5						
6	No.1 was enrolled May 10, 1899, on Choctaw card #1564 with					
7	his father and transferred to this card, Aug. 14, 1900					
	No.2 Enrolled Aug. 14th, 1900					
8	No.3 Enrolled April 20, 1901					
9	No4 Born Aug. 10, 1901; enrolled Sept. 18, 1902					
10	No1 and No2 have separated					
	For child of Nos 1&2 see NB (Mar 3, 1905) #527					
11						
12						
13						
14						
15						
16	No1 Beseville Ok 4/21/05			Date of Application		
17	No2 PO Boswell IT 4/29/03			for Enrollment.	Aug 14, 1900	

242

Choctaw By Blood Enrollment Cards 1898-1914

RESIDENCE: Choctaw Nation COUNTY.
POST OFFICE: So. McAlester, I.T.

Choctaw Nation

Choctaw Roll CARD NO.
(Not Including Freedmen) FIELD NO. **5343**

Dawes' Roll No.	NAME	Relationship to Person First Named	AGE	SEX	BLOOD	TRIBAL ENROLLMENT Year	County	No.
1481	1 Penny, Oren S	First Named	26	M	I.W.			
13535	2 " Annie	Wife	18	F	1/8	1896	Tobucksy	13005
13536	3 " Oren Seldon	Son	6wk	M	1/16			
13537	4 " Katherine S	Dau	1mo	F	1/16			
	5							
	6							
	7							
	8							
	9							
	10							
	11							
	12							
	13							
	14							
	15							
	16							
	17							

GRANTED
JUN 30 1905

ENROLLMENT
OF NOS. 2 3 & 4 HEREON
APPROVED BY THE SECRETARY
OF INTERIOR MAR 19 1903

ENROLLMENT
OF NOS. One HEREON
APPROVED BY THE SECRETARY
OF INTERIOR AUG 22 1905

TRIBAL ENROLLMENT OF PARENTS

	Name of Father	Year	County	Name of Mother	Year	County
1	Oren S Penny		Non-citizen	Catherine Penny		Non-citizen
2	Wm L. Wooley		Intermarried	Sarah Wooley	dead	Tobucksy
3	No.1			No.2		
4	No.1			No.2		
5						
6						

7 No.1 Enrolled Aug. 22d 1900
8 No.2 Enrolled Aug. 10th, 1899, and transferred from card #3344
to this card with husband Aug. 22d, 1900.
9 No.3 Enrolled Nov. 1st, 1900
10 No.2 on 1896 Choctaw roll as Annie Wooley
11 No.4 born Oct. 8th, 1901: Enrolled Nov. 7th, 1901
12 For child of Nos 1&2 see N.B. (Apr 26/06) card #276
" " " " " " (Mar. 3, 1905) " #389
13
14 See Choctaw card #3344 for previous enrollment of No.2
15
16
17 Aug. 22d, 1900

243

Choctaw By Blood Enrollment Cards 1898-1914

RESIDENCE:	Tobucksy	COUNTY.	**Choctaw Nation**			**Choctaw Roll**	CARD No.	
POST OFFICE:	Guertie, Ind. Ter.					*(Not Including Freedmen)*	FIELD No. **5344**	

Dawes' Roll No.	NAME	Relationship to Person	AGE	SEX	BLOOD	TRIBAL ENROLLMENT		
						Year	County	No.
13538 ₁	Flinchum, William	First Named	19	M	1/4	1896	Tobucksy	4027
IW935 ₂	" Ruby L	Wife	23	F	I.W.			
₃								
₄								
₅								
₆								
₇	ENROLLMENT OF NOS. 1 HEREON							
₈	APPROVED BY THE SECRETARY							
₉	OF INTERIOR Mar. 19, 1903							
10								
11								
12								
13	ENROLLMENT OF NOS. 2 HEREON							
14	APPROVED BY THE SECRETARY							
15	OF INTERIOR Aug. 3, 1904							
16								
17								

TRIBAL ENROLLMENT OF PARENTS

	Name of Father	Year	County	Name of Mother	Year	County
₁	Jas. W. Flinchum	Dead	Tobucksy	Julia A Flinchum		Tobucksy
₂	H.M. Foley		Non-Citizen	B.M. Foley		Non-Citizen
₃						
₄						
₅						
₆	No1 was enrolled Aug. 7, 1899 on Choctaw Card #3292					
₇	and transferred to this card Sept. 12ᵗʰ 1900					
₈	No.2 Enrolled Sept. 12ᵗʰ 1900					
₉	See testimony of No1 of July 16ᵗʰ 1900					
10	No.1 claims No.2 has deserted him, Oct. 26, 1900					
11	See testimony of May 1ˢᵗ 1902					
12						
13			For child of No.1 see NB 930 (Act Apr 26-06)			
14						
15						
16	No1 PO Box 516 Muskogee, I.T. 8/4/03					
17	No2 PO " 556 Tishomingo I.T. 11/10/03			Date of Application for Enrollment.	Sept 12ᵗʰ, 1900	

244

Choctaw By Blood Enrollment Cards 1898-1914

RESIDENCE: Skullyville   COUNTY. **Choctaw Nation**   **Choctaw Roll**   CARD NO.
POST OFFICE: Cartersville, I.T.   *(Not Including Freedmen)*   FIELD NO. **5345**

Dawes' Roll No.	NAME	Relationship to Person	AGE	SEX	BLOOD	TRIBAL ENROLLMENT		
						Year	County	No.
13539	1 Dobson, Leonidas	First Named	19	M	1/16	1896	Skullyville	3204
IW594	2 " Mary	Wife	18	F	I.W.			
	3							
	4							
	5	ENROLLMENT						
	6	OF NOS. 1 HEREON						
	7	~~APPROVED BY THE SECRETARY~~ OF INTERIOR MAR 19 1903						
	8							
	9							
	10							
	11	ENROLLMENT						
	12	OF NOS. 2 HEREON APPROVED BY THE SECRETARY						
	13	OF INTERIOR FEB -8 1904						
	14							
	15							
	16							
	17							

TRIBAL ENROLLMENT OF PARENTS

	Name of Father	Year	County	Name of Mother	Year	County
1	A.E. Dobson	Dead	Non-Citizen	Lama Dobson	1896	Skullyville
2	Annum Mangrum		" "	Mangrum		Non-Citizen
3						
4						
5						
6						
7	10/5/00 No.1 today transferred from Choctaw Card No 2546 No2 enrolled today					
8						
9						
10						
11						
12						
13						
14						
15						
16						
17					Oct 5/1900	

Choctaw By Blood Enrollment Cards 1898-1914

RESIDENCE: COUNTY. **Choctaw Nation**   **Choctaw Roll**   CARD NO.
POST OFFICE: Dwight P.O. Ind. Ter.   *(Not Including Freedmen)*   FIELD NO. **5346**

Dawes' Roll No.		NAME Care Jones Academy	Relationship to Person Named	AGE	SEX	BLOOD	TRIBAL ENROLLMENT		
							Year	County	No.
13540	1	Semple, Frank P	First Named	19	M	1/16	1896	Blue	11578
IW595	2	" Helen Mae	Wife	21	F	I.W.			
13541	3	" Alta Roberta	Dau	1wk	F	1/32			
	4								
	5								
	6								
	7	ENROLLMENT							
	8	OF NOS. HEREON APPROVED BY THE SECRETARY							
	9	OF INTERIOR							
	10								
	11	ENROLLMENT							
	12	OF NOS. HEREON APPROVED BY THE SECRETARY OF INTERIOR							
	13								
	14								
	15								
	16								
	17								

TRIBAL ENROLLMENT OF PARENTS

	Name of Father	Year	County	Name of Mother	Year	County
1	Chas. A. Semple		Blue	Minnie Semple		Blue
2	Wallace Hibbard		Non Citz	Sarah Hibbard		Non Citz
3	No1			No2		
4						
5						
6	No.1 Transferred from Choctaw Card Field No. 3598 Oct. 15th 1900					
7	Evidence of marriage to be supplied. Filed Oct. 15, 1900					
8	See testimony of No.2 Oct. 15th 1900					
	No.3 born Jan. 22, 1901: Enrolled Jan. 28, 1901					
9	For child of Nos 1&2 see NB (Mar. 3, 1905) #1167					
10						
11						
12						
13						
14						
15						
16				Date of Application for Enrollment. #2		
17	P.O. Caddo IT 11/18-04			Oct 15th, 1900		

Choctaw By Blood Enrollment Cards 1898-1914

RESIDENCE: Blue COUNTY. **Choctaw Nation** **Choctaw Roll** (Not Including Freedmen)
POST OFFICE: Bokchito, Ind. Ter.

Dawes' Roll No.	NAME	Relationship to Person First Named	AGE	SEX	BLOOD	TRIBAL ENR Year	County	No.
13542	1 Garland, Jack	First Named	17	M	3/4	1896	Blue	4905
IW 1040	2 " Jessie Lee	Wife	16	F	I.W.			
	3							
	4							
	5	ENROLLMENT OF NOS. 1 HEREON						
	6	APPROVED BY THE SECRETARY OF INTERIOR MAR 19 1903						
	7							
	8							
	9							
	10							
	11							
	12							
	13 Protest overruled by Department March							
	14 28, 1904							
	15							
	16							
	17							

TRIBAL ENROLLMENT OF PARENTS

	Name of Father	Year	County	Name of Mother	Year	County
1	Levi Garland	dead	Blue	Liffie Garland	dead	Blue
2	James Martin		Non-citizen	Jennie Martin		Non-citizen
3						
4						
5						
6	No 1 was enrolled Aug. 23d, 1899 on Choctaw card #3812					
7	and transferred to this card Nov. 28th, 1900.					
8	No.2 Enrolled November 28th, 1900					
9			ENROLLMENT			
10			OF NOS. 2 HEREON			
11			APPROVED BY THE SECRETARY OF INTERIOR OCT 21 1904			
12						
13	No.1 claims No.2 has deserted him. See letter of April 10, 1901.					
14						
15						
16			Date of Application for Enrollment.	Date of Transfer to this Card.		
17			Aug 22/99	NOV 28 1900		

247

Choctaw By Blood Enrollment Cards 1898-1914

RESIDENCE: Chickasaw Nation ~~COUNTY.~~
POST OFFICE: Newton, Ind. Ter.

Choctaw Nation

Choctaw Roll
(Not Including Freedmen)

CARD NO.
FIELD NO. 5348

Dawes' Roll No.	NAME	Relationship to Person First Named	AGE	SEX	BLOOD	Year	County	No.
13543	1 Scroggins, Lee		13	M	1/8	1896	Chickasaw Dist	11774
13544	2 " Columbus	Bro	11	M	1/8	"	" "	11775
13545	3 " Annie Bell	Sis	9	F	1/8	"	" "	11776
13546	4 " John F	Bro	8	M	1/8	"	" "	11777
13547	5 " May	Sis	5	F	1/8	"	" "	11778
	6							
	7							
	8							
	9							
	10							
	11	ENROLLMENT						
	12	OF NOS. 1 2 3 4 & 5 HEREON APPROVED BY THE SECRETARY						
	13	OF INTERIOR Mar. 19, 1903						
	14							
	15							
	16							
	17							

TRIBAL ENROLLMENT OF PARENTS

	Name of Father	Year	County	Name of Mother	Year	County
1	John Scroggins	Dead	White man	Susan Scroggins	Dead	Choctaw Roll
2	" "	"	" "	" "	"	" "
3	" "	"	" "	" "	"	" "
4	" "	"	" "	" "	"	" "
5	" "	"	" "	" "	"	" "
6						
7						
8	No1 on 1896 Choctaw Census roll as Lon Scroggins					
9	No3 " " " " " " Annie "					
10	No4 " " " " " " Jno F "					
	No5 " " " " " " Mary "					
11						
12	These children are now wards of Nettie Chandler, Choc. Care #28- P.O. Francis, I.T.					
13						
14						
15				Date of Application for Enrollment.		
16				Dec. 4, 1900		
17						

Choctaw By Blood Enrollment Cards 1898-1914

Choctaw Nation

Choctaw Roll *(Not Including Freedmen)*

CARD NO.
FIELD NO. **5349**

Dawes' Roll No.		NAME	Relationship to Person First Named	AGE	SEX	BLOOD	TRIBAL ENROLLMENT Year	County	No.
IW 596	1	Coleman, W.A.		37	M	I.W.	1896	Red River	14409
13548	2	" Lou Anna	Wife	31	F	1/8	1896	" "	2663
13549	3	" Romie	Dau	9	F	1/16	1896	" "	2664
13550	4	" Eddy	Son	7	M	1/16	1896	" "	2665
13551	5	" Nellie	Dau	5	F	1/16	1896	" "	2666
13552	6	" Tallie	Dau	4	F	1/16	1896	" "	2667
13553	7	" Dixie	Dau	1	F	1/16	1896	" "	
13554	8	" Oscar M	Son	2mo	M	1/16	1896	" "	
	9								
	10								
	11	ENROLLMENT OF NOS. 2 3 4 5 6 7 & 8 HEREON							
	12	APPROVED BY THE SECRETARY							
	13	OF INTERIOR MAR 19 1903							
	14	ENROLLMENT							
	15	OF NOS. 1 HEREON APPROVED BY THE SECRETARY							
	16	OF INTERIOR FEB -8 1904							
	17								

TRIBAL ENROLLMENT OF PARENTS

	Name of Father	Year	County	Name of Mother	Year	County
1	Marion Coleman	dead	Non-citizen	Minnie Coleman	dead	Non-citizen
2	Cal Morris	"	" "	Carrie Hampton	1896	Red River
3	No1			No2		
4	No1			No2		
5	No1			No2		
6	No1			No2		
7	No1			No2		
8	No1			No2		

9 No1 was admitted by Dawes Commission in 1896 as an intermarried
10 citizen: Choctaw case #753: no appeal.
Proof of marriage filed with Dawes Commission in 1897.
11 No.7 Affidavit of birth to be supplied. Recd May 6, 1899.
12 No.8 Enrolled May 24, 1900
13 Nos 1 to 8 inclusive were listed for enrollment April 24, 1899 on Choctaw
card #D.121 and transferred to this card and enrolled Dec. 5, 1900.
14 For child of Nos 1 and 2 see NB (March 3, 1905) Card #392.
15

#1 to 7
Date of Application for Enrollment

16   Enrolled Apr 24/99
17 PO Norwood   this Card   Dec. 5, 1900

Choctaw By Blood Enrollment Cards 1898-1914

RESIDENCE: Ch [redacted]
POST OFFICE: Harris, Ind. Ter.   (Not Including Freedmen)   FIELD NO. 5350
CARD NO.

Dawes' Roll No.	NAME	Relationship to Person First Named	AGE	SEX	BLOOD	TRIBAL ENROLLMENT		
						Year	County	No.
IW597	1 Stanford, Henry C		22	M	I.W.			
13555	2 " Sallie	Wife	15	F	1/16	1896	Red River	7582
13556	3 " Mary	Dau	1mo	F	1/32			
	4							
	5							
	6							
	7							
	8							
	9							
	10							
	11							
	12							
	13							
	14							
	15							
	16							
	17							

ENROLLMENT
OF NOS. 2 & 3 HEREON
APPROVED BY THE SECRETARY
OF INTERIOR MAR 19 1903

ENROLLMENT
OF NOS. 1 HEREON
APPROVED BY THE SECRETARY
OF INTERIOR FEB -8 1904

TRIBAL ENROLLMENT OF PARENTS

	Name of Father	Year	County	Name of Mother	Year	County
1	Mack Stanford	dead	Non-citizen	Prudy Stanford	dead	Non-citizen
2	Wyatte T. Kirby	1896	Intermarried	Kizzie Kirby	"	Red River
3	No.1			No2		
4						
5						
6	No.2 Enrolled April 28, 1899 on Choctaw card #1113					
7	and transferred to this card with husband					
8	Dec. 6, 1900					
	No1 Enrolled December 6th, 1900					
9	No.2 on 1896 Choctaw roll as Sallie E. Kirby					
10	No3 Born September 28. 1901: Enrolled November 1, 1901.					
11	For child of Nos 1&2 see NB (March 3, 1905) #882					
12						
13						
14						
15						
16	PO Isabel IT 9/12/05				for #1	
17	PO Kullituklo I.T. 11/26/02			Date of Application for Enrollment.	Dec. 6, 1900	

Choctaw By Blood Enrollment Cards 1898-1914

RESIDENCE:	Blue	COUNTY.					CARD NO.		
POST OFFICE:	Caddo, Ind. Ter.	**Choctaw Nation**				**Choctaw Roll** *(Not Including Freedmen)*	FIELD NO. **5351**		

Dawes' Roll No.	NAME	Relationship to Person	AGE	SEX	BLOOD	TRIBAL ENROLLMENT		
						Year	County	No.
IW598	1 Jones, Charles W	First Named	25	M	I.W.			
13557	2 " Lucetta	Wife	16	F	1/4	1896	Blue	1617
13558	3 " Frank W	Son	6wks	M	1/8			
13559	4 " Floyd	Son	3wks	M	1/8			
	5							
	6							
	7							
	8							
	9	ENROLLMENT OF NOS. 2 3 & 4 HEREON						
	10	APPROVED BY THE SECRETARY OF INTERIOR MAR 19 1903						
	11							
	12							
	13							
	14	ENROLLMENT						
	15	OF NOS. 1 HEREON APPROVED BY THE SECRETARY						
	16	OF INTERIOR FEB -8 1904						
	17							

TRIBAL ENROLLMENT OF PARENTS

	Name of Father	Year	County	Name of Mother	Year	County
1	Frank Jones	dead	Non-citizen	Eveline Jones		Non-citizen
2	Geo. A. Boydstum[sic]		Intermarried	Mary Boydstum	dead	Blue
3	No1			No2		
4	No1			No2		
5						
6	No.2 Enrolled on Choctaw card 3698 Aug. 22d. 1899 and					
7	transferred to this card with her husband December 6, 1900.					
8	No.1 Enrolled December 6th, 1900.					
9	No.2 on 1896 Choctaw roll as Lucy F. Boydston					
10	No.3 Enrolled Sept 21 1901					
11	No4 Born July 28, 1902, enrolled Aug. 19, 1902					
12	For child of Nos 1&2 see NB (Apr 26-06) card #757 " " " " " " " (Mar 3-05) " #1341					
13						
14						
15						
16					Date of Application for Enrollment.	Dec. 6, 1900
17						

251

Choctaw By Blood Enrollment Cards 1898-1914

RESIDENCE: Sans Bois   COUNTY. **Choctaw Nation**   **Choctaw Roll** *(Not Including Freedmen)*   CARD No.

POST OFFICE: Bower, Ind. Ter.   FIELD No. **5352**

Dawes' Roll No.	NAME	Relationship to Person First Named	AGE	SEX	BLOOD	TRIBAL ENROLLMENT		
						Year	County	No.
IW1041	1 McNeely, James C		43	M	I.W.	1896	Sans Bois	14853
13560	2 " " Ellen	Wife	29	F	1/4	"	" "	8990
DEAD.	3 " " Myrtie	Dau	12	F	1/8	"	" "	8991
13561	4 " " Julia F	Dau	7	F	1/8	"	" "	8993
13562	5 " " Edna	Dau	5	F	1/8	"	" "	8992
13563	6 Pearce, James E	Gr Son	1mo	M	1/16	"	" "	
	7							

ENROLLMENT
OF NOS. 1 HEREON
APPROVED BY THE SECRETARY
8
OF INTERIOR OCT 21 1904
9

10 ENROLLMENT
OF NOS. 2-4-5-6 HEREON
APPROVED BY THE SECRETARY
OF INTERIOR MAR 19 1903

13

14 No. 3 HEREON DISMISSED UNDER
15 ORDER OF THE COMMISSION TO THE FIVE
CIVILIZED TRIBES OF MARCH 31, 1905.
16

17

TRIBAL ENROLLMENT OF PARENTS

	Name of Father	Year	County	Name of Mother	Year	County
1	A.J. McNeely	dead	Non-citizen	Mary F. McNeely	dead	Non-citizen
2	William Monds	" "		Patsey Monds	dead	Tobucksy
3	No.1			No.2		
4	No.1			No.2		
5	No.1			No.2		
6	Jesse Pearce		non-citizen	No.3	dead	
7						

8 No.1 on 1896 Choctaw roll as Jas. C. McNeely
9 No.2 " " " " " Ellen McNealy
Surnames on 1896 roll as McNealy
10 No.1 was listed for enrollment Aug. 9, 1899 on Choctaw card #D.312
11 and Nos. 2,3,4 and 5 were enrolled Aug 2d, 1899 on Choctaw card #3134
12 Both of above cards cancelled and names transferred to this card Dec. 7th 1900
13 No3 was married Dec. 23, 1900 to Jesse Pearce non-citizen. Marriage license and
certificate filed April 3, 1902.
14 No.3 is dead. She died March 2, 1902, proof of death filed April 14, 1902.
15 No.6 born March 1, 1902. Enrolled April 14, 1902.

16

17   Date of Application for Enrollment.   Dec. 7, 1900

Choctaw By Blood Enrollment Cards 1898-1914

Choctaw Nation

Choctaw Roll *(Not Including Freedmen)*

CARD NO.
FIELD NO. 535

Dawes' Roll No.	NAME	Relationship to Person First Named	AGE	SEX	BLOOD	TRIBAL ENROLLMENT Year	County	No.
IW 1042	1 Neal, John W	First Named	42	M	I.W.	1896	Sans Bois	14896
13564	2 " Susan	Wife	33	F	1/2	"	" "	9537
13565	3 " Ira	Son	5	M	1/4	"	" "	9538
13566	4 " Green	Son	2	M	1/4			
13567	5 " Mamie	Dau	9mo	F	1/4			
DEAD.	6 " Edna P	Dau	2mo	F	1/4			
7								

No. 6 HEREON DISMISSED UNDER ORDER OF THE COMMISSION TO THE FIVE CIVILIZED TRIBES OF MARCH 31, 1905.

ENROLLMENT OF NOS. 2-3-4-5 HEREON APPROVED BY THE SECRETARY OF INTERIOR MAR 19 1903

ENROLLMENT OF NOS. 1 HEREON APPROVED BY THE SECRETARY OF INTERIOR OCT 21 1903

TRIBAL ENROLLMENT OF PARENTS

	Name of Father	Year	County	Name of Mother	Year	
1	James Neal	dead	Non-citizen	Jane Neal	dead	Non-c
2	Wm Walker	dead	Sans Bois	Louisa Walker	dead	Atoka
3	No.1			No.2		
4	No.1			No.2		
5	No.1			No.2		
6	No.1			No.2		
7						

8 No.1 Enrolled on Choctaw card D.495 and cancelled
9 and transferred to this card December 7th. 1900
10 Nos 2,3 and 4 Enrolled on Choctaw card #4782 Dec. 14th, 1899 and cancelled and transferred to this card December 7th, 1900. For child of Nos 1&2 see NB (Mar 3 1905) #636.
11 No.1 on Choctaw 1896 roll as John Neal.
12 No.5 Enrolled Sept. 17, 1901.
13 No.2 on Creek Card, Field No. 2936 as Susie Neil, Enroll her as a Choctaw as she will not appear on Creek final Roll.
14 No.6 Born April 16th 1902 Enrolled June 25th 1902
15 No6 Died Sept 13, 1902; Proof of death filed Dec. 23, 1902.
16

#1
Date of Transfer to this Card
Dec. 7, 1900

253

Choctaw By Blood Enrollment Cards 1898-1914

RESIDENCE: Towson COUNTY.
POST OFFICE: Doaksville, I.T.

Choctaw Nation

Choctaw Roll
(Not Including Freedmen)

CARD NO.
FIELD NO. **5354**

Dawes' Roll No.	NAME	Relationship to Person First Named	AGE	SEX	BLOOD	TRIBAL ENROLLMENT Year	County	No.
IW599	₁ Meggs, William		42	M	I.W.	1896	Nashoba	14819
13568	₂ " Jesse	Son	2	1/8				
13569	₃ " Elijah	Son	8mo	1/8				
	4							
	5							
	6							
	7							
	8							
	9							
	10							
	11							
	12							
	13							
	14							
	15							
	16							
	17							

ENROLLMENT
OF NOS. 2-3- HEREON
APPROVED BY THE SECRETARY
OF INTERIOR MAR 19 1903

ENROLLMENT
OF NOS. 1 HEREON
APPROVED BY THE SECRETARY
OF INTERIOR FEB -8 1904

TRIBAL ENROLLMENT OF PARENTS

Name of Father	Year	County	Name of Mother	Year	County
₁ George Meggs	dead	Non-citizen	Martha Meggs	dead	Non-citizen
₂ No1			Nancy I Meggs	"	Nashoba
₃ No1			" "	"	"

4
5 Nos 1,2 and 3 were listed for enrollment April 24, 1899
6 on Choctaw card #D.119, which is cancelled and applicants
7 transferred to this card Dec. 7th, 1900.
8 Mother of Nos 2 and 3 is No. 8617 on 1896 Choc. Roll Nashoba County.
9 Evidence of divorce between No 1 and Nancy C. Meggs filed Jany 2, 1903.
10 For child of No1 see NB (Apr 26 '06) #1160.
11
12
13
14
15
16
17 Oct [?]-03 - P.O. Kiomache[s|c] Tex

Date of Application for Enrollment. Dec. 7, 1900

254

Choctaw By Blood Enrollment Cards 1898-1914

	RESIDENCE: Atoka		
POST OFFICE: Legal, Ind. Ter.	COUNTY. **Choctaw Nation**	**Choctaw Roll** (*Not Including Freedmen*) ▮NO.	FIELD NO. **5355**

Dawes' Roll No.	NAME	Relationship to Person First Named	AGE	SEX	BLOOD	TRIBAL ENROLLMENT		
						Year	County	No.
13670	₁ Grubbs, John	Named	23	M	1/8	1896	Tobucksy	4692
IW600	₂ " Ity A	Wife	19	F	I.W.	1896	Atoka	6065
	₃							
	₄							
	₅							
	₆							
	₇							
	₈	ENROLLMENT						
	₉	OF NOS. 1 HEREON ~~APPROVED BY THE SECRETARY~~						
	₁₀	OF INTERIOR MAR 19 1903						
	₁₁							
	₁₂							
	₁₃							
	₁₄	ENROLLMENT						
	₁₅	OF NOS. 2 HEREON APPROVED BY THE SECRETARY						
	₁₆	OF INTERIOR FEB -8 1904						
	₁₇							

TRIBAL ENROLLMENT OF PARENTS

	Name of Father	Year	County	Name of Mother	Year	County
₁	Benj. F. Grubbs	1896	Tobucksy	Eliza C. Grubbs	1896	Inter-married
₂	Thos J. Howard		Non-citizen	Carrie Howard		Non-citizen
₃						
₄						

₅ ~~No.1 was listed for enrollment Sept. 5, 1899 on Choctaw card #4542, and transferred to~~
₆ ~~this card, Dec. 7, 1900.~~
₇ No.2 transferred from Choctaw card D. 523 and enrolled hereon with
 her husband, Dec. 7, 1900.
₈ ~~No.2 on 1896 Choctaw roll as Ida Howard: as a citizen by blood: tribal enrollment~~
₉ ~~said to be without authority of law.~~
₁₀ Thomas Howard, father, is applicant for identification as a
 Mississippi Choctaw, M.C.R. #130.

		Date of Transfer to this Card.	#1 Dec 7, 1900

Choctaw By Blood Enrollment Cards 1898-1914

RESIDENCE: Kiamitia   COUNTY.
POST OFFICE: Grant, Ind. Ter.

Choctaw Nation

CARD NO.
FIELD NO. 5356

Dawes' Roll No.		NAME	Relationship to Person First Named	AGE	SEX	BLOOD	TRIBAL ENROLLMENT		
							Year	County	No.
13571	1	Everidge, Joseph H		23	M	3/8	1896	Kiamitia	3811
IW601	2	" Mabel O	Wife	19	F	I.W.			
13572	3	" Helen Blanche	Dau	1mo	F	3/16			
	4								
	5								
	6								
	7								
	8	ENROLLMENT							
	9	OF NOS. 1 - 3 HEREON APPROVED BY THE SECRETARY							
	10	OF INTERIOR MAR 19 1903							
	11								
	12								
	13								
	14	ENROLLMENT							
	15	OF NOS. 2 HEREON APPROVED BY THE SECRETARY							
	16	OF INTERIOR FEB -8 1904							
	17								

TRIBAL ENROLLMENT OF PARENTS

	Name of Father	Year	County	Name of Mother	Year	County
1	Joseph W. Everidge	1896	Kiamitia	Susan Everidge	dead	Towson
2	William Oakes		Non-citizen	Jessie Oakes		Non-citizen
3	No 1			No 2		
4						
5						
6	No.1 was enrolled on Choctaw card #1526 May 10, 1899					
7	and transferred to this card Dec. 8th 1900					
8	No.2 Enrolled December 8th, 1900					
9	No.3 born Nov. 6, 1901. Enrolled Dec. 4, 1901					
10						
11						
12						
13						
14						
15						
16					Date of Transfer to this Card.	#1
17						Dec. 8, 1900

Choctaw By Blood Enrollment Cards 1898-1914

RESIDENCE: Towson   COUNTY. **Choctaw Nation**   **Choctaw Roll**   CARD NO.
POST OFFICE: Garvin, Ind. Ter.   *(Not Including Freedmen)*   FIELD NO. **5357**

Dawes' Roll No.	NAME	Relationship to Person First Named	AGE	SEX	BLOOD	TRIBAL ENROLLMENT		
						Year	County	No.
15171	1 Lewis, Joseph	First Named	12	M	Full			
	2							
	3							
	4							
	5							
	6							
	7							
	8	ENROLLMENT						
	9	OF NOS. 1 HEREON						
	10	APPROVED BY THE SECRETARY OF INTERIOR Mar. 26, 1904						
	11							
	12							
	13							
	14							
	15							
	16							
	17							

TRIBAL ENROLLMENT OF PARENTS

Name of Father	Year	County	Name of Mother	Year	County
1 Charles James	Dead	Louisiana	Cornelius[sic] Lewis	Dead	Louisiana
2					
3					
4 No1 is child of Louis Robinson and wife Cornelius, Full Blood					
5 Choctaws, who came with their family to Choctaw Nation from Louisiana in 1896. They died leaving Joe Lewis. They spoke					
6 Choctaw and very little English. See sworn testimony.					
7 Email Child, full blood Choctaw, who came with them from Louisiana.					
8 No1 admitted as a Mississippi Choctaw by Act of Council approved October 16th 1895.					
9 No.1 was enrolled on Choctaw Card #D.139 April 29 '99					
10 and transferred to this card					
11 Dec. 10th 1900					
12 The Email Child referred to above is on Choctaw Card #5358 as Email Charles, Dec. 10, 1900					
13					
14					
15					
16					
17				Date of Application for Enrollment. Dec. 10, 1900		

Choctaw By Blood Enrollment Cards 1898-1914

RESIDENCE: Towson   COUNTY. **Choctaw Nation**   Choctaw Roll   CARD NO.
POST OFFICE: Garvin, I.T.   *(Not Including Freedmen)*   FIELD NO. **5358**

Dawes' Roll No.	NAME	Relationship to Person	AGE	SEX	BLOOD	TRIBAL ENROLLMENT		
						Year	County	No.
13573	1 Charles, Email	First Named	28	M	Full	1896	Red River	2646
	2							
	3							
	4							
	5							
	6							
	7							
	8							
	9							
	10							
	11							
	12							
	13							
	14							
	15							
	16							
	17							

ENROLLMENT OF NOS. 1 APPROVED BY THE SECRETARY OF INTERIOR HEREON

TRIBAL ENROLLMENT OF PARENTS

	Name of Father	Year	County	Name of Mother	Year	County
1	Charles James	dead	Louisiana	Sallie Jackson		Towson
2						
3						
4						
5	No.1 was listed for enrollment on Choctaw card #D.117					
6	April 24, 1899 and transferred to this card Dec. 10, 1900					
7	No.1 admitted as a Mississippi Choctaw by act of Council approved October 16th, 1895 and copy of which is filed herewith.					
8	No.1 admitted in act as Emil Child.					
9	No.1 on 1896 Choctaw roll as M. T. Charles.					
10						
11						
12						
13						
14						
15						
16						
17				Date of Application for Enrollment.	Dec. 10, 1900	

Choctaw By Blood Enrollment Cards 1898-1914

RESIDENCE: Blue   COUNTY. **Choctaw Nation**   **5359**
POST OFFICE: Caddo, Ind. Ter.

Dawes' Roll No.	NAME	Relationship to Person First Named	AGE	SEX	BLOOD	TRIBAL ENROLLMENT Year	County	No.
13574	1 Airington Noah	First Named	22	M	1/8	1893	Blue	37
IW602	2 " Ellen	Wife	18	F	I.W.			
13575	3 " Willie Polee	Son	2mo	M	1/16			
13576	4 " Wiley Rap	Son	2mo	M	1/16			
	5							
	6							
	7							
	8							
	9							
	10							
	11							
	12							
	13							
	14							
	15							
	16							
	17							

ENROLLMENT
OF NOS. 1 - 3 - 4 HEREON
APPROVED BY THE SECRETARY
OF INTERIOR MAR 19 1903

ENROLLMENT
OF NOS. 2 HEREON
APPROVED BY THE SECRETARY
OF INTERIOR FEB -8 1904

	Name of Father	Year	County	Name of Mother	Year	
1	William Airington	1896	Blue	Belle Airington		Blue
2	Wiley Cariker		non-citizen	Martha E Cariker		non-citizen
3	No1			No2		
4	No1			No2		
5						
6						
7						
8						

TRIBAL ENROLLMENT OF PARENTS

9   No1 enrolled on Choctaw Card #3929 August 25, 1899 and
10   transferred to this card December 11, 1900.
   No.2 Enrolled December 11, 1900
11   No3 Born Feby 24, 1902: enrolled May 6, 1902
12   No4 Born Feby 24, 1902: enrolled May 6, 1902
13   Nos 3 and 4 are twins
   For child of Nos 1 and 2 see NB (Mar 3, 1905) #401
14
15
16   Date of Application for Enrollment.
17   Dec. 11, 1900

259

Choctaw By Blood Enrollment Cards 1898-1914

RESIDENCE: Choctaw Nation   COUNTY.

POST OFFICE: Shawneetown, I.T.   **Choctaw Nation**

Choctaw Roll *(Not Including Freedmen)*

CARD NO.

FIELD NO. 5360

Dawes' Roll No.	NAME	Relationship to Person First Named	AGE	SEX	BLOOD	TRIBAL ENROLLMENT		
						Year	County	No.
IW603	₁ Denson, Richard C		24	M	I.W.			
13577	₂ " Lula	Wife	16	F	1/2			
13578	₃ " Ruel Hopkins	Son	2wks	M	1/4			
	₄							
	₅							
	₆	ENROLLMENT OF NOS. 2-3 HEREON APPROVED BY THE SECRETARY OF INTERIOR MAR 19 1903						
	₇							
	₈							
	₉							
	₁₀	ENROLLMENT OF NOS. 1 HEREON APPROVED BY THE SECRETARY OF INTERIOR FEB -8 1904						
	₁₁							
	₁₂							
	₁₃							
	₁₄							
	₁₅							
	₁₆							
	₁₇							

TRIBAL ENROLLMENT OF PARENTS

	Name of Father			Name of Mother	Year	County
₁	Joe H Denson			▮attie Denson		Non-citizen
₂	Sim Farver	dead	Eagle	Helen Farver	dead	" "
₃	No.1			No.2		
₄						
₅						
₆	No.2 on 1896 Choctaw roll as Lula Farbee.					
₇						
₈	No.2 was enrolled April 18th, 1899 on Choctaw card #506 as					
₉	Lula Farver and transferred to this card with husband Jany 3d, 1901					
	Nos 1 and 2 were married Jany 1st, 1901					
₁₀	No.1 Enrolled Jany 3d, 1901					
₁₁	No.3 born Dec. 10, 1901: Enrolled Dec. 27, 1901.					
	For child of Nos 1 & 2 see NB (Apr 26-06) Card #446					
₁₂	" " " " " " " (Mar 3-05) Card #958					
₁₃						
₁₄						
₁₅						
₁₆	PO Idabel I.T. 4/1/05			Jan 3/01		
₁₇				Date of Application for Enrollment.	Date of Transfer to this Card. JAN -3 1901	

Choctaw By Blood Enrollment Cards 1898-1914

RESIDENCE: Tobucksy   COUNTY. **Choctaw Nation**   **Choctaw Roll**   CARD NO.
POST OFFICE: Cherryvale, I.T.   *(Not Including Freedmen)*   FIELD NO. **5361**

Dawes' Roll No.		NAME	Relationship to Person First Named	AGE	SEX	BLOOD	TRIBAL ENROLLMENT Year	County	No.
13579	1	Jefferson, Mary	Named	20	F	Full	1896	Tobucksy	13028
13580	2	" Wallace	Son	2	M	3/4			
13581	3	" Rosa	Dau	1	F	3/4			
13582	4	" Sweeney	Son	3mo	M	3/4			
	5								
	6								
	7								
	8								
	9								
	10								
	11	ENROLLMENT							
	12	OF NOS. 1,2,3 and 4 HEREON APPROVED BY THE SECRETARY							
	13	OF INTERIOR MAR 19 1903							
	14								
	15								
	16								
	17								

TRIBAL ENROLLMENT OF PARENTS

	Name of Father	Year	County	Name of Mother	Year	County
1	Wilson James	dead	Tobucksy	Malsey Williams	1896	Tobucksy
2	Simeon Jefferson		Chickasaw	No1		
3	" "		"	No1		
4	" "		"	No1		
5						
6	No1 On 1896 Choctaw Census Roll as Mary Williams					
7	No1 Is the wife of Simeon Jefferson on Chickasaw Card #1378					
8	~~Affidavit of birth of No3 to be supplied. Filed February 1st 1901~~ ~~No4 Born Sept 10 1902: Enrolled Dec 23 1902~~					
9						
10						
11						
12						
13						
14						
15						
16						
17	P.O. Carbon 12/23/02					Jany 28' 1901

261

RESIDENCE: Tobucksy
POST OFFICE: McAlester, I.T.

COUNTY. **Choctaw Nation**

Choctaw Roll
(Not Including Freedmen)

CARD No.
FIELD No. **5362**

Dawes' Roll No.	NAME	Relationship to Person	AGE	SEX	BLOOD	TRIBAL ENROLLMENT		
						Year	County	No.
13583	1 King, Susan	First Named	14	F	Full	1896	Tobucksy	7485
	2							
	3							
	4							
	5							
	6							
	7							
	8							
	9							
	10							
	11							
	12							
	13							
	14							
	15							
	16							
	17							

ENROLLMENT
OF NOS. 1 HEREON
APPROVED BY THE SECRETARY
OF INTERIOR MAR 19 1903

TRIBAL ENROLLMENT OF PARENTS

	Name of Father	Year	County	Name of Mother	Year	County
1	Watson King	dead	Sans Bois	Frances King	dead	Sans Bois
2						
3						
4						
5						
6						
7	No.1 is living with Jonas Peabody, enrolled					
8	on Choctaw card #4920					
9	No.1 Enrolled Jany 30. 1901 upon sworn statement of Simon E. Lewis					
10						
11						
12						
13						
14						
15						
16						
17						

Date of Application for Enrollment

JAN 30 1901

262

Choctaw By Blood Enrollment Cards 1898-1914

RESIDENCE: Choctaw Nation ~~COUNTY~~. **Choctaw Nation** Choctaw Roll CARD No.
POST OFFICE: Celestine Ind. Ter. *(Not Including Freedmen)* FIELD No. **5363**

Dawes' Roll No.	NAME	Relationship to Person First Named	AGE	SEX	BLOOD	TRIBAL ENROLLMENT		
						Year	County	No.
* 1	Stephens, William T	Named	65	M	I.W.	1896	Tobucksy	15040
2								
3								
4								
5	See White petition No. 35							
6	See Citizenship petition No. 2.							
7								
8								
9								
10								
11								
12								
13								
14								
15								
16								
17								

TRIBAL ENROLLMENT OF PARENTS

	Name of Father	Year	County	Name of Mother	Year	County
1	William Stephens	dead	non-citizen	Delilah Stephens	dead	non-citizen
2						
3						
4						
5						
6	No.1 was admitted by Dawes Commission in 1896 as an intermarried citizen					
7	Choctaw Case #837, appeal taken and No.1 admitted by U.S. Court for Central					
8	Dist of Ind Ter at So McAlester I.T. July 13, 1897, Court Case No 230. Copy of judgement filed April 1901.					
9	Judgement of U.S. Ct admitting No1 vacated and set aside by decree of					
10	C.C.C.C. Dec 17 '02					
11	No1 now in C.C.C.C. case # 18 Mc					
12	No.1 Denied by C.C.C.C. Oct. 20, 1904 in case #168 Mc					
13						
14						
15						
16						
17				Date of Application for Enrollment.	APR 1 1901	

Choctaw By Blood Enrollment Cards 1898-1914

RESIDENCE:	Reform school	COUNTY.							CARD NO.	
POST OFFICE:	Booneville, Mo.	**Choctaw Nation**				Choctaw Roll *(Not Including Freedmen)*			FIELD NO. **5364**	

Dawes' Roll No.	NAME	Relationship to Person Named	AGE	SEX	BLOOD	TRIBAL ENROLLMENT		
						Year	County	No.
13584	1 McGee, Tim	First Named	17	M	Full	1896	Atoka	4503
	2							
	3							
	9							
	10							
	11							
	12							
	13							
	14							
	15							
	16							
	17							

ENROLLMENT
OF NOS. 1 HEREON
APPROVED BY THE SECRETARY
OF INTERIOR MAR 19 1903

TRIBAL ENROLLMENT OF PARENTS

Name of Father	Year	County	Name of Mother	Year	County
1 Tim Falyia				dead	
2					
3					
4					
5					
6	No.1 was sentenced Feby. 13, 1901 to a term of five				
7	years in the reform school at Booneville, Mo.				
8	Application made by W. S. Farmer, by power of attorney				
	No.1 on 1896 Choctaw census roll as Tim Faliya[sic] .				
9	Information as to parentage to be supplied.				
10					
11					
12					
13					
14					
15					
16				Date of Application for Enrollment.		
17						Aug. 21, 1901

Choctaw By Blood Enrollment Cards 1898-1914

RESIDENCE: Atoka COUNTY. **Choctaw Nation** **Choctaw Roll** CARD NO.
POST OFFICE: Owl, Ind. Ter. *(Not Including Freedmen)* FIELD NO. **5365**

Dawes' Roll No.	NAME	Relationship to Person First Named	AGE	SEX	BLOOD	TRIBAL ENROLLMENT		
						Year	County	No.
15503	1 Turner, Albert P	First Named	30	M	1/8			
15504	2 " Charles M	Son	2mo	M	1/16			
IW1266	3 " Artie M	Wife	19	F	I.W.			
	4							
	5							
	6							
	7							
	8							
	9	ENROLLMENT						
	10	OF NOS. 3 HEREON						
	11	APPROVED BY THE SECRETARY OF INTERIOR DEC 30 1904						
	12	ENROLLMENT						
	13	OF NOS. 2 HEREON						
	14	APPROVED BY THE SECRETARY OF INTERIOR MAY 9 1904						
	15							
	16							
	17							

TRIBAL ENROLLMENT OF PARENTS

Name of Father	Year	County	Name of Mother	Year	County
1 John Turner	dead	claim Choctaw	Nancy M Turner		non-citizen
2 No.1			Artie M Turner		" "
3 Oliver Wiley		non citizen	Mollie Belle Wiley	dead	non citizen
4					
5					

6 No. 1 was admitted by Dawes Commission under act
7 of Congress of June 10, 1896: Choctaw citizenship case #295. No appeal as to No1
8 Evidence of marriage of No.1 and Artie M. Turner filed Oct. 30, 1901.
   No.2 born Aug 30, 1901. Enrolled Oct. 30, 1901.
9 No.1 is husband of Artie M. Turner on Choctaw card D#830
10 No.3 originally listed for enrollment Nov. 20, 1902 on Choctaw card #D-830:
11 transferred to this card Dec. 15, 1904. See decision of Nov. 26, 1904.
12
13 For child of Nos 1&3 see NB (Apr 26 '06) Card #1197
14   "   "   "   "   "   " (Mar 3, 1905) " # 638
15
16   #1&2
17 P.O. Tupelo IT 4/1/05   DATE OF APPLICATION FOR ENROLLMENT.   Oct. 30, 1901

265

Choctaw By Blood Enrollment Cards 1898-1914

COUNTY. **Choctaw Nation** Choctaw CARD No.
(Not Including) FIELD No.

Dawes' Roll No.	NAME	Relationship to Person First Named	AGE	SEX	BLOOD	TRIBAL ENROLLMENT		
						Year	County	No.
DEAD.	₁ Wade, Lucinda	DEAD	46	F	Full	1896	Tobucksy	13041
13585	₂ Nelson, Clarissa	Dau	14	F	"	1896	"	13042
13586	₃ Jefferson, Kitsie	Dau	11	F	"	1896	"	13043
	₄							
	₅							
	₆							
	₇	ENROLLMENT OF NOS. 2 - 3 - HEREON						
	₈	APPROVED BY THE SECRETARY						
	₉	OF INTERIOR MAR 19 1903						
	₁₀							
	₁₁	No. 1 HEREON DISMISSED UNDER						
	₁₂	ORDER OF THE COMMISSION TO THE FIVE CIVILIZED TRIBES OF MARCH 31, 1905.						
	₁₃							
	₁₄							
	₁₅							
	₁₆	For child of No2 see NB (Apr 26 '06) Card #455						
	₁₇							

ENROLLMENT OF PARENTS

	Name of Father	Year	County	Name of Mother	Year	County
₁						
₂				No.1		
₃	Jo. Jefferson	1896		No.1		
₄						
₅	No.2 on 1896 Choctaw census roll as Clarissa Wade					
₆	No.3 " " " " " " Kitsie Wade.					
₇	No.1 on 1893 Tobucksy county pay roll as Lucinda Wade. No.2 " " " " " " " Cassey Nelson.					
₈	No.3 " " " " " " " Kaitsie Jefferson					
₉	No.2 is at school at Tushkahomma female seminary.					
₁₀	Application for enrollment of Nos. 1,2 and 3 was made by Bradley Anderson, son of No.1, at Muskogee, Indian Territory, I.T. Nov. 16, 1901.					
₁₁	No.1 is now the wife of Herman C. Thurlow on Chickasaw					
₁₂	card #1543: were married June 4th, 1901. Jany 22d, 1902.					
₁₃	No1 Evidence of Death filed July 3rd 1902: Died Feb. 15" 1902.					
₁₄						
₁₅						
₁₆						
₁₇				Date of Application for Enrollment.	Nov. 16, 1901	

Choctaw By Blood Enrollment Cards 1898-1914

RESIDENCE: Sugar Loaf   COUNTY. **Choctaw Nation**   **Choctaw Roll**   CARD NO.
POST OFFICE: ~~Monroe~~, Ind. Ter.   *(Not Including Freedmen)*   FIELD NO. **5367**

Dawes' Roll No.	Savannah NAME	Relationship to Person First Named	AGE	SEX	BLOOD	TRIBAL ENROLLMENT Year	County	No.
IW1142	1 Garrison, Sarah E	First Named	45	F	I.W.			
	2							
	3							
	4							
	5							
	6							
	7							
	8							
	9							
	10							
	11	ENROLLMENT						
	12	OF NOS. 1 HEREON APPROVED BY THE SECRETARY						
	13	OF INTERIOR NOV 16 1904						
	14							
	15							
	16							
	17	See Choctaw 3062-3063-3064						

TRIBAL ENROLLMENT OF PARENTS

	Name of Father	Year	County	Name of Mother	Year	County
1	Joseph James	dead	non-citizen	James	dead	non-citizen
2						
3						
4						
5	No.1 was admitted as an intermarried citizen by Dawes Commission					
6	in 1896, Choctaw case #999. No appeal.					
7	No.1 was admitted as Mary M. Garison[sic]					
8	No.1 is the mother of Maud Killen on Choctaw Card #3062 and of Matilda Cox on Choctaw card #3064					
9	See statement of No.1 and that of her husband Lucious V. Garrison					
10	filed this day Feby. 21, 1902					
11						
12						
13						
14						
15						
16					Date of Application for Enrollment.	FEB 21 1902
17						

Choctaw By Blood Enrollment Cards 1898-1914

RESIDENCE: Sugar Loaf COUNTY.
POST OFFICE: Red Ok Ind Ter

Choctaw Nation

Choctaw Roll
(Not Including Freedmen)

CARD No.

FIELD No. **5368**

Dawes' Roll No.	NAME	Relationship to Person First Named	AGE	SEX	BLOOD	TRIBAL ENROLLMENT		
						Year	County	No.
13587	1 Colbert, Edmund		18	M	Full	1896	Sugar Loaf	7794
	2							
	3							
	4							
	5							
	6							
	7							
	8							
	9							
	10							
	11							
	12							
	13							
	14							
	15							
	16							
	17							

ENROLLMENT
OF NOS. 1 HEREON
APPROVED BY THE SECRETARY
OF INTERIOR MAR 19 1903

TRIBAL ENROLLMENT OF PARENTS

	Name of Father	Year	County	Name of Mother	Year	County
1	Thomas Colbert	Dead		Artemecy Colbert	Dead	
2						
3						
4						
5						
6	No 1 on 1893 Leased District pay roll Skullyville Co, page 11, #105 as Edward Colbert					
7	No.1 on 1896 Choctaw Census roll page 194, No 7794 as Edmund Loman.					
8	As to parentage and residence, see statement of No1 and that of William W Ish[sic] filed this day Feby 21, 1902					
9	For child of No1 see NB (Apr 26 '06) #1285					
10						
11						
12						
13						
14						
15						
16						
17				Date of Application for Enrollment.	Feby 21, 1902	

268

Choctaw By Blood Enrollment Cards 1898-1914

	RCE: Kiamitia COUNTY. **Choctaw Nation**							
	FFICE: Nelson Ind Ter					**Choctaw Roll** *(Not Including Freedmen)* CARD NO. FIELD NO. **5369**		

	NAME	Relationship to Person	AGE	SEX	BLOOD	TRIBAL ENROLLMENT		
						Year	County	No.
1	Smallwood, Lizzie	First Named	23	F	1/4	1896	Kiamitia	11525
2								
3								
4								
5								
6								
7		ENROLLMENT OF NOS. 1 HEREON APPROVED BY THE SECRETARY OF INTERIOR MAR 19 1903						
8								
9								
10								
11								
12								
13								
14								
15								
16								
17								

TRIBAL ENROLLMENT OF PARENTS

	Name of Father	Year	County	Name of Mother	Year	County
1	Robert Smallwood	1896	Kiamitia	Betsey Smallwood	Dead	
2						
3						
4						
5						
6	See testimony taken April 1, 1902					
7	No.1 also on 1896 Choctaw census roll as Eliza Smallwood page 297 #11525.					
8	No.1 on 1893 pay roll Kiamitia Co page 88 No 733 as Lizzie Smallwood.					
9	For child of No1 see NB (Apr 26-06) Card No 281					
10	" " " " " " (Mar 3-05) " " 839					
11						
12						
13						
14						
15						
16				DATE OF APPLICATION FOR ENROLLMENT		
17	PO Bennington IT 4/8/05					April 1, 1902

Choctaw By Blood Enrollment Cards 1898-1914

	Tobucksy COUNTY. **Choctaw Nation**	**Choctaw Roll** (Not Including Freedmen)	CARD No.
	So McAlester, I.T.		FIELD No. **5370**

	NAME	Relationship to Person First Named	AGE	SEX	BLOOD	TRIBAL ENROLLMENT		
						Year	County	No.
1	Crowder, Elizabeth		23	F	1/4	1896	Jackson	2753
2								
3								
4								
5								
6								
7								
8	ENROLLMENT							
9	OF NOS. 1 HEREON APPROVED BY THE SECRETARY							
10	OF INTERIOR MAR 19 1903							
11								
12								
13								
14								
15								
16								
17								

TRIBAL ENROLLMENT OF PARENTS

	Name of Father	Year	County	Name of Mother	Year	County
1	Wm J Crowder		Jackson	Betsey Crowder	dead	Jackson
2						
3						
4						
5						
6						
7	On 1896 roll as Lizzie Crowder.					
8						
9						
10						
11						
12						
13						
14						
15						
16				DATE OF APPLICATION FOR ENROLLMENT.	APR 24 1902	
17						

270

Choctaw By Blood Enrollment Cards 1898-1914

CE: Choctaw Nation	COUNTY. Choctaw ▮▮▮			Choctaw Roll *(Not Including Freedmen)*	CARD NO.
ICE: So. McAlester, I.T.					FIELD NO. **5371**

	NAME	Relationship to Person First Named	AGE	SEX	BLOOD	TRIBAL ENROLLMENT Year	C	No.
1	Russell, Dan	First Named	30	M	1/16	1893	Kiami▮	1
2								
3								
4								
5								
6								
7								
8								
9								
10								
11	ENROLLMENT							
12	OF NOS. 1 HEREON APPROVED BY THE SECRETARY							
13	OF INTERIOR MAR 19 1903							
14								
15								
16								
17								

TRIBAL ENROLLMENT OF PARENTS

	Name of Father	Year	County	Name of Mother	Year	County
1	James Russell		Kiamitia	Molsey Russell	dead	Towson
2						
3						
4						
5						
6						
7						
8						
9						
10						
11						
12						
13						
14						
15						
16				Date of Application for Enrollment.	JUL 31 1902	
17						

Choctaw By Blood Enrollment Cards 1898-1914

RESIDENCE: Choctaw Nation   COUNTY. **Choctaw Nation**   **Choctaw Roll**   CARD NO.

POST OFFICE: Lehigh Ind. Ter.   *(Not Including Freedmen)*   FIELD NO. **5372**

Dawes' Roll No.	NAME	Relationship to Person	AGE	SEX	BLOOD	TRIBAL ENROLLMENT		
						Year	County	No.
13591	1 Foster, Sallie	First Named	39	F	1/2	1896	Atoka	10552
	2							
	3							
	4							
	5							
	6							
	7							
	8							
	9							
	10							
	11							
	12							
	13							
	14							
	15							
	16							
	17							

ENROLLMENT OF NO. 1 APPROVED BY THE SECRETARY OF INTERIOR MAR 19 1903 HEREON

TRIBAL ENROLLMENT OF PARENTS

	Name of Father	Year	County	Name of Mother	Year	County
1	Aleck Folsom	Dead	Choctaw Roll	Jane	Dead	Chickasaw Roll
2						
3						
4						
5						
6	No(1) On Choctaw Roll 1896 as "Sallie Primer"					
7	No1 " " " No2 Page 403 as Sallie Primer					
8	No.1 originally enrolled on Chickasaw Card No. 114. Transferred to					
9	this card Oct. 15, 1902.					
10						
11						
12						
13						
14						
15					Date of Application for Enrollment	
16						
17					Sept 3rd 18	

| RESIDENCE: Pontotoc | COUNTY. | Choctaw Nation | Choctaw Roll | CARD NO. |
| POST OFFICE: Pontotoc Ind. Ter. | | | (Not Including Freedmen) | FIELD NO. 5373 |

Dawes' Roll No.	NAME	Relationship to Person First Named	AGE	SEX	BLOOD	TRIBAL ENROLLMENT Year	County	No.
13592	1 Anderson, Sampson		42	M	1/2	1896	Jacks Fork	527
	2							
	3							
	4							
	5							
	6							
	7 ENROLLMENT							
	8 OF NOS. 1 HEREON APPROVED BY THE SECRETARY							
	9 OF INTERIOR Mar. 19, 1903							
	10							
	11							
	12							
	13							
	14							
	15							
	16							
	17							

TRIBAL ENROLLMENT OF PARENTS

Name of Father	Year	County	Name of Mother	Year	County
1 Reuben Anderson	Dead	Choctaw Roll	Hettie Anderson	Dead	Chick residing in Choctaw N. 3rd Dist
2					
3					
4					
5					
6 No(1) also Choctaw Census Roll No 2 Page 21/					
7 " " Husband of Lizzie Anderson, Choctaw Roll Card #34.					
8					
9 No1 originally enrolled on Chick Card #205. Transferred to					
10 this card Oct. 15, 1902.					
11 For child of No1 see NB (Apr 26-1906) Card No.3.					
12					
13					
14					
15				Date of Application for Enrollment.	
16					
17				Sept 5" 1898	

Choctaw By Blood Enrollment Cards 1898-1914

	RESIDENCE: Pontotoc	COUNTY.					
POST OFFICE: Pontotoc Ind. Ter.							

Choctaw Nation

Choctaw Roll *(Not Including Freedmen)*

CARD No.

FIELD No. 5374

Dawes' Roll No.	NAME	Relationship to Person First Named	AGE	SEX	BLOOD	TRIBAL ENROLLMENT		
						Year	County	No.
13593	1 Anderson, William B.		46	M	1/2	1896	Jacks Fork	511
13594	2 Jefferson, Rosa	Dau	14	F	3/4	1896	Jacks Fork	513
13595	3 Anderson, Bessie	G.Dau	8	F	7/8	1896	Jacks Fork	514
	4							
	5							
	6							
	7							
	8							
	9							
	10							
	11	ENROLLMENT						
	12	OF NOS. 1 - 2 - 3 - HEREON APPROVED BY THE SECRETARY						
	13	OF INTERIOR MAR 19 1903						
	14							
	15							
	16							
	17							

TRIBAL ENROLLMENT OF PARENTS

	Name of Father	Year	County	Name of Mother	Year	County
1	Reuben Anderson	Dead	Choctaw Roll	Hettie Anderson	Dead	Chick residing in Choctaw N. 3rd Dist
2	No.1			Lizzie Anderson	"	Chickasaw Roll
3	Tom Anderson		Chick now on Choctaw Roll	Mary McCann		Chick residing in Choctaw N. 3rd Dist
4						
5						
6	No1 On Choctaw Roll 1896 as Wm B. Anderson					
7	" " Husband of Elsie Anderson Choctaw Roll #35					
8	" " On Choctaw Census Record No2, Page 21					
9	" 2 " " " " " " " "					
10	" 3 " " " " " " " "					
11	For child of No.2 see NB (March 3, 1905) #1045					
12	Nos 1, 2 and 3 originally enrolled on Chickasaw Card #206 Transferred to this card Oct. 15, 1902.					
13	No2 is now the wife of Sweeny Jefferson on Choctaw card #4536. Evidence of marriage filed Nov. 12, 1902.					
14						
15					Date of Application for Enrollment.	
16					Sept 5- 1898	
17						

Choctaw By Blood Enrollment Cards 1898-1914

	RESIDENCE: Choctaw Nation 3ʳᵈ Dist COUNTY.									

RESIDENCE: Choctaw Nation 3ʳᵈ Dist COUNTY. **Choctaw Nation** — **Choctaw Roll** CARD No.
POST OFFICE: Owl, Ind. Ter. *(Not Including Freedmen)* FIELD No. 5375

Dawes' Roll No.	NAME	Relationship to Person	AGE	SEX	BLOOD	TRIBAL ENROLLMENT		
						Year	County	No.
13596	1 Frazier, Kiliza	First Named	48	F	1/2	1896	Atoka	4488
5061	2 " Louisa	Dau	3	"	1/4			
	3							
	4							
	5							
	6							
	7							
	8	ENROLLMENT OF NOS. 1 HEREON APPROVED BY THE SECRETARY OF INTERIOR MAR 19 1903						
	9							
	10							
	11	ENROLLMENT OF NOS. 2 HEREON APPROVED BY THE SECRETARY OF INTERIOR FEB 16 1904						
	12							
	13							
	14							
	15							
	16							
	17							

TRIBAL ENROLLMENT OF PARENTS

	Name of Father	Year	County	Name of Mother	Year	County
1	On-no-pul-ley	Dead	Choctaw Roll	Salley	Dead	Choctaw Roll
2	Solomon Frazier	"	"	No.1		
3						
4						
5						
6	No1 the wife of Solomon Frazier on Choctaw Roll, Card #36					
7	" On Choctaw Census Roll No2. Page 191					
	No2 Evidence of Birth received and filed Feb. 26ᵗʰ 1902					
8						
9	Nos 1 and 2 originally enrolled on Chick. Card #210: transferred to this card Oct. 16, 1902.					
10						
11						
12						
13						
14						
15				Date of Application for Enrollment.		
16						
17				Sept. 5ᵗʰ 1898		

Choctaw By Blood Enrollment Cards 1898-1914

RESIDENCE: Choctaw Nation COUNTY. **Choctaw Nation** Choctaw Roll CARD NO.
POST OFFICE: Lehigh Ind. Ter. *(Not Including Freedmen)* FIELD NO. 5376

Dawes' Roll No.		NAME	Relationship to Person First Named	AGE	SEX	BLOOD	TRIBAL ENROLLMENT		
							Year	County	No.
DEAD	1	James, John Clay	DEAD	19	M	1/8	1896	Atoka	7301
13597	2	" Willie C	Bro	17	M	1/8	1896	Atoka	7302
13598	3	" Lorinda	Sis	15	F	1/8	1896	Atoka	7303
	4								
	5								
	6								
	7	ENROLLMENT							
	8	OF NOS. - 2 - 3 - HEREON APPROVED BY THE SECRETARY							
	9	OF INTERIOR MAR 19 1903							
	10	No.___1___ HEREON DISMISSED UNDER							
	11	ORDER OF THE COMMISSION TO THE FIVE							
	12	CIVILIZED TRIBES OF MARCH 31, 1905.							
	13								
	14								
	15								
	16								
	17								

TRIBAL ENROLLMENT OF PARENTS

	Name of Father	Year	County	Name of Mother	Year	County
1	Henry C. James		Choctaw Roll	Lorinda	Dead	Chickasaw Roll
2	" " "		" "	"	"	" "
3	" " "		" "	"	"	" "
4						
5	No1 On Choctaw Roll as "Johnie C James"; On Choctaw Census Record No2 Page 305					
6	" 2 " " " " "Willie " ": " " " " " " "					
7	" 3 " " " " "Lorindy " ": " " " " " " "					
8	No.1 Died Feb. 13" 1899; Evidence of death filed March 26" 1901					
9	Nos 1,2 and 3 originally enrolled on Chickasaw Card #247 and					
10	transferred to this card October 16, 1902.					
11						
12	For child of No3 see NB (Apr 26-06) Card #629					
13	" " " " " " (Mar 3-05) " #1200					
14	" " " No2 " " " " " " #1301					
15						
16						
17	PO Wapanucka IT 4/22/05			Date of Application for Enrollment.	Sept 6" 1898	

276

Choctaw By Blood Enrollment Cards 1898-1914

| RESIDENCE: Choctaw Nation 3rd Dist COUNTY. | | **Choctaw Nation** | | | | **Choctaw Roll** *(Not Including Freedmen)* | | |
| POST OFFICE: Calvin, Ind. Ter. | | | | | | | | |

Dawes' Roll No.	NAME	Relationship to Person First Named	AGE	SEX	BLOOD	TRIBAL ENROLLMENT		
						Year	County	No.
13599	1 Davis, Mary E	First Named	4	F	1/8	1896	Atoka	3629
	2							
	3							
	4							
	5							
	6							
	7							
	8							
	9							
	10							
	11							
	12							
	13							
	14							
	15							
	16							
	17							

ENROLLMENT
OF NOS. 1 HEREON
APPROVED BY THE SECRETARY
OF INTERIOR MAR 19 1903

TRIBAL ENROLLMENT OF PARENTS

Name of Father	Year	County	Name of Mother	Year	County
1 John W. Davis		Non-Citizen	Mary J Davis	Dead	Chickasaw Roll
2					
3					
4					
5					
6 No1 also on Choctaw Census Record No.2 Page 149					
7 No.1 Originally enrolled on Chick. card No 250; transferred to					
8 this card Oct. 16, 1902					
9					
10					
11					
12					
13					
14					
15				Date of Application for Enrollment.	
16					
17				Sept 6" 1898	

Choctaw By Blood Enrollment Cards 1898-1914

RESIDENCE: Choctaw Nation 3ʳᵈ Dist COUNTY. **Choctaw Nation** Choctaw Roll CARD NO.
POST OFFICE: Tuskahoma, Ind. Ter *(Not Including Freedmen)* FIELD NO. **5378**

Dawes' Roll No.	NAME	Relationship to Person First Named	AGE	SEX	BLOOD	TRIBAL ENROLLMENT		
						Year	County	No.
13600	₁ Anderson, Rogers		48	M	1/2	1896	Jacks Fork	484
13601	₂ " Raynie	Son	6	"	3/4	"	" "	489
DEAD	₃ " ~~Bonnie~~ ~~DEAD~~	"	~~14~~	"	~~3/4~~	"	" "	~~486~~
13602	₄ " Freeman	S Son	11	"	3/4	"	" "	487
13603	₅ " Willie	S Son	9	"	3/4	"	" "	488
13604	₆ " Osborne	S Son	16	"	3/4	"	" "	485
	₇							
	₈ ~~ENROLLMENT~~ OF NOS. 1-2-4-5-6 HEREON				No. 3 HEREON DISMISSED UNDER			
	₉ APPROVED BY THE SECRETARY OF INTERIOR MAR 19 1903				ORDER OF THE COMMISSION TO THE FIVE			
	₁₀				CIVILIZED TRIBES OF MARCH 31, 1905.			
	₁₁ No3 Died June 27" 1901: Evidence of Death filed July 3ʳᵈ 1902							
	₁₂							
	₁₃ Nos 1 to 5 inclusive originally enrolled on Chick. card No. 252 and transferred to this card Oct. 16, 1902							
	₁₄							
	₁₅ No6 transferred to this card from Chickasaw card #252 Dec. 31, 1902							
	₁₆							
	₁₇							

TRIBAL ENROLLMENT OF PARENTS

	Name of Father	Year	County	Name of Mother	Year	County
₁	Reuben Anderson	Dead	Choctaw Roll	Hettie Anderson	Dead	Chickasaw
₂	No.1			Kissie Anderson		Chick residing in Choctaw Natn
₃	No.1			Peggy		Chick residing in Choctaw N. 3ʳᵈ Dist
₄	Robert Anderson			Kissie Anderson		Chick residing in Choctaw Natn
₅	" "			" "		"
₆	" "			" "		"
₇						
₈	No1 On Choctaw Census Record No2 Page 20					
₉	" 2 " "	" " " "	On 1896 Choctaw Roll as "Rayney Anderson"			
₁₀	" 3 " "	" " " "	On 1896 Choctaw Roll as " Bunnie " "			
₁₁	" 4 " "	" " " "				
	" 5 " "	" " " "				
₁₂	Wife of No(1) and mother of (2), (4) (5) on Chickasaw Card #252: (now deceased)					
₁₃						
₁₄						
₁₅					Date of Application for Enrollment.	
₁₆					Sept 6" 1898	
₁₇						

278

Choctaw By Blood Enrollment Cards 1898-1914

RESIDENCE: Choctaw Nation COUNTY. **Choctaw Nation** Choctaw Roll CARD NO.
POST OFFICE: Guertie, Ind. Ter. (*Not Including Freedmen*) FIELD NO. **5379**

Dawes' Roll No.	NAME	Relationship to Person First Named	AGE	SEX	BLOOD	TRIBAL ENROLLMENT Year	County	No.
13605	1 Leader, Isabinda	First Named	32	F	Full	1896	Atoka Co	8296
13606	2 " Odis	Son	17	M	1/2	"	" "	8298
13607	3 " Aaron	"	13	"	1/2	"	" "	8299
13608	4 " Jim	"	3	"	1/2	"	" "	8300
13609	5 " Alice	Dau	20	F	1/2	"	" "	8301
13610	6 " Melinda	"	2	"	1/2	"	" "	8302
13611	7 " Mary	"	1 wk	"	1/2			
	8							
	9							
	10							
	11	ENROLLMENT						
	12	OF NOS. 1-2-3-4-5-6-7 HEREON APPROVED BY THE SECRETARY						
	13	OF INTERIOR MAR 19 1903						
	14							
	15	No1 Husband of, J M Leader on Choctaw Card 5636						
	16							
	17							

TRIBAL ENROLLMENT OF PARENTS

	Name of Father	Year	County	Name of Mother	Year	County
1	Aaron Frazier	Dead	Chickasaw Roll	Malinda James	Dead	Chickasaw Roll
2	J. M. Leader			No.1		
3	" " "			No.1		
4	" " "			No.1		
5	" " "			No.1		
6	" " "			No.1		
7	" " "			No.1		
8	No1 on Choctaw Census Record No2 Page 342: On 1896 Roll as "Isabina Leader"					
9	" 2 " " " " " " "					
10	" 3 " " " " " " "					
11	" 4 " " " " " " "					
12	" 5 " " " " " " "					
13	" 6 " " " " " " "					
	" 7 Born March 21st 1902: Enrolled April 1st 1902					
14	Nos 1 to 7 inclusive originally enrolled on Chickasaw Card #268 and transferred to this card Oct. 16, 1902.					
15						
16					1 to 6 inc	
17				Date of Application for Enrollment.	Sept 6" 1898	

279

Choctaw By Blood Enrollment Cards 1898-1914

Dawes' Roll No.		NAME	Relationship to Person First Named	AGE	SEX	BLOOD	TRIBAL ENROLLMENT		
							Year	County	No.
13612	1	Goer, Mary		29	F	Full	1896	Atoka	4969
13613	2	" Simon	Son	13	M	1/2	"	"	4970
13614	3	" Angeline	Dau	10	F	1/2	"	"	4972
13615	4	" Doney	"	6	"	1/2	"	"	4973
13616	5	" Henderson	Son	3	M	1/2	"	"	4971
13617	6	" Elmarina	Dau	3mo	F	1/2			
	7								
	8								
	9								
	10								
	11								
	12								
	13								
	14								
	15								
	16								
	17								

ENROLLMENT
OF NOS. 1 2 3 4 5 & 6 HEREON
APPROVED BY THE SECRETARY
OF INTERIOR   MAR 19 1903

TRIBAL ENROLLMENT OF PARENTS

	Name of Father	Year	County	Name of Mother	Year	C
1	Martin Stick	Dead	Chickasaw Roll	Viney Harris	Dead	Chicka
2	William Goer		Atoka Co. Choctaw Nation	No.1		
3	" "		" "	No.1		
4	" "		" "	No.1		
5	" "		" "	No.1		
6	" "		" "	No.1		
7						
8						
9						
10						
11	No1 Wife of William Goer Choctaw Roll Card #52					
	No1 On Choctaw Census Record No 2 Page 212					
12	" 2 " " " " " " " On 1896 Roll as "Simeon Goer"					
13	" 3 " " " " " " "					
	" 4 " " " " " " " On 1896 Roll as "Dany Goer"					
14	" 5 " " " " " " "					
15	" 6 Evidence of Birth received and filed Feb. 28" 1902					
16	Nos 1 to 6 inclusive originally enrolled on Chick. card #276. Transferr			Date of Application		
	to this card Oct [?] 1902					

Choctaw By Blood Enrollment Cards 1898-1914

RESIDENCE: Choctaw Nation COUNTY.

POST OFFICE: Conway, Ind. Ter.

Choctaw Nation

Choctaw Roll (Not Including Freedmen)

CARD No.

FIELD No. 5381

Dawes' Roll No.	NAME	Relationship to Person First Named	AGE	SEX	BLOOD	TRIBAL ENROLLMENT Year	County	No.
13618	1 Rushing, Caroline	First Named	17	F	Full	1896	Atoka	6008
13619	2 Rushing, Chas William	Son	2wk	M	1/2			
IW1143	3 " Joe	Husband	34	M	I.W.			
	4							
	5							
	6							
	7							
	8							
	9							
	10							
	11							
	12							
	13							
	14							
	15							
	16							
	17							

ENROLLMENT OF NOS. 1 - 2 - HEREON APPROVED BY THE SECRETARY OF INTERIOR MAR 19 1903

ENROLLMENT OF NOS 3 HEREON APPROVED BY THE SECRETARY OF INTERIOR NOV 16 1904

TRIBAL ENROLLMENT OF PARENTS

Name of Father	Year	County	Name of Mother	Year	County
1 Culberson Harris	Dead	Chickasaw Roll	Viney Harris	Dead	Chickasaw Roll
2 Joe Rushing		Non-Citizen	No.1		
3 Dennis Rushing	dead	" "	P. P. Rushing	dead	Non-Citizen
4					
5					

6   No1 On Choctaw Census Record No.2, Page 254

7   " Now the wife of Joe Rushing on Chickasaw Card #D.318   March 8" 1900

  No2 Enrolled Feb. 8" 1901

8   For child of Nos 1&3 see N B (Apr 26, 1906) Card No. 65

9   Nos 1 and 2 originally enrolled on Chickasaw Card No. 277. Transferred

10   to this card Oct. 16, 1902.

  No.3 transferred from Chickasaw Card #D-318, Oct. 31, 1904. See decision of Oct. 15, 1904

11   For Child of No1 see NB (March 3, 1905) #806

12

13

14

15

16   PO Ada IT 4/7/05

    Date of Application for Enrollment.   Sept. 7" 1898

17   No3 PO Jeffs[sic] I.T. 5/12/02

Choctaw By Blood Enrollment Cards 1898-1914

RESIDENCE:	Choctaw Nation	COUNTY.			**Nation**		**ctaw Roll** *luding Freedmen)*	CARD NO.	
POST OFFICE:	Owl, Ind. Ter.							FIELD NO. **5382**	

Dawes' Roll No.	NAME	Relationship to Person	AGE	SEX	BLOOD	TRIBAL ENROLLMENT		
						Year	County	No.
13620	1 Bond, Alice	First Named	22	F	Full	1896	Atoka	1755
13621	2 " Jesse	Son	2	M	1/2			
	3							
	4							
	5							
	6							
	7							
	8							
	9							
	10							
	11							
	12							
	13							
	14							
	15							
	16							
	17							

ENROLLMENT
OF NOS. 1 - 2 - HEREON
APPROVED BY THE SECRETARY
OF INTERIOR MAR 19 1903

TRIBAL ENROLLMENT OF PARENTS

Name	Year	County	Name of Mother	Year	County
1 Lawson	Dead	Chickasaw Roll	Klicey Roberts	1897	Chick residing in Choctaw N. 3rd Dist
2 Richard		Atoka Co Choctaw Roll	No.1		
3					
4					
5					
6					
7 No1 on Choctaw Census Record No.2, Page 71					
8 " 2 " " " " " " On 1896 Roll as "Jessie Bond"					
9 Nos 1 and 2 originally enrolled on Chick. card #336. Transferred to this card Oct. 16, 1902.					
10 No1 was married to Noah Burris Chickasaw card #200					
11 No.1 is the mother of Sloan Roberts on Choctaw care #5474					
12					
13					
14					
15				Date of Application for Enrollment.	
16					
17				Sept. 8" 1898	

RESIDENCE: Choctaw Nation County.
POST OFFICE: Guertie, Ind. Ter.

Choctaw Nation

Choctaw Roll
(Not Including Freedmen)

CARD NO.

FIELD NO. 5383

Dawes' Roll No.	NAME	Relationship to Person First Named	AGE	SEX	BLOOD	TRIBAL ENROLLMENT		
						Year	County	No.
13622	1 Pusley, Susan	First Named	40	F	Full	1896	Atoka	10545
	2							
	3							
	4							
	5							
	6							
	7							
	8							
	9							
	10							
	11							
	12							
	13							
	14							
	15							
	16							
	17							

ENROLLMENT
OF NOS. 1
APPROVED BY THE SECRETARY HEREON
OF INTERIOR MAR 19 1903

TRIBAL ENROLLMENT OF PARENTS

	Name of Father	Year	County	Name of Mother	Year	County
1	Aaron Frazier	Dead	Chickasaw Roll	Malinda Frazier	Dead	Chickasaw Roll
2						
3						
4						
5						

6 No1 On '96 Roll as "Susa Pusley: Also on Choctaw Census Record No 2 Page 403
7 No.1 Originally enrolled on Chickasaw Card No. 334. Transferred to
8 this card Oct. 16, 1902.
9 Wife of Jack Prisley, Choctaw card 3329. 11/20/02.

DATE OF APPLICATION
FOR ENROLLMENT. Sept. 7" 1898

Choctaw By Blood Enrollment Cards 1898-1914

<table>
<tr><td>RESIDENCE: Choctaw Nation <s>COUNTY.</s>
oma, Ind. Ter.</td><td colspan="7" align="right">Choctaw Roll
t Including Freedmen)</td></tr>
<tr><td rowspan="2">NAME</td><td rowspan="2">Relationship
to Person
First
Named</td><td rowspan="2">AGE</td><td rowspan="2">SEX</td><td rowspan="2">BLOOD</td><td colspan="3">TRIBAL ENROLLMENT</td></tr>
<tr><td>Year</td><td>County</td><td>No.</td></tr>
<tr><td>Gibson, Johnie</td><td></td><td>16</td><td>M</td><td>1/2</td><td>1896</td><td>Jacks Fork</td><td>5008</td></tr>
<tr><td>Louisa</td><td>Sister</td><td>13</td><td>F</td><td>1/2</td><td>"</td><td>" "</td><td>5009</td></tr>
</table>

ENROLLMENT
OF NOS. 1 & 2 HEREON
APPROVED BY THE SECRETARY
OF INTERIOR MAR 19 1903

TRIBAL ENROLLMENT OF PARENTS

Name of Father	Year	County	Name of Mother	County
1 Calvin Gibson	Dead	Choctaw Roll	Nancy Gibson	ckasaw Roll
2 " "	"	" "	" "	" "

6 No1 Also on Choctaw Census Record No.2 Page 214: On '96 Roll as "Johnie Gibson"
7 " 2 "   "   "   "   "   "   "
8 Nos 1 and 2 originally enrolled on Chick. card No. 435. Transferred to
~~this card Oct. 16, 1902.~~

Date of Application for Enrollment. Sept. 14" 1898

284

POST OFFICE: Guertie, Ind. Ter.		Choctaw Nation					(Not Including Freedmen)		

Dawes' Roll No.	NAME	Relationship to Person First Named	AGE	SEX	BLOOD	TRIBAL ENROLLMENT		
						Year	County	No.
13625	1 Lewis, Thompson	First Named	13	M	1/2	1896	Atoka	8344
13626	2 " Dickson	Bro	8	"	12	"	"	8345
	3							
	4							
	5							
	6							
	7							
	8	ENROLLMENT						
	9	OF NOS. 1 - 2 HEREON APPROVED BY THE SECRETARY						
	10	OF INTERIOR MAR 19 1903						
	11							
	12							
	13							
	14							
	15							
	16							
	17							

TRIBAL ENROLLMENT OF PARENTS

Name of Father	Year	County	Name of Mother	Year	County
1 John Lewis		Atoka Co Choctaw Roll	Al-lich-ta Lewis		
2 " "		" "	" "		
3					
4					
5					
6 No1 On Choctaw Census Record No2, Page 343					
7 " 2 " " " " " " On '96 Roll as "Dick Lewis"					
8 Father of (1) (2) John Lewis on Choctaw Card #4941					
Mother " " " Allichta Lewis acknowledged to be a full-blood Chickasaw					
9 but name not found on Chickasaw Roll Sept 8" 1898 See P.70 Chick Roll 1896,					
Ellicher Lewis, delinquent					
10 Nos (1) and (2) on Creek Card #3415					
11 Nos 1 and 2 originally enrolled on Chick. card #337. Transferred					
12 to this card Oct. 16, 1902.					
13					
14					
15				Date of Application for En	
16				Sept.	
17					

285

Choctaw By Blood Enrollment Cards 1898-1914

RESIDENCE: Pickens	COUNTY.		Choctaw Roll	CARD NO.		
POST OFFICE: Foster, Ind. Ter.	**Choctaw Nation**		*(Not Including Freedmen)*	FIELD NO. **5386**		

Dawes' Roll No.	NAME	Relationship to Person First Named	AGE	SEX	BLOOD	TRIBAL ENROLLMENT		
						Year	County	No.
13627	1 Bell, Eliza		25	F	1/2	1896	Tobucksy	7885
13628	2 Lawrence, Azzie Anna	Dau	3	"	1/4	"	"	7886
13629	3 Bell, Emma O	"	4mo	"	1/4			
13630	4 Gibson, Douglas	Bro	9	M	1/2	1896	Tobucksy	4690
13631	5 Bell, Delila Lucinda	Dau	4mo	F	1/4			
13632	6 " Grant	Son	1mo	M	1/4			
	7							
	8							
	9							
	10							
	11							
	12							
	13							
	14							
	15							
	16							
	17							

ENROLLMENT OF NOS. 1-2-3-4-5-6 HEREON APPROVED BY THE SECRETARY OF INTERIOR Mar. 19 1903

TRIBAL ENROLLMENT OF PARENTS

Name of Father	Year	County	Name of Mother	Year	County
1 Calvin Gibson	Dead	Choctaw Roll	Nancy Gibson	Dead	Chickasaw Roll
2 Osborne Lawrence		" "	No.1		
3 Grant Bell		non-citizen	No.1		
4 Calvin Gibson	Dead	Choctaw Roll	Nancy Gibson	Dead	Chickasaw Roll
5 Grant Bell		non-citizen	No.1		
6 W.G. Bell		" "	No.1		

7
8 No1 on Choctaw Census Record No.2 Page 331 Tobucksy Co: on '96 Roll as "Eliza Lawrence"
9 " 2 " " " " " " " " " " " "Anna Lawrence"
10 " 3 Evidence of birth received and filed Aug 4ᵗʰ 1902
11 " 4 On Choctaw Census Record No.2 Page 331 Tobucksy Co: Enrolled Sept 14 1898
12 " 5 Enrolled Nov 6ᵗʰ 1900
13 " 6 Born Feb. 2ⁿᵈ 1902: Enrolled March 22ⁿᵈ 1902
Nos 1 to 6 originally enrolled on Chickasaw Card #436. Transferred to
this card Oct. 16, 1902
14 For child of no 1 see NB (March 3 1905) #982
15
16 Date of Application for Enrollment.
17

{ No4 Enrolled Sept 15" 1898
Nos 1,2,3 " Sept 30" 1898
+ this notation placed
hereon Dec. 10 1912.

286

Choctaw By Blood Enrollment Cards 1898-1914

RESIDENCE: Pontotoc
POST OFFICE: Purcell, Ind. Ter.

COUNTY: **Choctaw Nation**

Choctaw Roll (Not Including Freedmen)

CARD NO. FIELD NO. **5387**

Dawes' Roll No.		NAME	Relationship to Person First Named	AGE	SEX	BLOOD	TRIBAL ENROLLMENT		
							Year	County	No.
13633	1	Moore, James E	First Named	19	M	1/8	1896	Atoka	8856
13634	2	" Nancy C	Sis	17	F	1/8	"	"	8857
13535	3	" Mary Jennie	Dau	1mo	"	1/16			
IW 1431	4	" Elizabeth	wife	19	F	I.W.			
	5								
	6								
	7	ENROLLMENT							
	8	OF NOS. 1-2-3 HEREON APPROVED BY THE SECRETARY							
	9	OF INTERIOR MAR 19 1903							
	10	ENROLLMENT							
	11	OF NOS. 4 HEREON							
	12	APPROVED BY THE SECRETARY OF INTERIOR JUN 12 1905							
	13								
	14								
	15								
	16								
	17								

TRIBAL ENROLLMENT OF PARENTS

	Name of Father	Year	County	Name of Mother	Year	County
1	Moore, J.B.	1897	Chick residing in Choctaw N. 1st Dist	Jennie		Roll
2	"	"	" " "	"		
3	No.1			Elizabeth Moore		Non-citizen
4	Lloyd T. Buckles		noncitizen	Hettie Buckles		non-citizen
5			For child of No.2 see NB (Mar 3 1905) #402			
6			" " "Nos1&4 " "		" " " #1354	

7 Surname of Nos 1&2 is More on 1896 Roll

8 J.B. Moore Father of (1) &(2) on Chickasaw Card #474   No4 As to names of parents see
 No1 On Choctaw Census Record No2 Page 357   General Office letter #10374-1905

9 No2 " " " " " " "

10 No1 Now the Husband of Elizabeth Moore non citizen: Evidence of marriage filed Aug 22nd 1902

11 " 3 Born July 23rd 1902: Enrolled Aug 22nd 1902

12 Nos 1,2 and 3 originally enrolled on Chick card #474 and transferred to this card Oct. 16, 1902.

13 No4 was married to James E. Moore, Aug. 1, 1901, but did not make personal application for
 enrollment as an intermarried citizen. July 19, 1904 the Secretary of Interior directed that a

14 letter written by her husband James E Moore Aug 20, 1902 be considered as an application.

15 Placed on this card Nov. 21, 1904.

		Date of Application for Enrollment.
16		
17 No4 PO Alex IT 2/20/05	Tishomingo IT as to No.4	Sept. 16" 1898

287

Choctaw By Blood Enrollment Cards 1898-1914

RESIDENCE: Choctaw Nation 1st Dist   COUNTY.   **Choctaw Nation**   Choctaw Roll   CARD No
POST OFFICE: Garland, Ind. Ter   *(Not Including Freedmen)*   FIELD No

Dawes' Roll No.		NAME	Relationship to Person First Named	AGE	SEX	BLOOD	TRIBAL ENROLLMENT		
							Year	County	No.
13636	1	Folsom, Arnold	First Named	54	M	3/4	1896	Sans Bois	3868
IW 1222	2	" Lizzie	Wife	30	I.W.	3/8	"	" "	24507
13637	3	" Clarence	Son	8	M	3/8	"	" "	3872
13638	4	" Cleveland	"	6	"	3/8	"	" "	3873
13639	5	" Prudence	Dau	3	F	3/8	"	ENROLLMENT	3874
DEAD	6	" Lela	"	i	"	3/8	OF NOS. 2 HEREON APPROVED BY THE SECRETARY		
13640	7	" Lewis F	Son	1mo	M	3/8	OF INTERIOR DEC 13 1904		
	8	ENROLLMENT							
	9	OF NOS. 1-3-4-5-7 HEREON							
	10	APPROVED BY THE SECRETARY OF INTERIOR MAR 19 1903							
	11	Nos 1 to 7 inclusive originally							
	12	enrolled on Chickasaw Card							
	13	No. 620. Transferred to this card Oct. 16, 1902.							
	14								
	15	No. 6 HEREON DISMISSED UNDER							
	16	ORDER OF THE COMMISSION TO THE FIVE CIVILIZED TRIBES OF MARCH 31, 1905.							
	17								

TRIBAL ENROLLMENT OF PARENTS

	Name of Father	Year	County	Name of Mother	Year	County
1	Willis Folsom	Dead	Choctaw Roll	Winnie Folsom	Dead	Chickasaw Roll
2	Lewis	"	Non-citizen	Mary Lewis	"	Non-citizen
3	No.1			No.2		
4	No.1			No.2		
5	No.1			No.2		
6	No.1			No.2		
7	No.1			No.2		

8 Lewis F son of Nos(1) & (2) born Nov 14 1899 on Card No D 300   See note Below No(7)
9 No1 on '96 Roll as "Arnold Folsum"; No1 Also on Choctaw Census Record No2 #164
10 " 2 Also on Choctaw Intermarried Roll Page 38: Marriage Certificate to be supplied
" 3 On 96 Roll as "Clarence Folsum"; No3 Also on Choctaw Census Record No.2 #164
11 " 4 " " " " "Cleveland Folsum"; No4 Also " " " " " "
12 " 5 " " " " "Prudence Folsum"; No5 " " " " " " " "
13 " 6 On Choctaw Roll as Lena Folsom
" 7 Born Nov 14" 1899 Transferred to Chickasaw Card #620 Feb 1st 1902
14 See affidavit of E. B. Harlan as to his being an ordained minister of the gospel filed July 3, 1903
15 No6 Died March 2, 1900. proof of death filed March 14, 1903.
16 For child of Nos 1&2 see NB (Mar 3, 1905) #624

Date of Application for Enrollment.

Sept. 26"1898

Choctaw By Blood Enrollment Cards 1898-1914

RESIDENCE: Choctaw Nation 1st Dist   COUNTY.

POST OFFICE: Stigler, Ind. Ter

Choctaw Nation

Choctaw Roll *(Not Including Freedmen)*

CARD NO.

FIELD NO. 5389

Dawes' Roll No.	NAME	Relationship to Person First Named	AGE	SEX	BLOOD	TRIBAL ENROLLMENT		
						Year	County	No.
IW604	1 Stigler, Joseph S	First Named	37	M	I.W.	1896	Sans Bois	15017
13641	2 " Mary	Wife	29	F	3/4	"	" "	11102
13642	3 " Edward Buckley	Son	10	M	3/8	"	" "	11103
13643	4 " Willie Grady	"	6	M	3/8	"	" "	11104
13644	5 " Hettie Lee	Dau	4	F	3/8	"	" "	11105
	6							
	7							
	8	ENROLLMENT OF NOS. 2-3-4-5 HEREON APPROVED BY THE SECRETARY OF INTERIOR MAR 19 1903						
	9							
	10							
	11	ENROLLMENT OF NOS. 1 HEREON APPROVED BY THE SECRETARY OF INTERIOR FEB -8 1904						
	12							
	13							
	14							
	15							
	16							
	17							

TRIBAL ENROLLMENT OF PARENTS

	Name of Father	Year	County	Name of Mother	Year	County
1	Edward Stigler		Non-citizen	Adeline Stigler	Dead	Non-citizen
2	Walker Folsom		Sans Bois Choctaw Roll	Hettie Folsom	"	Chickasaw Roll
3	No.1			No.2		
4	No.1			No.2		
5	No.1			No.2		

6

7 No1 On '96 Roll as J.S. Stigler: also on Choctaw Intermarried Roll Page 96

8 " 2 " " " " Mary " " " " Census Record No2 Page 417

9 " 3 " " " " Edward " " " " " " " " " "

10 " 4 " " " " Willie " " " " " " " " " "

11 " 5 " " " " Lela F " " " " " " " " " "

Nos. 1 to 5 inclusive originally enrolled on Chick. card #622 and transferred to this card Oct. 16, 1902.

12 For child of Nos 1&2 see NB (Mar 3, 1905) #637

13

14

15

16   Date of Application for Enrollment.

17   Sept. 26 '98

289

Choctaw By Blood Enrollment Cards 1898-1914

RESIDENCE: Choctaw Nation 1st Dist COUNTY.
POST OFFICE: Cowlington, Ind Ter.

Choctaw Nation

Choctaw Roll
(Not Including Freedmen)

Dawes' Roll No.	NAME	Relationship to Person First Named	AGE	SEX	BLOOD	TRIBAL ENROLLMENT Year	County	No.
13645	1 Folsom, Walker W	First Named	21	M	1/4	1896	Sans Bois	3880
IW 1043	2 " Leora	wife	19	F	I. W.			
13645	3 " Lloyd Ray	Son	3wks	M	1/8			
DEAD	4 " Olen William	"	1mo	M	1/8			
	5							
	6							
	7	ENROLLMENT						
	8	OF NOS. 1 - 3 - HEREON						
	9	APPROVED BY THE SECRETARY OF INTERIOR MAR 19 1908						
	10							
	11	ENROLLMENT						
	12	OF NOS. 2 HEREON APPROVED BY THE SECRETARY						
	13	OF INTERIOR OCT 21 1904						
	14	No. 4 HEREON DISMISSED UNDER						
	15	ORDER OF THE COMMISSION TO THE FIVE CIVILIZED TRIBES OF MARCH 31, 1905.						
	16							
	17							

TRIBAL ENROLLMENT OF PARENTS

	Name of Father	Year	County	Name of Mother	Year	County
1	Walker Folsom		Sans ois Co Choctaw Roll	Hettie Folsom	Dead	Chickasaw Roll
2	F. M. Greenlee		Non-citizen	V.E. Greenlee		Non-citizen
3	No.1			No.2		
4	No.1			No.2		
5						
6	No1 On '96 Roll as Walker Folsum On Choctaw Census Record Page 164 No2					
7	Married under U.S. Law in Choctaw Nation					
8	"3 Enrolled Nov 18" 1898					
9	"4 Enrolled June 3rd 1901 - No.4 Died Aug. 18, 1902. Proof of death filed Dec. 23, 1902					
10	Nos. 1,2,3 and 4 originally enrolled on Chick. card #626. Transferred to this card Oct. 16, 1902.					
11						
12	For child of Nos 1&2 see NB (Apr 26 '06) #1308					
13	" " " " " " " (Mar 3 '05) #403					
14						
15					#1 & 2 Date of Application for Enrollment.
16						
17	PO [Illegible] IT 1/12/03					Sept. 26"1898

Choctaw By Blood Enrollment Cards 1898-1914

RESIDENCE: Choctaw Nation 1st Dist ~~COUNTY~~
POST OFFICE: Stigler, Ind. Ter.

Choctaw Nation

Choctaw Roll
(Not Including Freedmen)

CARD NO.
FIELD NO. 5391

Dawes' Roll No.		NAME	Relationship to Person First Named	AGE	SEX	BLOOD	TRIBAL ENROLLMENT		
							Year	County	No.
13647	1	Coleman, Arian		28	F	1/4	1896	Sans Bois	2128
13648	2	" Bertha Marie	Dau	4	"	1/8	"	" "	2129
13649	3	" Bessie Neva	"	1	"	1/8			
13650	4	" Ola Gladys	"	4mo	"	1/8			
	5								
	6								
	7	ENROLLMENT							
	8	OF NOS. 1-2-3-4- HEREON APPROVED BY THE SECRETARY							
	9	OF INTERIOR MAR 19 1903							
	10								
	11								
	12								
	13								
	14								
	15								
	16								
	17								

TRIBAL ENROLLMENT OF PARENTS

	Name of Father	Year	County	Name of Mother	Year	County
1	Walker Folsom		Sans Bois Co Choctaw Roll	Hettie Folsom	Dead	Chickasaw Roll
2	Henry L Coleman		Non-citizen	No1		
3	" " "		" "	No1		
4	" " "		" "	No1		
5						
6	No1 Also on Choctaw Census Record No.2 Page 86 as Aaron Coleman					
7	" 2 " " " " " " " " Marie " On '96 Roll as Marie Coleman					
	" 3 " " " " " " " " Bessie "					
8	" 4 Enrolled May 24th 1900					
9	Nos. 1,2,3 and 4 originally enrolled on Chick. card #633. Transferred					
10	to this card Oct. 16, 1902.					
11						
12						
13						
14						
15	PO Box 84 Chickasha IT 4/1/05				Date of Application for Enrollment.	
16	No1 Coleman IT 11/1/04					
17	PO Haileyville 1/5/03				Sept. 26" 1898	

291

Choctaw By Blood Enrollment Cards 1898-1914

Choctaw Nation

Choctaw Roll *(Not Including Freedmen)*

CARD No. FIELD No. **5392**

Dawes' Roll No.	NAME	Relationship to Person First Named	AGE	SEX	BLOOD	TRIBAL ENROLLMENT Year	County	No.
13651	1 Coleman, Sarah Gaddy	Named	17	F	1/8	1896	Sans Bois	4633
13652	2 " Riley Buford	Son	5mo	M	1/16			
13653	3 Watts, Lillie	Sis	15	F	1/8	1896	Sans Bois	4655
13654	4 Coleman, Donnie B	Dau	3mo	"	1/16			
13655	5 " Ruby Almedia	"	3w	"	1/16			
13656	6 Watts, Carrie P	Dau of Nº3	2mo	F	1/16			
	7							
	8							
	9							
	10							
	11							
	12							
	13							
	14							
	15							
	16							
	17							

ENROLLMENT
OF NOS. 1-2-3-4-5-6 HEREON
APPROVED BY THE SECRETARY
OF INTERIOR MAR 19 1903

For child of No3 see NB (Apr 26-06) #319
" " " " 1 " " (Mar 3-05) #398

TRIBAL ENROLLMENT OF PARENTS

	Name of Father	Year	County	Name of Mother	Year	County
1	Arch Gaddy	Dead	Non-Citizen	Adeline Gaddy	Dead	Chickasaw Roll
2	Riley L. Coleman		" "	No.1		
3	Arch Gaddy	Dead	" "	Adeline Gaddy		Chickasaw Roll
4	Riley L Coleman		" "	No.1		
5	" " "		" "	No.1		
6	William F Watts		non-citizen	Nº3		
7						
8	No1 On Choctaw Census Record No.2 Page 197 as Sarah Gadd, On 96 Roll as Sarah Gaddy					
9	" 3 " " " " " " " " " " Liley "					
10	" 2 Affidavit of attending Physician to be supplied. Received Oct 11" 1898					
	" 4 Born Sept 6" 1899 Affidavit irregular and returned for correction Dec 14" 1899					
11	Returned Corrected and filed Feb. 24" 1900					
12	" 5 Enrolled Jan 16" 1901					
	Nos 1 to 5 originally enrolled on Chick card #627 Transferred to this card October 16, 1902					
13	No3 is now the wife of William F Watts, non-citizen. Evidence of marriage					
14	filed Oct. 24, 1902.					
	No6 Born Aug 19, 1902 enrolled Oct. 24, 1902.					
15						
16					#1 to 3	
17		DATE OF APPLICATION FOR ENROLLMENT.				Sept. 26" 1898

Choctaw By Blood Enrollment Cards 1898-1914

RESIDENCE: Choctaw Nation 1ˢᵗ Dist COUNTY. **Choctaw Nation** Choctaw (Not Including ▓▓▓) FIELD NO. **5393**
POST OFFICE: Cowlington, Ind. Ter.

Dawes' Roll No.	NAME	Relationship to Person	AGE	SEX	BLOOD	TRIBAL ENROLLMENT		
						Year	County	No.
13657	1 Folsom, Nathan	First Named	23	M	1/4	1896	Sans Bois	3832
	2							
	3							
	4							
	5							
	6	ENROLLMENT						
	7	OF NOS. 1 HEREON APPROVED BY THE SECRETARY						
	8	OF INTERIOR MAR 19 1903						
	9							
	10							
	11							
	12							
	13							
	14							
	15							
	16							
	17							

TRIBAL ENROLLMENT OF PARENTS

	Name of Father	Year	County	Name of Mother	Year	County
1	Walker Folsom		Sans Bois Choctaw Roll	Hettie Folsom	Dead	Chickasaw Roll
2						
3						
4						
5						
6	No1 On 96 Roll as "Nathan Folsum" Also on Choctaw Census Record No2 Page 163					
7						
8	No1 Originally enrolled on Chick card #636. Transferred to					
9	this card Oct. 16, 1902.					
10						
11						
12						
13						
14						
15					Date of Application for Enrollment.	
16						
17					Sept. 26" 1898	

RESIDENCE: Choctaw Nation COUNTY.
POST OFFICE: Burgevin, Ind. Ter.

Choctaw Nation

Choctaw Roll
(Not Including Freedmen)

CARD NO.
FIELD NO. 5394

Dawes' Roll No.	NAME	Relationship to Person First Named	AGE	SEX	BLOOD	TRIBAL ENROLLMENT Year	County	No.
13658	1 McDaniel, Mary		43	F	1/4	1896	Skullyville	9035
13659	2 " Thomas	Son	22	M	1/8	"	"	9036
13660	3 " Marvin	"	15	"	1/8	"	"	9037
13661	4 " James	"	12	"	1/8	"	"	9038
13662	5 " Mitchell	"	8	"	1/8	"	"	9039
13663	6 " Ruth	Dau	7	F	1/8	"	"	9040
13664	7 " Lula	"	4	"	1/8	"	"	9041
13665	8 McCurtain, Ben	Nephew	22	M	3/8	"	Sans Bois	9000
13666	9 " Randolph	Son of N°8	3mo	M	3/16			
Dead	10 McDaniel, Velma A	Dau of N°2	1mo	F	1/16			

No10 hereon dismissed under order of the Commission to the Five Civilized Tribes of March 31, 1905
Nos 1 to 9 inclusive originally enrolled on Chick. card No 638 Transferred to this card October 16, 1902
No10 transferred from Choctaw card No 2786 Oct 30 '02
No10 died Aug 12, 1902 Proof filed Dec 24, 1902

For child of No3 see NB (Apr 26 '06) #175
" " " " 2 " " (Mar 3 '05) #[?]
" " " No2 " " " " #1275

ENROLLMENT
OF NOS. 1-2-3-4-5-6-7-8-9 HEREON
APPROVED BY THE SECRETARY
OF INTERIOR Mar. 19, 1903

TRIBAL ENROLLMENT OF PARENTS

	Name of Father	Year	County	Name of Mother	Year	County
1	Willis Fulsom	Dead	Choctaw Roll	Sem-e-cha-che	Dead	Chickasaw Roll
2	Ed McDaniel		Choctaw residing in Chickasaw Dist	No.1		
3	" " "		" "	No.1		
4	" " "		" "	No.1		
5	" " "		" "	No.1		
6	" " "		" "	No.1		
7	" " "		" "	No.1		
8	Green McCurtain		Choctaw Roll	Rhoda Fulsom	Dead	Chickasaw Roll
9	No8			Clara McCurtain		Non-citizen
10	No2		Choctaw residing in Chickasaw Dist	Katie McDaniel	1896	Skullyville (I.W)
11						

No1 also on Choctaw Census Record No2 Page 361; Husband & father of her children Ed McDaniel Choc. Card 287
" 2 " " " " " " " " ; now the husband of Katie Folsom on Choc card #2786
" 3 " " " " " " " " ; now the husband of Commie McDaniel on Choc card #[?]
" 4 " " " " " " " " ; No 10 died Aug 12, 1902 Proof of death filed Dec 24, 1902
" 5 " " " " " " " "
" 6
" 7 " " " " " " " "
" 8 " " " " " " " " ; now the husband of Clara McCurtain non-citizen on
" 9 Born June 14, 1902 Enrolled Sept 11th 1902   Choctaw card #5767 9/16/02]
17 PO address of above now   Evidence of marriage filed Sept 11" 1902

Cowlington I.T. 2/11/01   No3 P.O. Durant IT 3/20/05

Date of Application for Enrollment. #1 to 8 Sept 26"

RESIDENCE: Choctaw Nation   COUNTY.   **Choctaw Nation**   **Choctaw Roll**   CARD NO.
POST OFFICE: Sans Bois, Ind. Ter.   *(Not Including Freedmen)*   FIELD NO. 5___

Dawes' Roll No.	NAME	Relationship to Person First Named	AGE	SEX	BLOOD	TRIBAL ENROLLMENT Year	County	No.
13667	1 Folsom, Elias	First Named	28	M	1/4	1896	Sans Bois	3829
DEAD	2 " Edler DEAD	Wife	22	F	I.W.	"	" "	14509
13668	3 Folsom, Irene	Dau	2	"	1/8	"	" "	3830
13669	4 " Willis	Son	2mo	M	1/8			
DEAD	5 " Vera	Dau	6wk	F	1/8			
13670	6 Folsom, Dennis	Son	1mo	M	1/8			
IW1144	7 " Delena	wife	22	F	I.W.			

No. 2 and 5   HEREON DISMISSED UNDER
ORDER OF THE COMMISSION TO THE FIVE
CIVILIZED TRIBES OF MARCH 31, 1905.

ENROLLMENT
OF NOS.   7   HEREON
APPROVED BY THE SECRETARY
OF INTERIOR   NOV 16 1904

11 No2 Died July 16, 1899 Proof of death filed Nov. 12, 1902
12 No5 Died Sept 15, 1902 Proof of death filed Nov. 12, 1902

ENROLLMENT
OF NOS.   1-3-4-6   HEREON
APPROVED BY THE SECRETARY
OF INTERIOR   MAR 19 1903

TRIBAL ENROLLMENT OF PARENTS

	Name of Father	Year	County	Name of Mother	Year	County
1	Willis Folsom	Dead	Choctaw Roll	Sem-e-cha-che	Dead	Chickasaw Roll
2	Matt Wade		Non-Citizen	Mary Wade		Non-citizen
3	No.1			No.2		
4	No.1			No.2		
5	No.1			Delena Folsom		Non-Citizen
6	No.1			" "		" "
7	Robert Priest	dead	non-citizen	Callie Blackwell		non-citizen

8 No1 On 96 Roll a Elias Folsum; Also on Choctaw Census Record No.2 Page 163
9 " Married to Delena Priest, non-citizen Feb. 1st 1900 Evidence of marriage filed April 10"1900
" Evidence of marriage between (1) & (2) received and filed March 29" 1902
10 " 2 On Choctaw Intermarried Roll Page 28 as Edlin Folsom Now Dead
11 " 3 On 96 Roll as Irene Folsum: Also on Choctaw Census Record No2, Page 163
12 " 4 Affidavit of attending Physician to be supplied: Evidence of Birth received and filed Sept 6 1902
" 5 Enrolled Dec 26" 1900 For child of Nos 1&7 see NB (March 3, 1905) #1056
13 " 6 Born July 10" 1902 Enrolled Aug 7" 1902
14 Nos 1 to 6 inclusive originally enrolled on Chick card No 639 Transferred to this card
15 Oct 11, 1902
Application made by No7 Nov 13, 1902: Placed on this card Sept 22d, 1904.   Da___ #1 to 6
17 PO Non IT 6/3/03   Sep___

Choctaw By Blood Enrollment Cards 1898-1914

RESIDENCE: Choctaw Nation ~~COUNTY.~~

POST OFFICE: Garland, Ind. Ter.

Choctaw Nation

Choctaw Roll
(Not Including Freedmen)

CARD NO.

FIELD NO. **5396**

Dawes' Roll No.	NAME	Relationship to Person First Named	AGE	SEX	BLOOD	TRIBAL ENROLLMENT		
						Year	County	No.
13671	1 Folsom, Frank	First Named	34	M	1/4	1896	Sans Bois	3857
	2							
	3							
	4							
	5							
	6							
	7							
	8							
	9							
	10							
	11	ENROLLMENT						
	12	OF NOS. 1 HEREON APPROVED BY THE SECRETARY						
	13	OF INTERIOR MAR 19 1903						
	14							
	15							
	16							
	17							

TRIBAL ENROLLMENT OF PARENTS

	Name of Father	Year	County	Name of Mother	Year	County
1	Willis Folsom	Dead	Choctaw Roll	Sim-cha-che	Dead	Chickasaw Roll
2						
3						
4						
5						
6	No 1 On 96 Roll as Frank Folsum					
7	" On Choctaw Census Record No2 Sans Bois co Page 164					
8	" Husband of Charlotte Folsom, Choctaw Roll Card No 288					
9	~~No.1 originally enrolled on Chickasaw Card No. 641: Transferred to this card Oct. 16, 1902~~					
10	For child of No.1 see NB (March 3, 1905) #841					
11						
12						
13						
14						
15						
16						
17				Date of Application for Enrollment.	Sept. 26" 1898	

Choctaw By Blood Enrollment Cards 1898-1914

	RESIDENCE: Choctaw Nation COUNTY.	POST OFFICE: Cartersville Ind Ter

RESIDENCE: Choctaw Nation   COUNTY. **Choctaw Nation**   Choctaw Roll (Not Including Freedmen)   CARD No. FIELD No. **5397**
POST OFFICE: Cartersville Ind Ter

Dawes' Roll No.	NAME	Relationship to Person First Named	AGE	SEX	BLOOD	TRIBAL ENROLLMENT Year	County	No.
IW605	1 Hickman, Eugene A	First Named	36	M	I.W.	1896	Sans Bois	14593
13672	2 " Lucy	Wife	31	F	1/8	"	" " "	5112
13673	3 " Chester	Son	12	M	1/16	"	" " "	5113
13674	4 " Gertie	Dau	10	F	1/16	"	" " "	5114
13675	5 " Manie	"	8	"	1/16	"	" " "	5115
13676	6 " Willis	"	4	"	1/16	"	" " "	5116
13677	7 " Hester	"	2	"	1/16	"	" " "	5119
13678	8 " Lucy	"	4mo	"	1/16			
13679	9 " Edwin L	nephew	19	M	1/4	1896	Sans Bois	5117
13680	10 " Frankie	"	15	"	1/4	"	" " "	5118
	11 ENROLLMENT							
	12 OF NOS. 2-3-4-5-6-7-8-9-10 HEREON APPROVED BY THE SECRETARY				ENROLLMENT			
	13 OF INTERIOR MAR 19 1903				OF NOS. 1 HEREON			

Nos 1 to 10 inclusive originally enrolled
on Chickasaw card #642. Transferred to
this card Oct. 16, 1902.

ENROLLMENT OF NOS. 1 HEREON APPROVED BY THE SECRETARY OF INTERIOR FEB -8 1904

	TRIBAL ENROLLMENT OF PARENTS						
	Name of Father	Year	County	Name of Mother	Year	County
1	Lad Hickman	Dead	Non-Citizen	Josephine Hickman		non-citizen
2	Peter McKinney	"	Choctaw Roll	Jency McKinney	Dead	Chickasaw Roll
3	No.1			No.2		
4	No.1			No.2		
5	No.1			No.2		
6	No.1			No.2		
7	No.1			No.2		
8	No.1			No.2		
9	Frank Hickman	Dead	Non citizen	Serena Hickman	Dead	Chickasaw Roll
10	" "	"	" "	" "	"	" "

1 No1 On Choctaw Intermarried Roll Page 40 All others on Choctaw Census Record No2 Page 218
1 No1 On '96 Roll as "E.A Hickman"
" 5 " " " " "Mary " "
" 8 Affidavit of attending Physician to be supplied: Received Nov 7" 1898
14 " 9 On 96 Roll as "Edmund Hickman"
15 " 10 " " " " "Frank " "
16 For child of Nos 1&2 see NB (Mar 3 1905) card #400.

Date of Ap for Enrol
Sept. 2

Choctaw By Blood Enrollment Cards 1898-1914

RESIDENCE: Choctaw								
POST OFFICE: Sans B		**Choctaw Nation** *(Not Including Freedmen)*			**Choctaw Roll**	CARD NO. FIELD NO. **5398**		

Dawes' Roll No.	NAME	Relationship to Person First Named	AGE	SEX	BLOOD	TRIBAL ENROLLMENT Year	County	No.
13681	1 Cooper, Becky	First Named	50	F	1/2	1896	Sans Bois	2075
13682	2 " Robert	Son	19	M	1/4	"	" "	2071
13683	3 Bohanan, Mary	Dau	14	F	1/4	"	" "	2080
14949	4 Cooper, Frances	Dau	12	"	1/4	"	" "	2081
13684	5 Bohanan, Silas W	Grand Son	2mo	M	1/8			
15596	6 Cooper, Henry E	Gr Son	2	M	1/8			

7 ENROLLMENT
OF NOS. 4 HEREON
APPROVED BY THE SECRETARY
OF INTERIOR Oct. 15 1903

10 ENROLLMENT
OF NOS. 1-2-3-5 HEREON
APPROVED BY THE SECRETARY
OF INTERIOR Mar. 19 1903

No6 born April 19, 1900 Application made
March 2, 1901. Final proof of birth filed
April 28, 1903.

15 ENROLLMENT
OF NOS. 6 HEREON
APPROVED BY THE SECRETARY
OF INTERIOR Sept 22 1904

TRIBAL ENROLLMENT OF PARENTS

	Name of Father	Year	County	Name of Mother	Year	County
1	Coley	Dead	Choctaw Roll	Rhoda Coley	Dead	Chickasaw Roll
2	Henry Cooper	"	" "	No.1		
3	" "	"	" "	No.1		
4	" "	"	" "	No.1		
5	Joseph Bohanan	"	" "	No.3		
6	No2			Sarah A Cooper		non citizen

7 No1 on 96 Roll as "Beckie Copper" on Choctaw Census Record #2 Page 84
8 Now wife of Israel Cooper Choctaw Card 289
9 No2 ——————— on Choctaw Census Record #2 Page 83 Now husband of
  Sarah A Mason, non-citizen Evidence of marriage filed March 6th 1901
10 No3 on Choctaw Census Record #2 Page 84 Now the wife of Joseph Bohanan
11 on Choctaw Card #2838: Evidence of marriage to be supplied: Filed Feb 13 1901
12 " 4 on '96 Roll as "Frances Cooper" on Choctaw Census Record #2 Page 84
   " 5 Enrolled Nov 21st 1900
13 Nos 1 to 5 inclusive originally enrolled on Chick. card #644. Transferred
14 to this card Oct. 16, 1902
15 For child of No3 see NB (March 3, 1905) #1426

16				Date of Application for Enrollment.	Sept. 26" 1898
17	PO Kinta IT				1 to 4

298

Choctaw By Blood Enrollment Cards 1898-1914

RESIDENCE: Choctaw Nation ~~COUNTY.~~
POST OFFICE: Sans Bois, Ind. Ter.   99

Dawes' Roll No.		NAME	Relationship to Person First Named	AGE	SEX	BLOOD	TRIBAL ENROLLMENT		
							Year	County	No.
13685	1	Cooper, Norris		25	M	1/2	1896	Sans Bois	2093
DEAD	2	" Frances	wife	19	F	I.W.	"	" "	14371
13686	3	" Maude	Dau	1	"	1/4			
	4								
	5								
	6								
	7								
	8	ENROLLMENT							
	9	OF NOS. 1 - 3 - HEREON							
		~~APPROVED BY THE SECRETARY~~							
	10	OF INTERIOR MAR 19 1903							
	11								
	12	No.____ HEREON DISMISSED UNDER							
		~~ORDER OF THE COMMISSION TO THE FIVE~~							
	13	CIVILIZED TRIBES OF MARCH 31, 1905.							
	14								
	15								
	16								
	17								

TRIBAL ENROLLMENT OF PARENTS

	Name of Father	Year	County	Name of Mother		
1	Henry Cooper	Dead	Choctaw Roll	Becky Cooper	1897	Choctaw
2	~~John Banks~~	"	~~Non-citizen~~	~~Mary Banks~~		~~Non-citizen~~
3	No1			No2		
4						
5						
6	No1 Also on Choctaw Census Record #2, Page 84					
7	" 2 " " " Intermarried Roll " 12: On 96 Roll as "Francis Cooper"					
8	Nos 1,2 and 3 originally enrolled on Chickasaw Card #645 and					
9	transferred to this card Oct. 16, 1902.					
10	~~No.2 Died Nov. 13, 1899: Evidence of death filed April 3, 1901~~					
11						
12						
13						
14						
15					Date of Application for Enrollment.	
16						
17					Sept. 26" 1898	

Choctaw By Blood Enrollment Cards 1898-1914

RESIDENCE: Choctaw Nation 3ʳᵈ Dist ~~COUNTY~~.
POST OFFICE: Stringtown Ind Ter

Choctaw Nation

(Not Including Freedmen) ~~5400~~

Dawes' Roll No.	NAME	Relationship to Person	AGE	SEX	BLOOD	TRIBAL ENROLLMENT		
						Year	County	No.
13687	1 Bond, Henry J	First Named	26	M	1/4	1896	Jack's Fork	1879
	2							
	3							
	4							
	5							
	6							
	7							
	8							
	9							
	10							
	11							
	12							
	13							
	14							
	15							
	16							
	17							

ENROLLMENT
OF NOS. 1 HEREON
APPROVED BY THE SECRETARY
OF INTERIOR MAR 19 1903

TRIBAL ENROLLMENT OF PARENTS

	Name of Father	Year	County	Name of Mother	Year	County
1	Jesse Bond		Jacks Fork Co ~~Choctaw Roll~~	Mary Bond		Chick residing in Choctaw N. 3ʳᵈ Dist
2						
3						
4						
5						
6						
7	No1 on 96 Roll as "Henry Bond"					
8	" ~~On Choctaw Census Record #2, Page 76~~					
	" ~~Husband of Lizzie Bond, Choctaw Roll Card #291~~					
9						
10	No.1 originally enrolled on Chick. Card #647. Transferred to this card Oct. 16, 1902.					
11						
12	For child of No1 see NB (Mar 3-1905) Card #191.					
13						
14						
15					Date of Application for Enrollment.	
16						
17					Sept. 26" 1898